Savo

Spiritual Moments

*The alchemy of transforming everyday
experiences into life changing events*

Colleen Foye Bollen

Savoring Life's Spiritual Moments:
The alchemy of transforming everyday experiences
into life changing events

Copyright © September 9, 2020 Colleen Foye Bollen

Turtle Island Press
PO Box 77598
Seattle, WA 98177
www.colleenfoyebollen.com

ISBN 978-0-9654384-1-4 (print)
ISBN 978-0-9654384-3-8 (ebook)
ISBN 978-0-9654384-2-1 (ebook)

Book design by Constance Bollen
Artwork by Colleen Foye Bollen
Author photo by Regina Szyskiewicz

Manufactured in the United States of America

First Edition

Note: This book is designed to provide information and motivation to our readers. The author of this book does not dispense medical advice or prescribe the use of any technique as a form of treatment for physical, emotional or medical problems without the advice of a physician, either directly or indirectly. This book is not a substitute for the advice of a licensed professional. The author expressly disclaims all responsibility for any liability, loss, risk, or injury resulting from the use and application of any of the contents of this book. The use of this book implies your acceptance of this disclaimer.

Contents

Contents

Chapter Seven — Divine Lessons

Chapter Eight — Reflection

Dedication

✢

To my adult children—

Spence & Melissa

Acknowledgments

THE JOURNEY OF WRITING THIS BOOK encompasses a lifetime of experiences. I owe a debt of gratitude to everyone who has influenced my personal, professional and spiritual growth.

Thanks to my many family members (the Foyes, Bollens, Parkers, and Marlows) and friends who listened to me talk about this book and my quest to publish it.

Many thanks go to the generous women in my first writer's critique group (back in 1988) who freely shared their wisdom and started me on my writing path.

Appreciation goes to two dearly departed friends, Lisa Jones, my college roommate and travel buddy; and Helen McDonald, my ace fan and vocal cheerleader. Both will sadly be reading the celestial version of this book.

An ocean of gratitude to my Hugo House critique group that nourished me as a writer and constantly pushed me to show, not tell: Phil Winberry, Paul Freeman, Frances Wood, Indu Sundaresan, Julie Hatfield, and others. More waves of thanks to Deidre Woods and Patti Piper, who both held a steadfast belief in me as a writer.

Gratitude to my ongoing dream group; my Jin Shin Jyutsu trade group; the Fab Five; the Naraya community; the Nines; North by Northwest Writers; Richards Bushnell, my former editor at *Sunset Magazine*; and my spirit guides, ancestors, and celestial helpers. Plus, giant applause to the *Commodore 64* computer that launched me on my writing career.

My manuscript would not have made it into your hands without the insightful editorial assistance of Marlene Blessing and expertise of my book designer, Constance Bollen.

Without the help of the aforementioned people, this book would still be a dream. I offer apologies and a bouquet of thanks to anyone I inadvertently left out.

As with all personal stories, there is no absolute truth. These stories reflect my memories and how I experienced events. In a quest for brevity, some of the storylines were altered or shortened. For reasons of privacy and anonymity, some names were changed.

Thank you to everyone holding my book in your hands. It is my sincere desire that this book helps you discover the magic of everyday life.

Introduction

YEARS AGO, I ATTENDED A SPIRITUAL WORKSHOP that inspired me to see the world from a new perspective. According to the presenter, I could achieve spiritual bliss by simply paying attention to the present moment.

Walking out of the auditorium, I was filled with fervor, ready to incorporate this new philosophy immediately. Amid a stream of other attendees, I stepped outside into a courtyard garden and saw the world anew. Colors were brighter. Pink blossoms on a rhododendron stood out against a pewter-colored sky and individual blades of grass swayed in a slight breeze. Chirping birds sang their notes distinctly and smells of roses laced the air. Climbing into my car, I felt confident that positive changes were imminent.

Then days, weeks, and months passed. For some inexplicable reason, I didn't apply the workshop's wisdom to my daily life. Instead I warehoused the presenter's sterling lessons in the recesses of my mind, essentially wasting the time and money I'd spent to acquire the knowledge.

I have played out this scenario more times than I care to admit. Despite having attended several workshops about spirituality, all of which touted the true way to enlightenment, I found my life remained unchanged.

Once, I attended a workshop about personal disarmament. The focus was on how to embody the peace you want to see in the world. The speaker explained how to rid ourselves of negative and violent emotions and become more caring and thoughtful in our interactions with other people.

Leaving the workshop, I was determined to exude peacefulness. But on the way home from the workshop, I encountered rush hour traffic. Within ten minutes of hitting the congested freeway, expletives leapt from my mouth as hot rodders zigzagged from one lane to another. This negativity left a nasty residue inside my body. By the time I arrived home, anger, not peace, had taken hold of me.

Eventually I grew tired of wasting time and money chasing after elusive illumination. This is not to say that the spiritual speakers didn't offer insightful advice; I just didn't apply their ideas to my everyday life.

That is when I made a deal with myself. Before spending more money on workshops, I would review my notes from previous seminars and implement what I had learned. After a trial period, if a particular technique or philosophy didn't work for me, I could drop it. But at least I'd know I had given it a chance.

As a writer, it was natural for me to jot down notes in a journal while combing through an assortment of rainbow colored notebooks and reviewing the wisdom I had collected at past workshops. My note taking paid off as I began identifying three reoccurring themes: living consciously by being in the here and now, breaking up problems into doable chunks, and focusing on the positive aspects of life.

After recognizing these themes, I picked one area of my life that created a significant challenge and applied my insights to working with that concern. Anger often hampered my ability to maintain a peaceful mind, so I chose to confront that emotion.

A key component of my anger was the flash point, that place where anger blocked out logic and consumed me physically, mentally, and emotionally. For example, when the hot rodders ticked me off after the workshop about personal disarmament, I found it hard to let go of my anger. Instead of returning to peaceful thoughts as the speaker had suggested, I spent my drive home ranting about stupid drivers. I felt consumed by aggression.

From that experience, and other similar incidents, I knew I didn't like the way I felt or behaved when anger took control. To improve my chances of mastering flash anger, I began breaking the process into doable chunks. Since my anger seemed to flare up without my conscious mind being engaged, I also focused on increasing my self-awareness by being more mindful of the here and now.

I made a commitment to work on anger management during a specific part of each day. That seemed easier than taking on every situation at the same time. Since anger while driving was one of my biggest challenges, I started there. This gave me short time segments to test my new theories in the privacy of my car.

What warning signs let me know anger was building? By paying close attention, I noticed my jaw tightened, a knot formed in my stomach, and heat rose from my chest to my face just before the flash point. With this knowledge, I created a mental buffer zone around my flash point. My goal was to short circuit the building anger so my fuse wouldn't instantly ignite. I did this by establishing guidelines for myself. When I felt my jaw tighten, my chest warm with anger, or my hands strangling the steering wheel, I applied one of two techniques.

The first was a tool used by many spiritual traditions: deep breathing. By taking three deep cleansing breaths, more oxygen entered my body, which reduced my stress level. The second technique was singing or humming for 30 seconds. Sound, in the form of singing or chanting, is used by most religions as a way to pray and praise God. I found these self-generated sounds shifted the vibration in my body, dissolved my anger, lifted my spirits, and balanced my emotions.

In addition to making physical and emotional changes, these two tools produced a tiny window of time where I could evaluate my options. Since there are times when anger is an appropriate response and times when it is out of place, these techniques gave me the mini-break I needed to distinguish between the two before I responded.

Implementing these techniques reduced my irritation with erratic drivers, but did not totally eliminate it. So I created what I call a "do over." When a curse escaped my lips, I used an imaginary eraser to wipe away the words. Then I mentally apologized to the driver and wished him or her a safe journey. Instead of passing my frustration on to other drivers by driving aggressively, I refocused my attention to positive things, such as having a running car and money for gas. My goal was not perfection; I just wanted to make conscious choices in my life instead of living on automatic pilot.

The more I worked on the three themes—living consciously by being in the here and now; breaking up problems into doable chunks; and being positive—the more adept I became at putting these spiritual themes into action.

Experiencing this progress in my own life created the desire to share what I had learned with other people. As luck would have it, this desire coincided with the birth of a Northwest publication called *New Spirit Journal*. I soon found myself writing a column that offered readers concrete examples of how the simple act of paying attention could turn ordinary events into valuable lessons. The column, which I titled "*Everyday Spirituality*," provided me with the impetus (and deadlines) to write essays about gaining spiritual insights while engaged in everyday situations.

Before long, I began dreaming about publishing a book of essays based on the same theme as my column. There was one problem: the original format focused too much attention on me. I needed a way to make readers the focus of the book.

After brainstorming and praying, the answer came to me during meditation. By adding a mixture of creative exercises and journaling ideas at the end of each story, readers could use my essays as a jumping-off point to get in touch with their own stories, spiritual truths, and life ambitions.

Addendum

The journey of writing this book began many years ago when I was married with children in elementary school. Flash forward a few decades and I am now unmarried with adult children. The stories are not in chronological order, so as you read this book my kids' ages will vary from story to story.

My former husband appears in many of the stories. After our divorce, I wrestled with how to keep stories that took place during our time together intact without confusing readers with references to husband or ex-husband. My solution is to simply call him Bo. I chose the name Bo to avoid commonly used names and because its meaning, "to live," felt like a positive way to honor our years together. Throughout the book, I refer to Bo as my partner. In actuality, Bo is my former husband.

Getting Started

How to use this book

THERE IS NO RIGHT OR WRONG WAY TO USE THIS BOOK. You can start at page one and work your way to the end or choose stories at random. My goal in publishing this book is to inspire readers to see beyond a series of everyday tasks and goals and to experience life as a spiritual adventure that incorporates the divine in all its aspects, from washing dishes to choosing a career.

At the end of each chapter, you will see a section called "Make It Your Story." These sections provide readers with the opportunity to tap into their reservoir of personal memories as they read and reflect on the stories in the book. By using the variety of activities and questions at the end of each essay, readers have an opportunity to explore how each theme resonates with their life experiences. The deeper they go with their own personal explorations, the more they can learn about savoring life's spiritual moments.

Everyday spirituality is a form of alchemy. Instead of turning common metals into gold, the goal of everyday spirituality is to transform commonplace activities into spiritually significant events. By recognizing the sacredness of everyday life, readers are better able to appreciate the threads of divine wisdom woven throughout their daily experiences.

Spirituality vs Religion

BEFORE WE START TALKING ABOUT SPIRITUALITY, let me briefly discuss the difference between spirituality and religion. While there is overlap, there are also differences. The points of similarity and difference tend to be subjective.

The larger differences show up in how people practice their chosen form of worship. Members of religious organizations, such as Christianity, Judaism, Buddhism, and Islam, tend to follow the specific teachings of a spiritual leader or leaders and adhere to specific rituals and rules.

Spirituality is born out of personal beliefs. It is an individual's way of infusing life with meaning. Instead of following preordained doctrines or rules, spirituality develops within a person. Inner guidance dictates how they relate to other people, animals, nature, and the world around them. A person's spiritual beliefs can have their origins in religion, be inspired by nature, or evolve after a spiritual revelation. At its core, spirituality is about finding one's own path rather than following the specific teachings of an established religion, group, or individual.

About The Author

Spiritual Journey

I WAS BORN INTO AN IRISH-CATHOLIC FAMILY. In Catholic tradition, children from birth to adulthood attend regular church services. There is no Sunday school for children. Everyone attends mass together. The term "growing up in the church" takes on a literal meaning within the Catholic faith.

I took to Catholicism, its rules and the Ten Commandments, like a dolphin to the open sea. It was my element and I embraced it fully.

Beginning in elementary school, I thought about becoming a nun (a community of religious women who dedicate themselves to poverty, chastity, and obedience to church doctrine). Later, if things worked out, I'd become the first Saint Colleen. In addition to grace before each meal, nightly prayers, the sacrament of confession, catechism classes (similar to Sunday school, but held on Saturday), and Sunday mass, I also did extra prayers called indulgences. The book of indulgence prayers worked like an eraser. Any sinful behavior, such as lying to a teacher or stealing extra cookies at home, could be washed away by saying prayers from the book. According to church doctrine, unconfessed sins were added up at the time of death. The total number of sins determined the amount of time a person had to spend in purgatory, heaven's waiting room. By saying the right prayers, I could shave anywhere from 15 to 300 years off my time in purgatory. At the rate I was praying, I could easily have gone straight to heaven without passing go or stopping in purgatory.

It was a good plan, until I began attending my first Catholic school. Saint Mary's Academy was not just a religious school, it was the same all girls' high school my mother and her two older sisters had attended. With a few exceptions, all of the teachers were nuns. One of my teachers had taught my mother decades earlier. After spending time with nuns on a daily basis, I changed my views on joining a nunnery. While some of the nuns were pleasant, several were mean and vindictive. As a whole, it was not a group I wanted to spend my life living and working with.

During my high school years, there were many changes within the church. The biggest transformation was the switch from masses spoken in Latin to the native language of the congregation. This change made the masses more accessible to millions of parishioners, who, like me, did not speak Latin. Instead of endearing me to the faith, understanding what the priest said raised concerns and questions. Why were women supposed to be subservient? How did endless servings of guilt help us become better Catholics? If we were supposed to care for the poor, why did the church amass massive wealth? I tried to appease myself and keep my faith alive through active involvement in the growing folk mass movement and attendance in a teen group lead by a Jesuit brother.

Even with regular participation in church activities, I continued questioning the Catholic Church. Once the chinks started forming, there was no sacred territory. I questioned church rules, priests' sermons, and the general premises of my up-until-then unquestioned faith. I made serious efforts to forgive the church's imperfections, but the cracks in the Catholic armor kept growing.

Then, one Sunday while I was attending college, I deliberately missed mass. My world did not crash down around me, and I found I enjoyed curling up in my cozy bed for an extra hour of sleep much more than going to church. So I skipped church the next Sunday, and the one after that. Breaking the rule on regular church attendance opened the doors to breaking other rules. Why did a bunch of celibate old men have the right to tell me not to use birth control? What did eating meat on Fridays have to do with my relationship with God? The more I questioned, the more uncomfortable I became with some of the church's beliefs.

Gradually, my disinterest in church attendance turned into an aversion that encompassed all aspects of the Catholic Church and religion in general. I wasn't cavalier about turning my back on the Catholic Church. It felt like I was breaking up with a core part of myself. I fretted and searched deep into my being to see if I could find a way to stay with the church.

My intense religious beliefs turned into adamant disbelief. After years of unquestioning devotion, I developed a severe allergy not only to my faith, but to anything even faintly religious. For the next twenty years, I reacted strongly anytime someone mentioned the words God or Jesus, often by leaving the room or literally breaking out in a rash. Psychologists say love and hate are only separated by a breath. I blew out my candle of passion for Catholic Church and wandered in the void left behind.

Then in 1997 a dear friend, Helen, was dying of cancer. During my visits to her condo I was introduced to people from a variety of spiritual and religious backgrounds. I began the summer with my aversion to anything hinting of God fully intact, racing from the room when spiritual subjects came up in conversation or breaking out in a rash if I delayed my exit. During that summer, I was living in the trenches of life, where death was no longer an abstraction.

A few weeks after Helen lost her ability to talk, a group of healers showed up at the condo. They held hands and circled around her as she lay on a massage table. Standing off to the side, I closed my eyes and sent good thoughts to Helen. With my eyes shut, I saw Helen rise off the table. She looked down on the gathering of healers and said, "Thank you so much for doing this, but I don't want to come back."

Personally experiencing that unexplainable phenomenon shook me to my core. If someone else had told me about it, I would have poopooed their story. As I tried to come to terms with what I had witnessed, a simple question came to my mind: "If that could happen, what else could happen?" And, with those words, the floodgates to spiritual awareness opened. I no longer ran from the room when people spoke about God-stuff. I listened and learned from everyone who came to help Helen through her final journey. I received a crash course in spiritual practices from people with widely different religious and spiritual persuasions. That summer turned my world on its axis. I went from anti-religious to having my life center around spirituality. I started reading every book I could find about spirituality and regularly attending workshops.

Healing Arts Story—
Discovering Jin Shin Jyutsu®

THE YEAR WAS 2002. I was getting ready for my first trip to Mexico that would reach beyond the partying towns of Tijuana and Juarez when a dream changed the course of my life.

A few weeks before my departure, I dreamt a friend had a book I should read before my trip. At that time, I had been a member of an ongoing dream group for seven years. In the past, a precognitive dream prompted me to put new batteries in my house's smoke detectors the night before a fire engulfed my home. Another dream identified the source of my chronic abdominal pain as series of appendicitis attacks; something numerous doctors had been unable to diagnose. I knew the power of dreams and the importance of paying attention to my newest installment.

The next morning, I called my friend to ask if she had a book about Mexico. She said, "No, but I have a book about the indigenous Mayan culture called *The Mayan Factor*."

The next day I got a copy of the book and began reading. As I read what turned out to be a very esoteric book, I understood less than ten percent of the information. I comprehended individual words: planet, Mexico, seasons. But the concepts, such as galactic patterns and morphogenetic fields, flew over my head.

Chapter after chapter I waded through the pages, searching for why my dream maker wanted me to read that book. Midway I found my answer in an illustration of the ancient Mayan calendar. Unlike our Gregorian calendar, it is a large square with 260 smaller squares and Mayan glyphs (pictures). On each side of the Mayan calendar was the outline of a human body, marked with 26 dots along left and right side. One showed the location of dots on the front of the body and the other the back view.

My eyes locked onto the illustration; my breathing slowed.

Continuing to read, I learned that the dots represented the 26 energy activation points that are a part of a healing art called Jin Shin Jyutsu. (It is pronounced, Gin, as in the drink; Shin, the lower part of your leg and Jyutsu, similar in sound to the martial art.)

I was mesmerized. My body began to vibrate. Intuitively, I knew that illustration was the reason my dream maker wanted me to read the book. I understood on a deep level that a single picture and a few words of explanation had just created a benchmark moment in my life.

As planned, I flew to Mexico. While there I toured Chichén Itzá, a sacred Mayan ruin and one of the Seven Wonders of the World. The day of my tour was scorching hot. I slathered myself with sun lotion, wore a big brimmed hat, and drank lots of water. But it was still too hot. Like M&Ms in the hot sun, I was melting.

Hundreds of tourists swarmed the site. The pyramid at the center of the site was covered with people climbing its 91 steps in the blazing sun. My eyes stung from sweat dripping down my forehead. I needed to find somewhere cool, out of the sun and away from the crowds.

I wandered through rows of ancient stone columns covered with carved serpents and past the remains of buildings built in 600 AD. Farther down the path, I found a bathhouse Mayans had used for healing and spiritual purification. Its stone walls and ceiling created an inviting place to rest.

Sitting on the ground with my back against the cool stone wall, I slowed my breathing and slipped into a meditative state. Within minutes, I heard an inner voice tell me, "We are not kidding, you need to learn Jin Shin Jyutsu." My body filled with same vibration I had felt staring at the illustration in *The Mayan Factor*. I sat in the stillness that followed absorbing the voice's message.

Returning home, I began researching Jin Shin Jyutsu on the Internet. As luck would have it, a five-day training session was being held in three months across town from my home. Based solely on my body's reaction to the illustration in *The Mayan Factor* and my inner voice's urging, I plunked down several hundred dollars for my first five-day workshop. In hindsight, I realize I should have prepared for the class. But I did not talk to anyone about Jin Shin Jyutsu, read an introductory book, or receive a treatment. The only thing I knew was that the healing art involved 26 energy points.

With no foundational knowledge about Jin Shin Jyutsu, every bit of information was new. And the volume was overwhelming. I learned the 26 points I'd seen in *The Mayan Factor* were called safety energy locks. Each safety energy lock was part of a depth. Each depth was associated with specific organs, a planet, an astrological sign, numerology, a taste, a color, a tone, a mineral, a day of the week and more. For eight hours a day, I learned how to use gentle touch to facilitate the flow of energy to unblock disharmonies within the body, mind and spirit. I learned treatments connected to each of the 26 safety energy locks, 12 organs, and other flows for harmonizing the body's energy. Plus, I was introduced to pulse reading, body reading, and the history of Jin Shin Jyutsu. And let's not forget the technical side, how to implement all this knowledge in a way that best served clients.

Just when I thought I couldn't hold another piece of information, we shifted from the complex aspects of Jin Shin Jyutsu to simple self-help flows.

My brain relaxed as I learned we each have the innate ability to harmonize ourselves. By simply holding my fingers, one at a time, I could help bring healing, health, and wholeness to my total being. I could give myself a bear hug, while visualizing my breath going down the front of my body on the exhale and up my back on inhale, to balance myself physically, mentally, emotionally, and spiritually. Or I could employ numerous other self-help holds. It turned out Jin Shin Jyutsu was incredibly complex and startlingly simple; I could choose which part to focus on.

Talking with my classmates, I found out some of them had been studying Jin Shin Jyutsu for more than two decades and they were still learning new things. It became obvious that I could study this system for the rest of my life and still not know everything. As a lover of learning, that was a plus for me.

This story is just one example of how paying attention to clues from the universe and my inner wisdom changed my life path. I could have chosen to ignore the promptings to study Jin Shin Jyutsu. And, if I had ignored these gentle nudges, my life would have continued skipping forward, but I can't imagine what it would look like.

By embracing the opportunity to study and practice Jin Shin Jyutsu, I gained a cherished community of friends and a healing art that benefits myself and others in profound ways. Over the years, the philosophy and practice of Jin Shin Jyutsu has become an intricate piece of my day to day life and a core part of how I live my life. I am eternally grateful to my dream maker for devising a way to introduce me to the art of Jin Shin Jyutsu.

Joy

Spirituality and Stress

SUNSHINE WARMS MY BACK as I wander through the college campus in Seattle. I stop for the umpteenth time to consult the campus map. To my left, a young man with curly locks plays an acoustic guitar as a parade of other students stroll past him. Surrounded by a forest of identical brick buildings, I feel my stress level rising. I have five minutes to make it to my appointment. And, according to the map, I passed my destination five buildings back. Reminding myself that getting upset won't get me there any faster, I stop to appreciate and give thanks for the white and pink cherry blossoms forming canopies over the walkways. Then I retrace my steps.

It had been a year since I filled out a questionnaire regarding spirituality and stress in exchange for a five-dollar gift card for espresso. At the request of the questionnaire's author, an assistant psychology professor, I am now about to do a more in-depth interview on the same subject.

My life is frequently blessed by clusters of stressful events. It is not unusual for several events, such as the death of a friend, family issues, and a job transition, to occur concurrently. I use the word "blessed" deliberately.

While I don't enjoy stress, I have come to realize that stressful events have helped temper my abrasive personality traits. Over the years, like metal forged over a fire, my rough edges have been smoothed. In the past if a stranger yelled at me, I hollered back twice as loud. Now I usually stop, take a deep breath and calmly respond. I also exchanged my list of hard and fast beliefs for a more open minded attitude. Like bamboo, I stand strong against the winds of fate by being flexible.

Stepping into the assistant professor's book-lined office, I take the seat facing the window. Outside, cherry blossoms cascade like confetti onto the sidewalk. After hearing a brief explanation of the project, I sign a consent form allowing my statements to be used in her research paper. Then we begin the interview.

Instead of giving me a list of questions to answer, she asks only one question, "How do you use your spirituality to handle stress?"

At first I am stymied. How can I explain something that is such an intricate part of my life? I incorporate spiritual practices into everything I do, not only stressful situations. Just that morning I had prayed for divine assistance in finding a parking space on the crowded college campus. When retracing my steps while searching for her office, I remembered to pause and feel gratitude for flowering trees.

I ask for guidance and consciously appreciate nature's beauty not because these actions make me a good person, but because they make me feel good. During college, there was a darkness inside me that manifested in negative, even suicidal thoughts. I could take any situation or comment and find the negative. Reversing the poles of my thinking has been a laborious process that took many years to accomplish; one I am still working on. The first step was noticing my thoughts. Step two involved taking responsibility for my thoughts. No one could make me think a certain way. No matter what they did or didn't do, I chose how to respond.

Mindfulness is the third key to my spiritual practice. As I go through my day, my intention is to make the people I interact with feel better after our contact than they did before we interacted. I consciously strive to bring humor into each transaction with a cashier or service provider and to make them laugh or at least smile.

When someone is rude or cuts me off on the freeway, I work on remembering that we all have issues we are dealing with. The erratic driver may have just learned they have an illness or fought with a loved one. Their action most likely has nothing to do with me, so I don't take it personally. Usually, but not always, I can let their behavior pass without reacting. If I do curse them as they race by me, I quickly apologize and send them a blessing for a peaceful day.

As I recount the ways I incorporate spirituality into my life, I tell my interviewer that my goal is not to be Pollyannaish about life. It's not that I see everything in a positive light, but I am working to calm my inner chatter and live more peacefully. That means I take action where I can, while recognizing some things are out of my control. Being positive has a decidedly selfish facet. I am the one who most benefits from my upbeat attitude. The outside world has no knowledge of what I am doing. It's my inner world that vibrates with joy.

Driving home, I mull over the interview. Reciting the ways I integrate spirituality into my life gave me an uplifting feeling. With the interviewer's prodding, I articulated practices that have become so fluid they are second nature to me. Although I was ostensibly doing the interview to help the assistant professor with her research paper, she helped me articulate my beliefs. As I reviewed the key ways of using spirituality to deal with stress and everyday situations (notice my thoughts, take responsibility for my reactions, be mindful, and pray), my mind taps into its deep reservoir of songs. Soon I am singing a refrain from an old 1940s song by Bing Crosby: "You've got to accentuate the positive, eliminate the negative, latch on to the affirmative and don't mess with Mister In-Between." Today those are still good words to live by.

❧ Make it your story

Many of the steps I took to create a calmer and more positive inner landscape fall into the mindfulness category. I began by paying attention to my thoughts. During that period, a friend offered this insight: "Thoughts are like trains; just because it passes through the station/mind, it doesn't mean you need to jump on." In other words, just because a thought passes through my mind, it doesn't mean I need to believe it or engage with it.

Mindfulness starts by noticing your thoughts. Once you are aware of your thinking, pay attention to how the thoughts make you feel. If a thought is negative, make a shift that will stop that line of thinking. Things that have worked for me are: singing (mentally or out loud), noticing details in the world around me, and intentionally changing dark thoughts to positive or silly ones.

Bryon Katie, an author and speaker who teaches a method of self-inquiry known as "The Work," uses four questions to help people evaluate their thoughts. I paraphrased two of the questions to help myself avoid the murky places negative thinking can take me. The first question I ask myself is, "Is it true?" That question allows me to query the validity of what I am thinking. Is the story true or am I making it up?

For instance, I recently thought a friend was avoiding me, and started making up a story about the situation. Then I caught myself. I asked myself if the story was true. The immediate answer I got was no; it was a fabrication of my imagination.

Other times, I initially believe my story is true. That's when the second question comes in handy. "Can I guarantee it's true?" Let's take the same situation. I ask myself if it is true that my friend is avoiding me. After pondering the question, I decide it is true. As proof, I cite three instances when she declined offers to get together. Then I ask myself if I can guarantee my assumption is true. While I may think it is true, I cannot guarantee it. At that point, I find it best to get clarification. In this situation, I called my friend. She told me she was working double shifts and didn't have time to visit with friends. She wasn't avoiding me, she was overbooked.

If shifting your thinking doesn't work, try asking yourself the two questions. With practice, these techniques will help you shift your mind out of automatic thinking and into mindfulness.

Blessings

THE SHARP SMELL OF SMOKE WOKE ME out of a deep sleep. Opening my eyes, I saw pulsating flames engulfing the bedroom. Seized by panic, my heart took up the beat of an African drum. Strong and loud. A whispery voice from deep within me could barely be heard above its booming beat. Instinctively, I followed the voice's advice, "Heat rises, stay low to the ground. Get people out first. Leave things behind. Call 911 after you're out of the house." Impaired by thick smoke and searing heat, I clung onto my partner Bo and our baby and dashed out the front door.

Then I woke up.

It had all been a dream; a nightmare to add to my growing list of waking ordeals. In the past six months, I had quit my job and became a first-time mom, and Bo was suddenly laid off from work. Sleepless and stressed, I desperately needed relief from life's tribulations, not invasive nightmares. Looking for the positive, I used the dream's prompting to install new batteries in my home's smoke detector.

One high point during this stressful period was my mom's visit to meet her new granddaughter. Before my nightmare, she had flown up from California and taken over kitchen duty. Dressed in her green-flowered muumuu, she performed kitchen magic. As I tended Melissa's constant feedings and diaper changings, the aroma of comfort foods lulled me back to treasured childhood memories.

Tucked into Mom's suitcase, beside her cold cream and bottles of vitamins, was the baptismal gown my four siblings and I had worn. After all these years, the white silk kimono, covered with tiny embroidered bows, was still purity itself. The long pleated undergown and the lace-edged bonnet were immaculate. At my mother's urging, we called the local church and set a date for Melissa's baptism.

Days later, the once-familiar smell of spicy frankincense whiffed through a heavy wood door, as we stepped into the church. The organ's deep chords vibrated through our bodies. This baptism was an offering to my mother.

Dressed in the family heirloom, Melissa cooed quietly while blessings and fluttering hands passed over her head. Mom stood in proud attendance.

Bo and I held Melissa's head as she was immersed in the ancient ritual, irreverently known as "the dunking." Not partial to cold water, Melissa let out an ear-piercing scream. Taking her from our arms, Mom rocked her with a gentle swing and sway of her hips. Tilting her head toward Melissa's ear she whispered, "You'll be just fine, sweet-stuff."

Mom beamed as she held her granddaughter for post-baptismal photos. Melissa was cute, she had good strong lungs, and she wouldn't go to hell for lack of a proper baptism. What more could a grandma ask for?

None of us knew that would be the last time we'd all be together as a family. Mom headed back down to California feeling slightly tired. Weeks of rest left her weaker, not stronger, and her doctors requested hospital tests.

Within a month, she was dead. Cancer had spread undetected throughout her body and no amount of modern medicine or old-fashioned prayers could keep her on this earth.

Dizzy with grief, I mourned the loss of my mom. Just when I needed her advice, the wisdom she'd gained raising five kids, she was snatched away from me. I would grow into motherhood without my role model. My daughter would grow into womanhood without knowing her grandma's hearty laugh and lame jokes.

Depression tried to lure me into its quicksand. For Melissa and Bo, I struggled to remain semi-sane. Bo was going through his own grief, and Melissa's safety and well-being were dependent on my keeping a finger hold on sanity. My daughter's constant needs were my salvation. By focusing on her, I could escape the despondency that surrounded me.

Christmas loomed ahead. Yet the joy of the season and my daughter's first Christmas eluded me. My belief in miracles was at an all-time low. I forced myself through the motions, buying gifts and taking Melissa to see Santa.

The morning after my fire dream, Melissa and I spent the day in the attic as I wrapped presents and listened to different versions of "Jingle Bells" and "Silent Night". Remnants of the dream stubbornly clung to my psyche. Mentally, I relived our escape from the fire and planned out better routes. Unaware of her mother's preoccupation with disaster, Melissa giggled the day away, decorating herself with leftover bits of paper and ribbon. A small space heater kept us warm while snow clouds formed outside. By day's end, I had accomplished a lifetime goal. I finished wrapping gifts before Christmas Eve.

That night the first snowflakes of the year covered the ground. It looked as if we were going to have a rare white Christmas in Seattle. I eagerly anticipated seeing Melissa's reaction to this cool white stuff. Dawn seemed too far away.

In the dark hours between night and morning, our smoke detector started beeping. "Damn it," I fumed. "Why is it waking me up with its blasted beeping?"

Floating into consciousness, I opened my eyes to a room filled with smoke. My mind raced back to the night before and my nightmare about a house fire. Was I now having serial fire dreams?

My eyes stung and my nose was clogged with blackness; this was the real thing. Bo and I raced around our house searching for the fire's source. He checked the basement and I raced to get Melissa. Pausing outside her bedroom, I checked the attic stairs.

Opening the door I saw blistering flames engulfing the stairs that shared a common wall with my baby's room, right next to where she was sleeping. Slamming the door against the hissing fire, I grabbed Melissa out of her crib and raced out the front door with Bo.

Glancing back over our shoulders, we saw the kitchen, right next to our daughter's room, explode into flames. Words slowly stumbled out of my mouth, "If the alarm had gone off a few minutes later, our baby would be caught behind that wall of flames."

Within minutes the fire department arrived. Neighbors poured out of their homes with offers of hot coffee and blankets. Lost in shock, we stood in the bone-chilling snow watching sizzling flames engulf our house.

A flashback of the fire nightmare played out in my mind. Could it have been a warning? A message from my mother? The thought alternately sent shivers up my arms and a glow of warmth to my heart. Without a doubt the dream had prepared me for our house fire. Reviewing fire safety lessons and planning our exit route sped our escape.

We survived the house fire with our family, including Tammy Cat, together and safe. With what little emotions I had left, I gave heartfelt thanks for the miracle of our survival and for the dream I had originally scorned.

I longed to hear my mom's comforting voice, but had to be content with her ethereal presence. Internally, I could hear her whisper soothing words. The tone of voice and cadence were just as I remembered; the only thing missing was Mom's physical presence.

In the light of day, Bo and I returned to assess the house's damage. There we learned the fire was caused by the combustion of a cheap extension cord attached to the attic space heater.

As we stepped through the doorway, the smell of smoke overwhelmed us. It was like walking through thick smog; our eyes burned and our lungs filled with lingering smoke. Devastation was everywhere. Rooms that hadn't burned were scarred with smoke damage. With leaden legs, we slowly surveyed the remains of our worldly possessions.

Tears streamed down my cheeks as I found my smoke-damaged wedding dress, roasted family recipes, fire-scented letters and piles of melted toys. Ghostly images of picture frames and figurines were silhouetted against a backdrop of black, smoke streaked walls.

As Bo and I gingerly climbed the fire-damaged steps to the attic, little drifts of snow fell through the few remaining rafters. This had been my refuge, the place I'd stored all my childhood treasures after my mom's sudden death. It was also the heart of the fire.

Picking through charred remains, I found little to salvage. Books, files and those beloved stuffed animals I saved for my yet-to-be-born children, were all destroyed. The caustic smell of smoke permeated the damaged remains.

I found a fire-scorched box that held the family baptismal gown my mother had brought up for Melissa's christening. Before tossing it into the trash pile, I felt compelled to peek inside. Opening the blackened lid, my fingers picked up flakes of burned cardboard. But inside the tissue paper was miraculously unsinged. Lifting my family's gown, a stillness embraced me, just like it used to when my mom would whisper, "Don't worry, sweet stuff, you'll be just fine." My breathing slowed as I brushed off my hands and gently traced the gown's tiny, embroidered bows.

✂ Make it your story

Sometimes in our darkest hours, grace slips into our lives. In Leonard Cohen's song, "Anthem," he wrote, "There is a crack, a crack in everything. That's how the light gets in."

After the house fire and my mother's death, fear became a frequent visitor. One thing that slowed down the avalanche of panic was mentally going back into fire-damaged attic. Picturing the pristine family baptismal gown and hearing my mom's reassuring voice reminded me that grace was present in my life. And, although it did not always feel like it, a force beyond my comprehension was watching over me.

Have you experienced the feeling of being cracked—depleted or bottomed out—and experienced a moment of grace? A time when, if only for a second, you believed in the possibility that things in your life might eventually improve? If you have, tuck that memory away for safe keeping. You can use it as a lifeline when the world feels like it is crashing down. The memory can remind you that, at any moment, you might receive a blessing or an answer to your prayers that pierces your despair with an arrow of joy.

If you are currently searching for a grain of grace to help you climb out of despair, try talking with a therapist or friend about your concerns. Journaling is another way to express your feelings and figure out your next step. During times of stress, normal activities like eating, sleeping, and exercise can become magical elixirs that keep you grounded, healthy, and better able to deal with your challenging situation.

In Pursuit of Hope

MY FRIEND JULIE AND I SAT ON HER FRONT PORCH catching the last splashes of sunlight before the golden orb slipped behind her neighbor's rooftops. As we chatted about spirituality and her divinity classes at a local university, Julie produced a notebook and a pen. "Tomorrow I'm facilitating a class discussion about hope," she said. "Can you help me brainstorm ways to regain hope in times of grief, despair, or disappointment?" With pleasure, I agreed.

We struggled for a few minutes on where to start, finally deciding we needed a definition of hope. After more discussion, we defined hope as, "having the desire or ability to raise one's spirits or emotional state of being."

Both of us had read several books touting the importance of positive thinking and counting one's blessings to overcome despair. While we agreed that those are two powerful ways to regain a sense of hope, we wanted to compile a list of other tools people could use in the face of a life crisis, such as the death of a beloved pet, being jilted by the love of one's life, or failing an important exam.

Julie, a part-time disc jockey, put music at the top of the list. We concurred that listening to music, playing an instrument, and singing all could reopen the door to hope.

Research has proven that music aids the body's healing process by stimulating the release of endorphins, the body's natural painkillers. If music can accomplish that for physical traumas, it seemed logical that it could also help ease grief, heartbreak, and disappointment.

Chocolate was also high on our list of ways to generate feelings of hope. Studies have found that chocolate, like music, releases endorphins. A few bites of chocolate containing up to 70 percent cocoa butter can stimulate feelings of optimism and happiness.

Any list about raising one's spirits had to mention friends. Julie and I knew intuitively that talking with friends helps us feel better. Researchers at the University of California in Los Angeles confirmed our intuition with a study that showed talking about one's feelings with another person decreased grief, anger, and pain and promoted better health.

Physical activity is one of my favorite ways of easing my mind, so I added it to the list. There is something magical about dancing, swimming, or walking that takes my mind off my troubles. In addition to providing a distraction, exercise also improves the body's use of oxygen and reduces mental sluggishness, a common byproduct of despair.

No divinity student can talk about raising hope without mentioning prayer. We agreed that reciting conventional prayers from established religions or even having an informal one-on-one chat with the Divine also improved one's sense of well-being. The numerous research projects that studied the benefits of saying prayers and the long history of people asking for Divine intercession were sufficient endorsements. Prayer was added to the list.

We completed our list with a whimsical choice, eating potato chips. In the past, we had both found the intense crunch of biting into a potato chip helped cure the "down-in-the-dumps" syndrome by releasing anxiety and frustration. The salty aftertaste filled us with a sense of well being. Of course, there are no studies to support a link between potato chips and hope. We justified our decision by connecting the experience of munching on potato chips with carefree childhood memories of picnics, lounging at the beach, and watching cartoons on television.

Later, while driving home, I realized everyone's spiritual toolbox holds different methods for regaining hope. Some differences would be the result of cultural or spiritual beliefs; others would be the result of individuals' personal experiences. The most valuable part involves each person exploring and being aware of what triggers feelings of hope for them.

✣ Make it your story

A spiritual toolbox can help you maintain hope in the face of grief, despair or disappointment. This is a list of things and activities that help buoy your spirits when adversity metaphorically slams you to the ground. You can think of the tools as the equivalent of a security blanket or beloved stuffed animal that calms your nerves and provides a sense of wellbeing.

The creation of a spiritual toolbox is best done in good times. Crises and the companying stress adversely affect cognitive thinking, making it difficult to think clearly. With a pre-packed toolbox, you have options at your fingertips; things you have already tested that you know provide solace. Through trial and error, you will see how much relief each tool provides. It is good to have a variety of options, because no one tool will work in every situation. In addition to the suggestions mentioned in the essay, you can also try: knitting, coloring, journaling, hugs, and gardening.

Make a list of what you will put in your spiritual toolbox.

Tapping into the Power of Music

IMAGINE A FORCE SO POWERFUL it can calm wild animals, yet so gentle it can mend a broken heart; a force that reduces stress, increases creativity, and enhances learning. What is this magical force? Music.

Whether you sing, play an instrument, or just enjoy listening to music, you have probably experienced the powerful connection between songs and significant life events. It's as if music leaves an emotional residue in our brains. All it takes is a few notes from certain songs to trigger mental screenings of past experiences.

Songs are reminders of lost loves, summer vacations, and major life transitions. Familiar songs, like "Happy Birthday," are so ingrained in people's psyches that some stroke victims who have lost their ability to speak can still sing them. Music therapists and speech pathologists use a therapeutic process called "melodic intonation" therapy to help patients with communication disorders caused by brain damage. Using rhythmic patterns, intonations, and patients' subconscious reservoir of songs, therapists stimulate activity in multiple areas of the brain in an effort to help restore speech. Patients start by singing sentences. Slowly, the singsong rhythm is reduced and the sentences move closer to regular speech patterns.

Hospitals worldwide are harnessing the power of music by allowing surgical patients to listen to their choice of music in operating rooms. Even though patients aren't consciously aware of the music during surgery, it affects them on a subliminal level by helping to slow down their breathing and creating a sedative response that allows doctors to reduce the use of anesthesia. After surgery, music aids the healing process by stimulating the release of endorphins, the body's natural painkillers, and reducing the need for chemical painkillers.

Music also helps stimulate creativity, aids learning, and improves spatial intelligence. Researchers at the University of California Irvine discovered that music improves concentration and enhances our ability to make intuitive leaps. By activating both the creative right brain and the more logical left brain, music enables us to find more creative solutions to our problems and tasks. Board-certified music therapists use music to help people with addictions, anger management, behavior problems, eating disorders, and self-esteem issues.

Chris James, founder of the International School of Sacred Sound, is dedicated to finding ways that the healing power of music can recreate harmony within people, between people, and between people and the planet. James has found that self-generated sounds, whether it is playing an instrument or singing, has an immediate effect on our body and our consciousness. Off-key singers will be happy to learn that he believes the intent behind one's singing is more important than the quality of the singing. This means amateurs and professional singers are on equal ground when it comes to using their voices for healing.

In addition to singing and chanting, James also stresses the power of listening. "I think it's a mistake to measure sound and music solely by what we put out, what we broadcast, what we play, and what we say or sing. We receive sound through our skin, through our bones, through air conduction, and perhaps subtly in other ways. I believe there is great value in learning how each individual actually receives sound."

To appreciate how the human body responds to sound, we first need to understand that the atoms making up our bodies are mostly empty space. With or without discernible environmental sounds, our atoms are in a constant state of oscillation. When sounds are introduced to the environment, the atoms change their vibrational frequency in accordance with the sound's frequency. The energy of these new frequencies alters our breath, pulse, blood pressure, muscle tension, skin temperature, and other internal rhythms.

We can get a visual image of how sound affects the human body by picturing grains of sand on a drumhead. Tap on a drum and the sand dances across the drumhead. Similarly, the vibrations of music and sound create a dance through our bodies' cells, tissues, and organs.

Although musical preferences affect the results one gets from listening to specific music, there are general beliefs about which types of music are most helpful. According to these guidelines, Mozart is one of the best composers to listen to when studying. Gregorian chants are relaxing, uplifting, and beneficial to our physical, mental, and spiritual well being. On both mental and spiritual levels, the classical guitar lifts one into a higher realm of consciousness. Because jazz structurally moves into chaos and from chaos creates order, it is the optimal music to listen to when grappling with issues that do not lend themselves to simple linear solutions.

Not everyone agrees with these musical prescriptions. Don Campbell, author of *The Mozart Effect* and founder of the Institute for Music, Health, and Education in Boulder, Colorado, died in 2012, but his work remains relevant. Campbell recounted a study done at a Dallas burn clinic with children that had severe burns. "Playing my CD, *Crystal Meditations*, increased the pain," he said. "However, playing Michael Jackson, rock music, or rap music decreased the pain." For this reason, it is worth experimenting with different types of tunes, including music from other countries, to learn what kinds of music works best for each individual. Whatever music we choose, like a potter shaping clay, the sound will sculpt us both inside and outside.

☙ Make it your story

Experiment with the healing power of your voice using these three vocal exercises:

1. Tone the vowels a, e, i, o, u—Unlike singing, toning has no a melody or rhythm. It involves holding the vocal sound of a single vowel for an extended period of time. Toning each vowel balances the physical body and the chakras. How long and loud you tone a vowel is up to you.

2. *Chant "Om" — This sacred sound is often called the cosmic sound of the universe. Use a simple melody for the chant. Repeatedly chanting "Om" brings the body, mind, and spirit into alignment.*

3. *Sing the* Do, Re, Mi *song from the movie* The Sound of Music. *Repeat this song three to four times and its rhythm will activate the energy in the spine and balance all the chakras.*

Practice daily musical exercises. Try out different ways you can incorporate music into your day by singing, playing an instrument, or listening to music. Notice what kind of music makes you feel happy, energized, creative, or relaxed. Look for ways to add more music into your life.

Jury Duty

WHEN THE JURY SUMMONS ARRIVED in the mail, I silently cheered. Unlike many people, I looked forward to serving on a jury. Being self-employed, I could have gotten excused from duty. But my writer-self saw it as an opportunity to experience a slice of life outside my normal day-to-day existence.

On the appointed date, I took an hour and a half bus ride to the regional courthouse in Kent, almost 20-miles south of my home. Although the journey required me to wake up two hours earlier than usual, there were perks. The bus meandered through areas around Puget Sound that were unfamiliar to me. Passing the back of industrial warehouses painted with several twelve-foot murals, I marveled at the artists' ingenuity. Farther along, I passed the Green River and caught peek-a-boo views of Mount Rainier.

After checking in with the jury office at 8:30 a.m., I took a seat in a blue flowered chair in the jury room and, along with 155 other potential jurors, waited quietly. Finally, an hour later, a judge arrived, delivered a welcoming speech, and played a video about how to be a good juror. Then a clerk instructed us to say hello to the person next to us.

As everyone introduced themselves to their neighbors, the room filled with chatter. To my left, I met Jody, electronic parts distributor, and to my right, Kat, an office manager.

At 11:30 a.m. the clerk reappeared and informed us that the attorneys were still not ready to interview prospective jurors. Instead of waiting until noon, she told us to take a 90-minute lunch break. Jody, Kat, and I decided to eat together at the mall across the street.

It was a glorious sunny day, the first after many days of cold, overcast weather. After spending our morning confined to the jury room, we unanimously chose an outdoor cafe. Once we had ordered lunch, the conversation turned toward our day's experience as jurors.

Jody was beside herself with fidgety energy. Angry about the hours of seemingly fruitless waiting, she called the time spent in the jury room a colossal waste of time. There were piles of work on her desk and sitting idly was driving her nuts.

Kat gushed about how much she loved jury duty. She enjoyed the break from work, undisturbed reading time, a long lunch break, and basking in the sunshine. In fact, Kat was so jubilant she could easily have been mistaken as a person on vacation.

As for me, I was completely absorbed in all aspects of my jury experience. A confirmed people watcher, I could not ask for better surroundings than the jury room. The 155 jurors spanned the age spectrum, from early 20s to late 60s. A rainbow of skin hues suggested a broad cross-section of cultures and races.

I enjoyed watching a cluster of people begin the day with their eyes locked on their laptops, who, as the morning wore on, began talking to each other more than keyboarding. All around, I saw women who entered the room alone chatting with their neighbors. Most of the men ignored their seatmates. The younger and older men alike focused on their cell phones or other electronic devices.

Mulling over what I was seeing in the jury room, plus Jody and Kat's comments, I was reminded of a Carlos Castaneda quote: "The trick is in what one emphasizes. Either we make ourselves miserable, or we make ourselves happy. The amount of work is the same."

All 155 of us were taken away from our everyday routines and dropped into the same situation. Yet, responses to the summons and hours of waiting varied greatly. A flexible mindset was a key ingredient for enjoying the experience. In many ways, our stints at jury duty were a microcosm of everyday life. The saving grace, when we are stuck in situations we can't change, is often a shift of attitude.

❧ Make it your story

Although we usually think outside forces have the power to make us happy or sad, it is really an inside job. Our emotional reality is more dependent on our attitude then it is on anything outside of us. If it rained on our picnic or our boss yelled at us, we can't change the reality of what happened. Our power is in choosing how we are going to react. Dwelling on the negative reinforces downbeat thinking. Instead, we can focus our thoughts on what can be learned from the experience to make sure it doesn't happen again. This is not naive thinking. It is acknowledging that something went wrong and, instead of wallowing in negative self-talk, using the situation as a learning experience.

One way to keep your positive attitude in good working order is to find something to do every day that you enjoy and that makes you feel good about yourself. That way you always have a positive in your day to focus on. The triad of gratitude, curiosity, and humor can also work wonders on staving off negativity. Individually or together, they create magical potions for eradicating bad moods.

His Holiness the Dalai Lama

A STRING OF GRAY SEPTEMBER DAYS in Seattle was finally broken by a glorious sunny afternoon. Unfortunately, my bi-monthly writers critique group's meeting began just as the sun broke through the clouds. Straining to keep my mind focused on writing, I kept glancing out the second-story windows at the sapphire sky.

As soon as the two-and-a-half-hour meeting adjourned, I bolted outside for a stroll around the Capitol Hill neighborhood. Walking by Victorian-style houses, I passed sunflowers with their faces turned towards the sun, a backyard gardener picking juicy red tomatoes, and a floppy-eared mutt lounging in the shade. After working up a sweat trekking up and down the hilly section of town, I stopped in a local food co-op for a cool drink. At the checkout counter, I saw His Holiness the Dalai Lama, with a pensive smile, on the cover of a magazine. Below his photograph were the words "Contemplating Anger, Cultivating Peace." Picking up the magazine, I looked at the price, and then counted the change in my pocket. Darn, I thought, I didn't have enough money to cover the cost. Maybe, I thought, the public library would have that issue.

On my 20-mile drive home through Seattle's ubiquitous traffic congestion, the Dalai Lama's face kept flashing across my mind. Ever since I had heard him give a talk in Portland, Oregon, I had been partial to his message about personal disarmament: that each person needs to develop inner peace before there can be world peace. One of my spiritual practices was applying that principle to my daily interactions.

By the next day, I had convinced myself that I had to have my own copy of the magazine; a library loan would not suffice. Even though Seattle's traffic put my teeth on edge, I manufactured an errand near the food co-op. On the freeway, I tap-danced on the brakes as I inched my way through a river of brake lights.

I purchased a few items at the co-op, grabbed a copy of the magazine, and then checked out. As the cashier bagged my groceries, we chatted about the newest set of condos going in up the street.

Brake tapping my way back home, I tried to keep a positive attitude. After all, I had His Holiness riding along with me in a brown paper bag on my passenger seat.

Back home, I looked forward to kicking back in a comfortable chair and reading His Holiness' wise words. Emptying the bag, I found my three organic apples, a package of firm tofu, and a bag of animal crackers, but no magazine. I dashed out to search the car and found nothing under the seats or in the trunk. No magazine.

The cashier had neglected to put my magazine in the bag. Her oversight meant I had endured bumper-to-bumper traffic for naught. Even if I could prove that I purchased the magazine, it would still require another round-trip drive through gridlock traffic to pick it up.

In an instant, the calmness I gained through my morning spiritual practice of prayer and meditation vaporized. I transformed into a modified version of The Incredible Hulk, the Marvel comic book character who undergoes a transmogrification and morphs into a seven-foot-tall green monster when under stress. It only took a millisecond for me to shift from calm to livid.

I called the cashier every unpleasant name I could think of, plus a few I created on the spot. Thankfully, no one was home to hear me rant about the long trek it took to purchase the blankety-blank magazine.

Lost in my tirade, it took a full minute before I could see the craziness of my behavior. I purchased the magazine to read the Dalai Lama's sage words about personal peace, yet there I was ready to punch out the cashier for her minor mental slip.

Halting my rant, I reached for a bottle of calming lavender aromatherapy and took a dozen deep cleansing whiffs. Then I said a prayer for the cashier and one for myself. With my insides still quaking, I called the store and asked how I could get a copy of the magazine I had purchased. No problem, the manager told me, just stop in before the cashier gets off work and she'll have it ready for you.

Ah yes, no problem for them, I thought. But I had to make another trip across town.

With the car radio station set to my favorite sing-along channel, I headed back to the store. Singing all the way there kept any leftover emotional demons at bay. Once I reached the co-op's neighborhood it took only a couple of minutes to park and run into the store. As an antidote to my earlier rant, I made a point of being polite and gracious to the cashier.

The Dalai Lama's smiling face confronted me as I drove home. I could almost hear him chuckling. It is one thing to have peaceful thoughts in peaceful times and another to hold onto the feeling of grace when faced with aggravation. Mulling over my earlier emotional explosion, I was reminded of a story the Dalai Lama often tells about a Tibetan monk who spent eighteen years in a Chinese gulag or prison. After his release, he told the Dalai Lama that on a few occasions he faced danger. "What kind of danger?" His Holiness asked. The monk replied that on a few occasions he faced the danger of losing compassion toward his Chinese jailers.

If that monk could forgive the Chinese for eighteen years of imprisonment, I could certainly forgive the cashier for her memory lapse. And forgive myself for not noticing her slipup.

As a reminder to practice personal disarmament, I have kept the magazine on my desk. Every day for two years I saw the picture of His Holiness the Dalai Lama and told myself it is not enough to read sage words; the important part is putting the ideas into action in my daily life.

❧ Make it your story

Maintaining your peace of mind in times of stress takes effort and practice. Here are four ideas to help you succeed:

1. Learn to differentiate between things you do and do not have control over.

In my story I could not change the fact that I arrived home without my magazine. Unfortunately, I could not magically make the magazine appear. The areas I could control were my response to the situation and how I wanted to remedy the situation.

2. Don't punish yourself.

If you lose your cool and have an outburst, like I did, don't waste time berating yourself. There is nothing to gain by making yourself feel worse. Once you recognize that you spinning out of control—stop. Change your behavior and your thoughts by focusing on positive things.

3. Don't assume the changes you've made in your behavior are permanent and unshakable.

You may decide to keep your temper in check, and then explode when life spins out of control. A commitment to making changes in your life is one thing; implementing the changes is another. The process can be very difficult and it takes time. Accept that change can be slow. It may take a few tries (or a lot of tries) before a new behavior sticks.

4. Cherish small successes.

Celebrate the moments when you succeed. Noticing the small wins along the way gives you a feel-good moment and helps build momentum for more wins.

Gratitude

Dolphin Dreams

WHILE OTHER YOUNG GIRLS DREAMT of ballet dancing into the arms of a handsome prince, I dreamt of swimming side by side with my dream companions, dolphins.

My yearning began while writing a school report in fourth grade. As I filled my blue-lined tablet with dolphin facts, my imagination shimmered with the possibility of living like a dolphin. I conjectured mental images of me chasing a boat at 20 knots, holding my breath for 15 minutes as I dove 500 feet down into the depths of the ocean, or better yet, actually becoming a dolphin.

Even then, water was my element of choice. In my memory, there is no time when I did not know how to swim. It was as natural as breathing. Although I could maneuver through the water using several different strokes, my favorite was frog-kicking underwater.

As a child, my dream of becoming a dolphin did not seem that far-fetched. After all, dolphins aren't like fish who breathe in the water. From my reading, I knew they needed air from above the water's surface to survive. Just like when I swam, they had to surface periodically and breathe in fresh air. As conscious breathers, they chose when they would take each breath. On land my breathing was automatic, but in the water, I too chose when to breathe.

Although I grew up in Southern California, just blocks from the ocean, parental rules during my pre-teen years didn't permit me unlimited access to the open waters of the Pacific Ocean. Our backyard swimming pool became my water sanctuary. At age nine, after proving my swimming abilities and assuring my mother I wouldn't drown, she let me swim in the pool by myself.

Night swimming especially enthralled me. Lights imbedded in the pool walls illuminated the water. Reflecting off the blue walls, the water became bluer than blue; heavenly blue.

Many nights I stood in the cool evening air and jumped into the warm, heated water of our pool. After a few laps on the water's surface, I switched to my passion, underwater swimming. Taking a deep breath, I filled my lungs and dove under the surface. Bubbles, reminiscent of the effervescent ocean froth dolphins play in, filled my wake.

Then I switched it up and dove to the bottom of the pool, where I stayed underwater until my air ran out and my lungs were deflated, empty. Sometimes I held my breath so long; there was a slight pain in my chest as my lungs hungered for air.

A sensuous, liberating life opened up for me under the water. At times, I sat cross-legged on the bottom of the pool, casually pretending it was my natural world. Other times I closed my eyes and rolled and spun. Spinning like a toy top gone wild, I focused on my one wish, that when I opened my eyes I would be a dolphin swimming in the open sea with a pod of companions by my side.

I even dreamt up an imaginary way to communicate with my water friends, the dolphins. I was too far away from dolphins to tap into their sophisticated sonar transmissions. Besides, that skill was beyond this two-legged's abilities. But maybe, I thought, I could use water to send them messages. In my mind, I filled my underwater world with a cappella singing and spoken words, then imagined the pool water, saturated with my messages, evaporating in the California sun. In my imagination, I saw the message-filled water becoming raindrops and falling into the Hawaiian waters where dolphins swam. If I couldn't be a dolphin, I wanted to believe I could at least communicate with them.

Forty years after writing that school report, I fulfilled my life fantasy of swimming with the dolphins at a weeklong dolphin seminar on the Big Island in Hawaii.

At Honokohau Harbor, two and a half miles north of Kailua-Kona, I met the boat's guide, who went by the name Captain, and a group of swimming mates onboard a 27-foot Zodiac. The Zodiac was a large rubber boat with two huge motors fastened on the back. It had open sides and a roof rack filled with life jackets.

Within thirty minutes of leaving the harbor, we saw dozens of dolphins swimming on both sides of the boat. Captain slowed the boat to match the pace of the dolphins as they gracefully arched in and out of the water. We stopped a hundred feet offshore in a small bay, Kealakekua Bay, a well-known hangout for local dolphin pods.

In preparation for my swim, I zipped up my shorty wetsuit and pulled on my mask, snorkel, and fins. Sitting on the rim of the boat, I listened as Captain went over the rules one more time. Finally, the other swimmers and I jumped into the water. Pandemonium prevailed as we spread out away from the boat, each looking for dolphins to play with.

Breathing in the salt-laced air, I glanced around until I found a pod of dolphins. Knowing wild dolphins can live for 50 years, I was hoping one or two of this group was alive when I was in grade school. I quickly flutter-kicked within a few feet and called out. "Did you get my messages? The ones I sent oh so many years ago?" Two dolphins carrying scars along their backs from years at sea turned their heads my way and smiled. My heart heard them answer, "Yes."

⚘ Make it your story

The secret of making dreams come true
can be summarized in four C's.
They are Curiosity, Confidence, Courage, and Constancy;
and the greatest of these is Confidence.
—Walt Disney

To make your dreams come true, start by declaring what you want. Don't worry about picking your one and only true dream. As you progress toward your goal, stay curious and flexible. Take small steps and pay attention to shifts in your plan. Maybe you thought about being a freelance life coach and along the way you realize your strengths and lifestyle are better suited to 9-5 job with healthcare benefits and a retirement plan. Or you might set out to be a book author and discover that you enjoy short piece work more than long projects. Dreams are meant to be fine-tuned as you move forward along your path.

"Fake it till you make it." Even if you lack confidence, act as if you have it. Create mental images of yourself doing a scary task with ease and grace. The stronger your belief in yourself, the more capable you will act. Start small and work your way up to big actions.

Fear can be a stumbling block for any dream. Instead of giving in or becoming immobilized, acknowledge the fear. Then apply courage. Ask yourself what is worse, stepping outside your comfort zone to pursue your dream or giving up on your dream and yourself?

If things don't go the way you had hoped, sidestep the "woe is me" syndrome. Instead take time to review your dream. Is it still what you want? Do you want to make adjustments or totally rewrite your dream? Whatever you chose, don't panic. Even if you put a lot of time and energy into something that did not work out the way you wanted it to, you learned valuable lessons. Use what you have learned to revamp your path to success.

If you need inspiration, look to other's success stories. Reading stories about other people's achievements can be reassuring and inspiring.

A Time to Give, a Time to Stay Home

AT FIRST GLANCE, MY ADDICTION LOOKED BENIGN. I was not physically hurting anyone with my behavior and what I did was not only legal, it was encouraged. I was a volunteer-aholic, also known as a do-gooder or someone who works for no pay.

I volunteered at my kids' schools, church, political campaigns, and umpteen causes, including environmental, community, and human rights. My volunteer positions have run the gamut from chairperson to classroom aid to general gofer. In my quest to be helpful, I had attended as many as six volunteer meetings in a single week and still yearned to do more.

My need to volunteer dates back to my parents. By example, if not intent, they raised me to be a volunteer. My dad was a council member and mayor of my hometown. My mom served her stint as president of a children's hospital auxiliary and spend years volunteering for her kids' schools and scouting troops.

I began volunteering in third grade as caretaker of the kindergarten's rabbit. In junior high school, I helped fourth graders learn to read. By high school, I had entered the political field and stuffed envelopes for a presidential campaign. College in the 1970s was full of political movements happy to help my volunteer spirit bloom. But it was parenthood that sent me over the top. Adding school volunteering to an already bursting agenda of meetings took me into the danger zone. I no longer volunteered a few weeks out of the month. Instead, I was volunteering every week, sometimes several times a week and other times several times in one day.

My volunteerism probably would have gone unchecked, if it weren't for a casual comment made by another mom. A group of moms and I were having coffee (after a meeting, of course). It was our third school meeting that week, and the conversation easily turned to our other volunteer work. Soon we were comparing schedules. One woman lamented the fact that we spend so much time in meetings, doing things for our kids, that we had little time to be at home with our children.

While charitable work is a noble obsession, I began to question my priorities. Do the world's needs outweigh my family's desire to have me stay home more nights than I am out? Is there a balance between saving the world and satisfying my family?

As I thought back on the past week, the truth of her statement knocked me off my do-gooder's pedestal. I was spending only a few hours a week with my family, most of it at the dinner table. After dinner, I went to meetings and didn't return home until the kids were in bed.

My family had complained about my compulsive volunteering for years, saying I gave more to others than I gave to them. Although my intentions to give back to organizations that helped my family and me were good, I knew I had gone too far. Spurred on by my long-standing dislike for people who take but don't give back, I allowed a virtuous pastime to turn into an addiction. The facts were inked in on my calendar. Although my kids' elementary school required parents to volunteer ten hours a month, I had penned in 40-plus hours of commitments for one month alone. Adding in my other causes, I could see why the calendar's boxes for each date were never big enough to hold all my activities.

Slowly, with my family reminding me that it was okay to say "No," I began to change. How much I changed depends on whom you talk to. One night when I told my family I was enjoying life as a reformed volunteer, they quickly counted off my four volunteer positions. Only slightly deflated, I pointed out that I no longer attended weekly committee meetings. I even had an occasional week with no outside commitments.

✂ Make it your story

How do you allocate time? Do your family, friends and work get equal dibs on your 24 hours? Is there a slice of your day left over for alone time?

Create a visual image of how you spend your time using a pie chart. First, draw a circle. Then make a pie wedge for each key area of your life. These can include chores, commuting, family time, physical activity, relaxing, socializing, working, volunteering, or whatever else fills your days. Make thin slices for areas that are allotted a little time, and big slices for areas that take up a lot of your time. If you want, jot down the percentage of time each area receives.

After looking at your finished pie chart, explore the balance (or lack of balance) in your life. If there are changes you would like to make in how you use your time, write out an action plan. Then list what steps you can take to make those changes occur.

Hidden in Diapers

PIVOTAL MOMENTS ARE TIMES IN MY LIFE when my world shifted off its axis. Many of these events, such as childbirth, marriage, and career changes had elements of anticipation, preparation, and expected periods of adjustment. Although the ripple effects—how the event affected every corner of my life— usually came as a surprise, the core event was known in advance.

Other life-changing moments were more covert. Like undercover agents, they moved in without drawing attention to themselves. Their outward appearance offered no hints that normal life was about to take a detour . . . forever.

The birth of my first child was an expected pivotal moment. Like most new parents, I experienced a huge rift between life before baby and life after baby. Every aspect of my daily life shifted. While many of the changes were expected (less sleep and volumes of crying), a few of them took me by surprise (overwhelming love and my momma bear determination to protect her).

By the time I had two kids, ages five and two, I was living in the moment, but not in any Zen sense of the phase. It was more like riding an errant wind, being tossed from one mini-crisis to another. As each problem arose, such as figuring out how to calm a colicky-teething baby or forgetting to buy food for a dinner party, I focused fully on the task at hand. Potential problems lurking around the corner had to wait their turn. There was precious little routine in my daily life.

The one reoccurring event I could count on happened every Tuesday when a stranger and I made our weekly exchange. I dumped a bag of stinky, soiled cloth diapers on my front porch. An anonymous delivery driver for a cloth diaper service replaced my skunk-perfumed deposit with a week's supply of clean, fresh-smelling diapers.

Once a month, a copy of the diaper service's newspaper came nested in the pile of 90 newly delivered cotton diapers. The arrival of this newsletter filled with articles written by and for parents, was like having a good friend over for coffee. As I read about sleepless nights, cooking with a babe in arms and toddler around the legs, and other people's playgroup fiascos, I felt understood and comforted by the writers' words.

The weekly diaper routine continued month after month, year after year. Except for a brief diaper-free hiatus between my first and second child, there were no changes and no surprises, just dependable service. In the winter of 1988, there was no fortune cookie clue telling me my life was about to change.

Then it happened. One day, as I perused a new issue of the diaper service's newspaper, I found a short, four-line announcement for a moms' writing group. "Babies welcome," the ad read. With no need to track down a daytime babysitter, I decided to drop in and check out the other moms' writings. As a closet-writer who had not written in years, I had no intention of sharing my paltry compositions.

I arrived at the writers' meeting late and unshowered, with my two disheveled kids in tow. Unstrapping my kids from their car seats, I fantasized about the scene inside the white 1940s bungalow. I pictured moms sitting around a kitchen table eating coffeecake and sharing short stories they wrote for their own amusement.

Wrong. It turned out to be a meeting of high-powered-women/mothers/ writers who juggled parenting and household duties with writing articles, hitting publishing deadlines, and communicating with editors. And, from what I could surmise, they did it all better than I managed two kids, a house, and zero writing. The women wowed me. I wanted to rub up against them until a magical transference occurred and gifted me with their time-management skills.

The pleasure of being around six women dynamos compelled me to attend their monthly meetings. Time after time, I watched in awe as they helped each other fine-tune sterling pieces of writing. When asked about my lack of submissions, I crossed my fingers behind my back and made up excuses. I never told them the truth, that I had never written anything for publication.

Finally, out of guilt, I gave myself an ultimatum. If I was going to continue attending the writers' meetings, I had to try writing and submitting an article for publication.

Breaking a cardinal writing rule (never call editors), I telephoned the editor for the diaper service newsletter. When I asked about upcoming topics, she said she was looking for a piece about picky eaters. I knew right away that was going to be my topic. My oldest child was a champion in that department.

After setting up my old electric typewriter on the dining room table, I wrote my essay using my high school hunt-and-peck typing style. Then I cut up the pages with scissors and rearranged the paragraphs. After going through that process a dozen times, I glued down the final paragraphs and took the essay to a professional typist.

A few weeks after dropping off my finished piece with the editor, I got a call saying my essay would be published. Hanging up the phone, I danced in the backyard, hooting and hollering in excitement. For payment, I received one free month of cloth diapers. But the bigger reward came a month later when I saw my name under the article's title.

It only took one byline and I was hooked. Like an addict, I needed a steady flow of fixes. My drug of choice was the rush of adrenaline that came with each new byline.

It has been decades since I wrote my first article. My kids are not only out of diapers, they are both adults. In hindsight, I could say the pivotal moment that spun my career path toward writing was the day I read that tiny ad in the diaper service's newspaper. Or maybe, the turning point was set in motion when I chose cloth diapers over disposable diapers. Either way, it was a small act with big consequences.

✐ Make it your story

Small actions can have big effects. Dale Carnegie's book, How to Win Friends and Influence People, *originally started with a few notes on a piece of paper and short talk. He turned his talk into a book that has now sold more than 15 million copies.*

Many of we have had experiences where we were delayed leaving our house and thereby missed a car accident on our route. After 9/11, many people reported missing their train and not arriving for their jobs in the Twin Towers until after the tragedy. Sometimes a small mishap (spilling coffee on a white blouse or needing to stop and change a dirty diaper) turns out to be the best thing that could have happened to us.

Think of the times small actions/decisions in your life that have had big consequences. Have you ever taken a small step in one direction, only to look back and see that it changed your life's course?

A Meditation on Chocolate

CHOCOLATE PLAYED AN INTRICATE ROLE in my childhood. I was blessed to live within walking distance of a candy store that made scrumptious hand-dipped chocolates. Weekly outings to the store left me with an assortment of chocolate-coated memories.

Each week on allowance day, I made a beeline down to the Jo's Candy Cottage. Inside, the aroma of chocolate was so thick it saturated the air. Staring wide-eyed into display cases filled with assorted butter creams, golden caramels, almond bark, hunks of pure chocolate, and more, I fretted over my many choices.

Often, I bought a sizable chunk of dark semi-sweet chocolate, large enough to fill my palm, held it up to my nose, and breathed in its fragrance. After that came the first bite. Letting my teeth sink into the dense delight, I allowed the smooth chocolate to coat my mouth, saturate my taste buds. My mental chatter melted along with the chocolate and I slipped into a Zen-like moment.

My mind entered a stillpoint similar to the space between breaths, only expanded. On the inhale, my abdomen swelled, pushing the concept of time outside of my awareness. Exhaling I tuned into my body, feeling an aliveness, a joyful quivering, in my cells.

In the time it would take to sing "Happy Birthday," chocolate-induced endorphins, commonly known as the body's "feel good" chemical and nature's pain killer, begin soaring through me. The endorphins worked to help relieve minor pain, slow and deepen my breathing, and produce a feeling of well-being.

My love of chocolate has continued beyond childhood. In my thirties, I started entering and winning chocolate competitions with entries of orange chocolate truffles, caramel-walnut-cheesecake brownies, mousse-filled red velvet cupcakes, and many more. I perfected several recipes in my dreams. While I slept, my inner baker created different versions of that year's dessert entry, altering the ingredients, measurements, and cooking time. Once the recipes passed the dreamtime taste test, I created it in real time. Then my family and friends, all of whom were happy to be my guinea pigs, offered critiques and suggestions for perfecting the recipe.

If all of that is not enough reason to justify my love of chocolate, recent research done by the National Academy of Sciences shows that my favorite confection is also good for my heart. Chocolate contains chemicals that help improve circulation and reduce blood pressure. All of these positive consequences give credence to the claim that chocolate is a comfort food.

⚘ Make it your story

Try the following chocolate meditation. You will need a piece of quality chocolate, and a place where you won't be disturbed for three minutes.

- *Break off one square of chocolate.*
- *Holding it in your hands and feel its silky texture as it begins to melt from the warmth of your fingers.*
- *Take a few deep breaths. Smell the aroma of the chocolate.*
- *Pop the square in your mouth.*
- *Indulge your inclination to lick chocolate traces left on your fingers.*

- *Close your eyes and take relaxing deep breaths as you allow the chocolate to melt completely.*
- *Be in the moment, fully experiencing the flavor, texture and sensuality.*
- *Slowly open your eyes and bring your awareness back to your surroundings.*
- *Pause for a moment and enjoy the surge of endorphins.*

After you have tried the chocolate meditation you might be inclined to change the old adage about apples and doctors to, "An ounce of chocolate a day keeps the doctor away."

Be Happy—Be Grateful

If the only prayer you ever say in your whole life is "Thank You," it will be enough.
Meister Eckhart

WHEN YOU EXPERIENCE A NEGATIVE EVENT, how long does it take to bounce back? What about when something wonderful happens in your life? How long do you linger in the happiness? In both situations, your emotions naturally fluctuate toward the more tense side of the emotional scale. But once the spike in emotions dissipates, you invariably will return to your "normal state." This is your happiness baseline.

In a study on the psychology of gratitude, psychologists Michael McCollough and Robert Emmons found that although the ability to release strong emotions (negative or positive) is genetically influenced, it is not fixed. You have the ability to change how long you stay in a funk and how long you ride the wave of happiness. In other words, you have the ability to increase your happiness baseline. The key is gratitude.

The gratitude study divided several hundred participants into three groups. All the groups were told to keep a daily diary. The first group was asked to write down five things for which they were grateful. Group two was instructed to write down five hassles. The third group was not limited to positive or negative events; they were told simply to list any five events.

Study participants who daily wrote out their list of gratitudes increased their happiness baseline by around 25 percent. They bounced back more quickly after experiencing adversity and were able to stay at a higher level of happiness regardless of outside circumstances.

In addition, participants who focused on gratitude reported higher levels of alertness, creativity, enthusiasm, determination, and optimism than those in the other two groups. They experienced less depression and stress, and made more strides toward achieving their personal goals. And that's not all. They also developed a stronger immune system and stronger social relationships than those people who didn't practice gratitude.

I have experienced the power of gratitude in my own life. Several years ago, I learned a daily gratitude practice from a life coach. She suggested that each day I share, with a friend or in writing, these four aspects of my day: what were my expectations for the day; what went right; what went wrong; and what topped my list of gratitudes.

Over the years, this exercise has become a ritual. This simple structure for sharing the day's events allows me to name the many ways I am feeling blessed. The routine of this practice has helped me become more aware of the amazing bounty in my life. Sometimes there are special reasons for being grateful, such as a visit with my adult children, a trip, or a work-related success. But my more frequent gratitudes are more mundane: clean water to drink, a comfortable place to sleep, and the ability to not only fill my stomach, but choose what I want to eat.

Practicing gratitude has made a difference in my life. In years past, I was a bit of a walking storm cloud. Even when something positive happened, I could (and often would) dampen people's enthusiasm by pointing out negative aspects of their joyful news. Since I began my gratitude practice I tend to focus on the positive side of life. This translates into more upbeat thoughts flowing through my mind. When crises occur—and they surely do—I bounce back faster. My happiness baseline has risen to a point where I notice physical changes in my body when negative thoughts start percolating in my mind. I have found that gratitude begets more joy and happiness in my life.

❧ Make it your story

One way to tap into the power of gratitude is to have a daily check in with a friend. Share the four check-in points I listed before: your expectations for the day; what went right; what went wrong; and what is your top gratitude. If you don't want to share with another person, you can write your comments in a gratitude journal.

Sometimes we take our blessings for granted or forget to look at the positive side of something that is not perfect. Here are two approaches for reflecting on gratitude:

- ***Wanting what you have:** This means finding the positive side of life situations, even if they are not exactly how you would like them to be. For instance, if you get a regular paycheck from a job you dislike or find boring, you can focus on friends you have at work, skills you are learning, or what your income allows you to purchase (lodging, food, clothing, or training to find a new job).*

- ***Communicating gratitude:** This involves thanking people who assist you. Wave at drivers who let you into their lane. Thank the grocery clerk for checking your eggs for breakage before putting them in your shopping bag. Smile at the person moving her backpack so you can sit down on the bus. Being generous with thank-yous improves everyone's day.*

Investigate different ways of counting your blessings and expressing your gratitude. Keep what works for you and toss out what doesn't work. Over time you will have a higher happiness baseline and more joy in your heart.

A Wink from God

WHAT'S A COINCIDENCE? For me, it is a conjunction of events that appear to be accidental, yet at the same time feel cosmically planned or arranged. For example, on the first anniversary of 9/11, the New York State Lottery's daily three number pick was 9, 1, 1.

A story from the book *Phenomena: A Book of Wonders* by John Michell and Robert J. M. Rickard reports on an even more bizarre example of coincidence. "Two brothers in Bermuda were killed by the same taxi and driver, carrying the same passenger, while riding on the same moped in the same street, but exactly one year apart."

In his book *The Celestine Prophecy*, James Redfield suggests that paying attention to coincidences will "start you on your path to spiritual truth." Squire Rushnell, writer and television producer, calls coincidences "God

Winks." He believes these seemingly chance events are meant to reassure us as we travel along life's path.

The following message, which came to me while I was deep in meditation, reaffirmed that concept: "No major overall life plan is needed. Go step by step, using coincidences like a trail of breadcrumbs. You will know you are on the right path when you notice serendipitous and coincidental occurrences."

That insight struck home in the summer of 2005, when I took a solo car trip from Seattle to Northern California to attend a spiritual retreat and visit the giant Redwoods. This was before I had a phone with GPS. Having spent most of my life map-challenged, I was concerned about doing my own navigating. That fear soon dissipated when hawks began appearing overhead every time I seriously questioned my bearings. Sometimes a single hawk, other times a pair of hawks, appeared above the road, as if to say, "follow us and you'll do just fine." And I did, allowing the hawks to lead me until I found a landmark or road sign that confirmed my direction. During my two-week adventure, the hawks appeared daily to reassure me. They were divine signposts, escorting me to my destinations.

Coincidences sometimes remind me to trust my intuition. For example, on a recent Sunday I woke up with an overwhelming craving for sweet potatoes. As I read the comics, I daydreamed about sweet potato tacos with grilled onions and spicy avocado cream sauce. Then, turning to the news section, I saw a startling notice. Puget Sound blood centers were down to a one-day supply of blood. Although blood centers are normally closed on Sundays, two centers opened their doors to help curb the crisis. Even though both centers were in unfamiliar neighborhoods, I knew I had to find my way to one of them and donate blood.

Before hopping on the freeway, I stopped at a grocery store and purchased my sweet potatoes. Stashing them in the trunk of my car, I headed to the blood center. After several wrong turns, a stop to call for better directions, and a few more wrong turns, I finally arrived at the center. Inside I found a lobby crowded with donors. The receptionist told me they had initially expected a total of 30 people. By the time I arrived, they had already processed 75 donors.

Ten minutes later, a nurse took me into a room for a pre-donation interview and blood test. For the first time ever, I was rejected due to a low blood iron count. The nurse told me to go home and eat iron-rich foods, such as meat, greens, or sweet potatoes. While disappointed I would not be able to give blood, I was elated that my body intuitively knew I needed iron. Hence, my craving for sweet potatoes.

In his book, *When the Impossible Happens*, psychiatrist Stanislav Grof doesn't discount coincidences; however, he does warn against making decisions based solely on them. Grof recounts stories where people based their choices to date or marry solely on magical coincidences that occurred and not on long-term compatibility. In those cases, the relationships did not hold up over time.

I agree with his point of view. As much as I love "winks from God," it is important to base major life decisions on several different factors, not just coincidences.

Some people would go further than Grof and call my sweet potato story a meaningless happenstance. They might even insist that people are hardwired to tie anomalies together and create meaning. And that way of perceiving life probably works well for them. I choose to interpret unique happenings differently. Instead of pooh-poohing coincidences that tumble into my life, I use them to reinforce my belief in the magical quality of life. For me these kinds of stories are spiritual breadcrumbs that guide me on my life's journey.

✀ Make it your story

As the Greek philosopher Epictetus is quoted as saying, "It's not what happens to you, but how you react to it that matters." You can choose to see the magic in coincidences, dismiss them as accidental occurrences, or take the middle ground and use them as one part of your decision-making process.

Play with different viewpoints: getting caught up in the enchantment of coincidences, only paying attention to what you can explain and using caution to decipher "winks from God." See which way resonates the best with you? Do coincidences provide you with a trail of breadcrumbs that help you clarify your options or resolve specific issues? Or do you find coincidences to be meaningless? Are you more comfortable heeding Grof's warning and adding other factors into your decision-making process?

Rusty's Tomatoes

I AM A TOMATO SNOB. In my estimation, the only tomatoes worth eating are vine-ripened summer tomatoes; no hothouse ones for me. My favorites are homegrown cherry tomatoes plucked off the vine on a hot summer day and immediately popped into my mouth. I love the way my teeth break through the fleshy skin, then sink into the warm juicy center. The sweet taste combined with acidic overtones is heavenly.

The reason I bring up tomatoes is because they played a key role in my introduction to Rusty. My son Spence and I had attended a church brunch to enjoy the company of the congregation and talk with Jane, who had recently arrived in Seattle from Ecuador. Spence planned on studying aboard in Ecuador, and we both hoped Jane could offer some useful advice. The seating arrangements placed my son and me on either side of Jane. With a hall packed tightly with tables, it was necessary to take turns going up to the buffet. Jane and my son's lively conversation about Ecuadorian geography and politics kept us entertained during the long wait.

When it was our table's turn to dish up our food, Jane and Spence broke off their talk mid-sentence. We rose as a group and went up to the buffet. The serving tables were laden with an assortment of homemade quiches, roasted vegetables, fresh fruit salads, and tossed green salads. The smell of oven-roasted potatoes and fresh baked rolls whetted my appetite as I filled my plate and headed back to our table. Soon, the rest of my table companions rejoined me, except Jane. She had gotten sidetracked by other friends and never returned to our table. Although I was surprised and a little miffed that Jane wandered away without an explanation or good-bye, I knew dwelling on my disappointment would ruin the gathering. Instead I turned my attention to the scrumptious food and the other people around the table.

Before I even finished my slice of asparagus quiche, a late-arriving woman with a solid build, steel gray hair, and a hot-red walker came in and took Jane's place. I had seen this middle-aged woman sitting quietly at the back of the church, but had never spoken with her. She introduced herself as Rusty. Because she was unable to walk without assistance, a member of the church prepared a plate of food and brought it to her.

As we chatted, Rusty told me she'd recently been critically ill, but was doing much better. When she noticed tomatoes on my plate, her brown eyes lit up. "Boy, those look good," she commented. I told her I had eaten some and they looked better than they tasted. "That might be, but they sure look good to me. I live in a nursing home and we don't get tomatoes very often." Having relatives who lived in nursing homes, I knew that was true. I offered to get tomatoes for her. At first she declined, but after I repeated my offer, she acquiesced.

Returning to the buffet line with a clear plastic cup, I picked about half a dozen cherry tomatoes out of the salad. Rusty loved them. "I know you don't think they have much taste, but they are a real treat for me," she said.

As she munched on the tomatoes, Rusty and I shared stories about our church's main tenet, meditation, and how it had helped us through serious illnesses. I told her I began meditating when I was temporarily unable to walk, drive, or even hold a book. Since I had often wanted to try meditation, but had never found the time, I decided my physical condition provided me with the perfect opportunity to establish a practice. Years later, I was still hooked.

Rusty said that even when she was very ill, she always sat in her meditation spot. "I might not actually meditate, but I always show up and see what happens." She told me meditation was the highlight of her days. "It is how I stay in touch with the Divine."

Delighted to have met Rusty, I was looking forward to talking with her after the next Sunday's church service. Smiling to myself, I half hoped Rusty would think of me as "the tomato lady."

Two days later, Jane emailed me to say she'd enjoyed meeting Spence and to apologize for wandering away from our table. When I told her about Rusty taking her place at the table, she wrote back saying Rusty had died the day after the brunch. In shock, I reread her email half a dozen times.

Unwilling to believe Rusty was dead, I called the church and learned Rusty had been rushed to the hospital the day after the gathering and had died. I felt simultaneously saddened and blessed when I heard about Rusty's passing. The grief was for Rusty and the lost opportunity to develop a friendship. The poignancy of our brief time together felt like a blessing.

The incident at the church brunch was a prime example of me initially thinking something unpleasant had happened, when in fact, life was giving me a gift. My job was to be open to receiving it. If Jane had not abandoned our table, I never would have gotten to spend one of Rusty's last hours with her. Nor would I have discovered how meditation helped her in times of health and illness. If I had spiraled into a funk when Jane vacated her chair, I could easily have ignored Rusty's presence and missed the opportunity to present her with those last tomatoes. The day required me to keep a positive attitude for it to unfold the way it did.

✂ Make it your story

When I enter a situation with a set agenda and am unwilling to accept any alternative outcomes, I close myself off from serendipitous moments. By pre-determining how things are going to happen, I miss the magical things happening right in front of me.

What's your typical response when plans change? Do you embrace spontaneous adjustments or are you threatened by change? Try substituting your typical way of doing an activity for something new, such as changing where you get your morning coffee or carpooling instead of driving solo. How does the shift influence your outcome? Did implementing a substitution spark new ideas or insights?

Pick one day to deliberately pay attention to the big and small things happening during your day and how you react. Notice what occurs in the periphery of your main activities. As you commute to work, notice how many green lights you get and how many red lights. Do you notice a difference in your body or thoughts when the light is red instead of green? Once the feeling or thought comes into your awareness, do you hold on to it or let it go?

Is there anything out of the ordinary happening? Is there road work; a detour; people dressed in unusual outfits; or a rainbow in the sky?

Pay attention to how you respond when something goes awry. Can you see the positive aspects of the change? Do you get angry?

Write down key observations. Would you like to be more observant throughout your day? Are you satisfied with how you respond to unexpected events? Jot down ideas that can help you make desired changes.

Adrenaline Junkie

THE FREIGHT TRAIN PULLED OUT of the Interbay railyard and followed the tracks north through a ravine, then across the Lake Washington Ship Canal along an old drawbridge. From the doorway of a boxcar, I saw hundreds of sailboat masts at Shilshole Bay Marina. Miles of Puget Sound stretched out to the horizon. With nothing blocking my view, it was like watching a wide-screened movie from the first row. As the boxcar swayed beneath my feet and the musical clickety-clack of the steel wheels on the track played a melody for my ears, I basked in the wonder of my childhood fantasy coming true.

Growing up across the street from railroad tracks, I spent my childhood watching freight trains make evening runs through my hometown in California and dreaming about riding the rails. I loved everything about the freight trains: their dusty exteriors, the smell of hot metal as the brakes hissed to a stop, the clanking noises boxcars made when coupled or uncoupled, and the loud whooo whooo of the whistle. During my formative years, train sounds serenaded me to sleep.

My first teaching job after graduation from college was with at a school for children with disabilities, located adjacent to a freight yard. Every morning on my way to work, I passed lines of freight trains awaiting journeys to distant places. Sounds from the freight yard pierced my classroom walls and revived my yearning to ride the rails.

Although I had often dreamt about hopping a train, as a girl it never seemed possible. Then I talked with a fellow teacher, Sage. She was the first woman rail rider I had ever met. When she regaled me with stories about her weekend rail adventures, the idea of hopping a freight train changed from a childhood fantasy to burning desire. After talking to Sage, I decided if she could do it, so could I. The combination of a racing heart, tangible fear, and an adrenaline boost were big selling points.

My addiction to adrenaline rushes started as a teenager when I slipped a Hershey bar into my pocket at the local five-and-ten cent store and felt my heart do flip-flops as I slunk out the door. In college, friends and I raced side by side down the freeway. With my foot pressed against the gas pedal, I fed off the simultaneous thrill of speeding and the fear of a collision. Hitchhiking across Europe after graduating from college, I thrived on daily doses of electrifying anxiety and fear.

The common denominator between all these adventures was adrenaline rushes. Engaging in risky activities filled my body with intense, gripping energy that initially jazzed me up, but then dropped me into a pit of exhaustion. The only way back up was another shot of heart-pounding adrenaline.

Before my first rail trip, Sage and I reviewed the options and decided it would be best to start with a short 230-mile jaunt between Seattle and Spokane. If all went well, we'd leave Friday and be back at work on Monday. For me, the thought of joining the ranks of hobos was like being admitted into an exclusive club. Going with Sage added to the excitement.

Although she was about my height, five-six, Sage projected a larger-than-life presence. With her unconventional teaching style and casual attire, Sage was a maverick. Instead of creating a typical classroom setting with rows of desks, she used her workspace to replicate a home-like environment. There she taught adults with disabilities basic survival skills, such as grooming, dressing, and simple household tasks. Due to her charisma and excellent results, the ordinarily cautious administration reluctantly tolerated her unorthodox approach.

At school, Sage consistently wore hiking boots, weathered jeans, and a dark colored tee shirt. A red bandana, laid flat across her forehead and tied in the back, kept her black shoulder length hair pulled back. She cemented her status as workplace rebel when she changed her name from Suzie to Sage and dared anyone to criticize her right to rename herself.

The morning of my first rail ride, Sage was at the freight yard when I arrived. "Good to see you have a sense of time," she said. "Timing is critical. The train may be late, but a hobo better not be. Let's get going. The yard man already told me which train to catch."

Sage swung her backpack, with a sleeping bag bungee-corded to the bottom, over her shoulder and headed toward a line of trains. She scurried between two boxcars like a little kid racing over sawhorses. Suddenly she stopped and turned to face me. "Sorry, I forgot to give you a few pointers. This is one of the most dangerous parts of training. When you move from one track to another, first throw your stuff over the coupling, where the box-cars are connected together, then climb onto the ladder that hangs off the back of the boxcar and drop off the other side."

Her instructions ended with a worrisome caution: "I've seen old-time hobos get caught by a jolt from a car moving when they weren't expecting it. Sent them flying off the train faster than a coyote chasing a jackrabbit."

I followed Sage, my heart pounding in my chest, feeling like a jackrabbit being chased by a wild coyote. Images of being maimed or killed haunted my thoughts as I climbed, with great caution, between the boxcars.

Sage found an empty boxcar and we climbed in. From the inside, it looked like a weather-beaten shed. Looking around the back of the car, Sage found a clump of material she called brake linings. Using it to peg open the door, she said, "Train doors don't open from the inside. If the door closed there'd be no way out."

Setting down our backpacks and sleeping bags on the grimy floor, Sage and I stood in the doorway. Moments later, the train whistle blew and the sound of air hissed down the brake lines. A jolt shuddered through the train and we grabbed hold of the metal handles positioned at each side of the doorway. Beaming with joy, I let out a big whoop. My first rail trip had begun.

Three hours later, I found myself desperately trying to reclaim that feeling of ecstasy. We were stranded in the Cascade Mountain Range, miles from any town. The car we'd been riding in got bumped onto a sidetrack halfway up Stevens Pass. The rest of the train went on without us. A brakeman working at the site told us we would have to wait an hour or so for another train to come through.

There we sat, in the middle of a mountain range, with no train in sight and few provisions. The brakeman moved on to his next job, leaving us alone. Sage took a deck of cards out of her pack and began shuffling them. Before playing a few hands of gin rummy, I surveyed the dense evergreen forest and quivered. "Please," I prayed, "don't let there be any wild animals searching for an easy meal."

As we waited, the temperature took a nosedive, along with my mood. I began to question the wisdom of my quest. What was I doing out here surrounded by nothing but forest pretending to be a hobo? When would I stop seeking life-threatening adventures?

After an icy two-hour wait, another freight train stopped to drop off railcars. Our new train had no empty boxcars, so we climbed aboard an open-sided car used to transport automobiles. What our ride lacked in warmth it made up for with spectacular scenery. As the train chugged through the mountains, we passed cascading waterfalls, droopy-topped western hemlock, towering cedars, and grazing deer. The 360-degree view of calendar-perfect scenery brought the smile back to my face. I didn't even mind when cold gusts of wind slapped my face and a late spring snow formed drifts along the metal edges of the car. Wrapping my sleeping bag around my shoulders, I sang "This Land Is Your Land" at the top of my lungs.

Just before twilight turned to night, our train pulled into Wenatchee, a small town on the eastern side of the Cascades. Sage talked the worker at the train depot into letting us sleep in the lobby. After a dinner of peanut butter and jelly sandwiches, we tossed our sleeping bags on the floor and crumpled up our jackets into pillows. Tired as I was from the trip, it still took a while to fall asleep on the hard tile floor.

About five the next morning, the same depot worker woke us up. "A train heading straight through to Spokane leaves in ten minutes," he announced. Gathering our gear, we made a quick bathroom stop and then raced out to the tracks. Luck was on our side. We found an empty boxcar and settled in for the ride.

The train arrived in Spokane around noon. We checked into a cheap motel, then spent the remainder of the day touring the city. Walking around town felt delicious after sitting on hard train floors for two days, plus a night in the train depot.

Rested, we set off on our return trip to Seattle the next morning. We arrived at the Spokane freight yard before seven and found a rail worker willing to point us toward the Seattle bound train.

As we crossed over the first set of railroad tracks, two men with tattered jackets, ripped jeans, and scraggly beards spotted us and started running our way. From a distance, it looked like they both outweighed us by at least a hundred pounds.

Thinking only of escape, we climbed through boxcars, backtracked, and circled around long lines of cars, trying to lead them away from our destination. Once the men were out of sight, we circled back and climbed aboard our train.

Minutes after the freight pulled out of the yard, Sage realized we had mistakenly boarded the wrong train. "Dang! We must have gotten turned around trying to elude those men," she said. "This train is heading south to Pasco, one of the worst freight yards around. It's full of bulls."

"What's a bull?" I stammered.

"Railroad police. They'll toss us in jail if they catch us on this train."

Jail! That was a slap of reality. I could not comprehend why someone would want to put me in jail. The rail jaunt was just for fun. Who was I hurting?

"What's the surprise?" Sage said, sensing my confusion. "You knew before you started that it's illegal to ride the rails."

"Jaywalking is illegal," I replied. "But I don't expect to go to jail for doing it."

For the next hour, Sage stewed in the corner. Saying she needed time to think, she refused further conversation. My heart pounded so loudly it scared me. I longed for something to distract my mind from jail scenes, but all I could see were handcuffs and orange jail jumpsuits.

Sage finally emerged from her corner. "I am furious with those men," she said stomping her foot. "If it weren't for them we'd be heading home. Now we're in deep trouble. Our only hope is to act like first-time riders and hope they let us off with a slap on the wrist. Remember to act remorseful."

After the train stopped in Pasco, we waited a few minutes before jumping out. Knowing there was no way to sneak by the bulls, we adjusted our backpacks and walked toward the station house, a quarter mile down the line.

"Hey, you two. Stop right there. I want to talk to you," a loud voice called out.

As we looked around for a body to go with the voice, a big, burly man with a pig shave came up behind us. With muscles like a wrestler, he looked to be at least six-foot-three and 250 pounds.

"Saw you two jump out of that boxcar," he said, giving us a good looking over. "You going to deny it?"

"Nope," Sage said.

"Well, that's good. You look out of place here. Too clean and well dressed to be regulars. What are young women like you doing on a train?"

"Nothing." Sage replied.

"Real talkers, aren't you?" he barked. "I've a couple of choices here. I could leave you two out here for the old tramps to pick apart. Know how much you're worth to them?" he demanded. "About two bottles of wine. They could roll you easy. You are like damn turtles with those backpacks on. One push and neither of you could get up."

As he continued his rant, I searched my mind for a way out of this mess.

"Maybe I should have the police come get you," he threatened. "What do you think? Heck, you two are so green it hurts me just to think what might happen to you." His voice softened ever so slightly. "What's your story, anyway?"

Seizing the opening, I pleaded our case. "This was our first time riding the rails. If you let us go, I promise we'll never do it again," I said, turning to Sage to get her confirmation. She nodded in agreement and added, "We're teachers with no business being here. Please, let us go."

Without warning, tears gushed from my eyes. They came from fear, but once they started, I realized they might gain us some sympathy.

Taking a step back, the bull said, "OK, I'll give ya'll a break. But just this once. I'll even drive the two of you to the bus station. But, if I ever see you again, I'm going to make sure you get double time in jail. You may not think you were doing any wrong, but riding the rails is illegal. And dangerous. Go home and leave the rails to the tramps." After thanking him for his leniency, we turned and gave each other a hug.

We'd escaped jail time, but the stress from our adventure drained me emotionally and physically. On our way back to Seattle, I was surprised to realize I didn't mind being bumped from the rails to a bus. Although I dared not admit it to Sage, I was happy to be traveling on a safe and dependable mode of transportation.

Of course, the scenery from the bus couldn't compare with that from a freight train. And the adrenaline thrill wasn't there. But that was fine. As much as I loved the feel of the train's gently rocking movement, nostalgia-inducing sound effects, and the breathtaking views, I knew I could never ride the rails again.

Turning to Sage I said, "I think my hobo days are over. Riding the rails requires nerves of steel. Something this weekend taught me I don't have."

"One run in with the bulls is no reason to give up," she responded. "I was just sitting here planning our next rail trip. Maybe we could try a week's excursion south to Oregon or California."

Hearing Sage say she wanted to go on another trip with me was flattering. But I had to be honest with myself. Riding the rails scared the bejeesus out of me.

"There is probably no way you'll understand, Sage, but I need to swear off trains and every other life-threatening adrenaline rush. I have to stop risking my life while I still have a life to live."

"That's just fear talking. In a week or so you'll be craving another adventure."

In a way, Sage was right. Within a week, I wanted an adrenaline fix. For the first time, instead of giving in to my urge, I continued exploring the reasons behind my constant need for thrills.

After months of self-examination and journal writing, I realized my cravings were related to stress and drama. I had a stressful job teaching infants with multiple disabilities. The non-profit organization employing me was always surfing dangerously close to the financial edge. The ratio of children to teachers was high, and resources for equipment and training were low. The only thing that was plentiful was pressure from the administration, parents, and we teachers to perform miracles.

My personal life wasn't much better. I constantly created dating situations filled with drama. The result was emotionally wrenching.

Then, in my free time, I free-based adrenaline by taking unnecessary risks, like riding freight trains. All told, I was living a recipe for disaster. Keeping company with people who lived on the edge, like Sage, kept adrenaline powering through my veins. Tension had become so commonplace for me that I had forgotten how stress-free living felt.

Knowing that some stress was unavoidable, I began looking for benign activities and challenges that would satisfy my need for excitement. In place of my high-risk adventures, I substituted white-knuckle rides at amusement parks and public speaking. After marrying and giving birth to my two children, I realized their high fevers, grabs for sharp objects, and dashes into the street guaranteed me regular shots of adrenaline.

Even with my new alternative ways to get adrenaline rushes, I still missed the daredevil intensity of my former lifestyle. Then, when I was in my forties, I found something that significantly reduced my craving for adrenalin rushes. It was so counterintuitive I could hardly believe its potency. My remedy was meditation.

The act of sitting and focusing on my breath created new, unfamiliar sensations throughout my body. After twenty minutes of conscious breathing, I felt my inner core fill with feelings of warmth, expansion, and liveliness. As stress melted away, I could almost sense my body's cells waking up to joy.

Meditation was the antithesis of an adrenaline rush. Yet, it had its own magnetism. The more I meditated, the more I wanted the peaceful feeling that came with deep meditation. Floating in a sea of tranquility, I found my stillpoint, an inner balance. From that place, I was in harmony with the world around me, and more importantly, with myself.

As I began meditating on a daily basis, a major shift occurred. I felt truly satisfied living without massive doses of adrenaline. Instead of squeezing stressful situations for all the adrenaline I could get, I found joy in noticing potentially taxing situations and figuring out how I could remain tranquil.

I still keep a few lightweight sources of adrenaline in my life, such as solo travel, public speaking, and roller coasters. But my desire for peace of mind now outweighs my cravings for adrenaline.

✂ Make it your story

As my story illustrates, putting oneself in dangerous situations for the rush of adrenaline can be deadly. It's no surprise that research finds similarities between the brains of drug users and adrenaline-seekers. After all, adrenaline junkies are also addicted to getting a high. The drug of choice differs, but it is still chemically based. When people get scared, their bodies release endorphins and dopamine. And, the more fearful they are, the bigger the release of chemicals they get.

What is your attitude toward adrenaline rushes? Do you generate stress, fear, and anxiety to keep your life exciting?

If you identify as an adrenaline junkie and want to change, look for safe ways to get the same rush. This is called developing a positive addiction. According to Dr. William Glasser, author of the book Positive Addiction, the key elements of a positive addiction are: something noncompetitive that you devote an hour a day to; easy to do without great mental effort; can go it alone; has some type of value to you (physical, mental or spiritual); requires no pressure to excel; offers an escape from self-criticism. Options for positive addictions include, but are not limited to: fitness classes, journaling, meditating, running, and yoga. Whether or not your choice is a part of this list is unimportant. The key is to find an activity that works for you.

Inspiration

Angel at the Wheel

WHEN MY PARTNER BO AND I decided to play hooky from work, I never dreamed our adventure would end in a roadside ditch.

It was Friday, February 1, 2007. With Bo at the wheel, we drove out of Seattle and headed north on Interstate-5. Our destination was the upper Skagit River for a day of eagle watching. This area, located in Washington's North Cascade Mountain Range, boasts one of the largest wintering populations of bald eagles in the lower 48 states. Local newspaper reports claimed 500 of these majestic birds had been spotted along an 11-mile stretch of the river.

Taking the exit to State Route 20, we headed east towards Burlington. The rows of strip malls lining the freeway gave way to small towns, then sweeping views of hills, fields, and farmland, all with a backdrop of evergreens.

Just past eleven, we stopped outside the town of Rockport at the Milepost 100 Rest Stop. Located right next to the Skagit River, the rest stop offers spectacular views of eagles feeding on the chum salmon that return each year to spawn on the river's gravel bars. Unfortunately, we had forgotten our binoculars at home. Using the less-than-ideal zoom settings on our cameras, we managed to spot six large birds flying above a distant hillside. Based on their long wingspans and graceful soaring flight patterns, we identified the birds as eagles. The cottonwoods, alders, and big-leaf maple trees along the banks of the Skagit River were bare of eagles, as well as leaves.

Up the road, we continued our quest at the Marblemount Fish Hatchery. But we were skunked. Supposedly, the eagle watching was the best in decades. Yet, in our two hours of searching, we'd only seen a few raptors, and those from afar.

Reversing direction, we headed west on State Route 20 to find a restaurant. It was well past our normal lunchtime and we were ravenous. Then we noticed a rusty 1940s tow truck parked in an empty field. The lure of getting some unusual photographs overrode our hunger. We pulled off the highway and spent a delightful half hour photographing the truck's orange rust juxtaposed against bare blackberry vines and the cornflower blue sky.

Back in the car, Bo accelerated to the posted 50 mph speed limit. Within minutes, we were back at Milepost 100. Craning my head to look out Bo's window, I hoped to see eagles swooping down to capture salmon. Instead, I saw a man and woman with binoculars and wondered if they were having better luck than we had.

Just then, a bump sounded from beneath the car. Swinging my gaze back to our side of the road, my eyes were drawn to the ground outside my passenger window as our car's front tires crunched the dirt. Frightened, I yelled at Bo, "Stop rubbernecking. Pay attention to the road, not the eagles."

Bo neither responded nor righted the car. Instead, he stared straight ahead; his arms were taut as boards, his hands like vice grips on the steering wheel. From his profile, I saw a determined "nothing will deter me" look on his face.

My brain scrambled to make sense of what was happening. Just two minutes earlier, Bo and I had been talking. Everything was fine. Now he was acting like a robot and driving us into a ditch. What was going on?

As those thoughts raced through my mind, the car tipped at an angle and slid sideways down a three-foot embankment. At the bottom, the car righted itself and came to rest a few feet from a church's driveway and inches from its 4x4 signpost. The car was planted between two metal posts, with wire fence running along the right side of the car.

The instant the car settled, I turned toward Bo, ready to demand an explanation. Instead, I gasped at his white complexion, his head tipped back against the headrest and eyes rolled upward. Grabbing his shoulders, I shook him and yelled. No response.

Panic gripped my mind. "Is this how it ends," I thought. Was my partner of 25 years dead? Fear flooded my chest and I almost stopped breathing. I had heard plenty of stories about people being fine one second and dead the next. Knowing this was a possibility, I tried to suppress my distress and stay focused on my critical task, getting Bo help.

Still unsure if Bo was alive or dead, I sprang into action. I turned off the car's engine, grabbed my cell phone from my purse, and scampered up the embankment. Dashing across the highway, I headed straight for the couple I had seen eagle watching at the rest stop. I needed help dealing with the situation, whatever it turned out to be.

With shaking hands, I dialed 911 while simultaneously screaming, "Help!" It took a few shouts before the couple heard me and turned around. I quickly explained the situation to them as I waited for the emergency switchboard's response.

My inability to answer the dispatcher's first question confirmed my level of confusion. "Where are you?" she asked. "I don't know," I answered. "The place where people watch eagles." Turning to the couple I asked them, "Do you know where we are?" Thankfully, they did. I told the dispatcher my location and explained that my partner had passed out while driving down State Route 20. As she was asking about injuries, I looked over at the car. Bo was standing outside the driver's door.

Cell phone in hand, I sprinted back across the highway. The couple followed close behind. Assured that an aid car was on its way, I turned to Bo and gave him a hug. He said he felt woozy, so with the couple's help, I settled him into the back seat of our car.

Unable to contain my question a second longer, I asked, "What happened?" He said, "I felt a buzz inside my head and thought to myself, I should pull over. Then I passed out."

Weaving the pieces together, I pictured our car coursing down the highway, with Bo passed out and me in panic mode. Who had been driving? Neither of us. How did the car slow down and maneuver itself down an embankment, without flipping? There seemed to be only one explanation, Bo's guardian angel had taken over the wheel.

Not only did the angel get us safely off the road, he positioned the car equal distance between the two metal posts, missed the fence, and avoided colliding with the hefty 4x4 signpost. To flaunt his divine talent, the angel stopped the car in front of the church's driveway so we could return to the highway without the need of a tow truck. But the angel's biggest accomplishment was veering off the right side of the highway. Had the car gone across the highway, it would have run into the three-foot-wide concrete block in front of the rest stop, hit a massive cedar tree, or plunged into the Skagit River.

A few minutes later, we heard a siren. The aid car technicians leapt from their vehicle and rushed over to Bo. They listened to his description of blacking out, checked his vital signs, and completed an extensive checklist. Bo aced all their tests. Uncertain why he'd passed out, the technicians signed off on his care, told him to see his doctor the following day, and sent us on our way.

I took over the driving and, at Bo's request, pulled into the rest stop across the highway. "I need a few minutes to steady my nerves," he said.

Climbing from the car, Bo and I sat down on top of a picnic bench. No longer interested in eagles, we stared blankly in the direction of the river. In halting sentences, we recounted our versions of the incident, marveling at our brush with near disaster.

As I drove home, I kept one eye on the road and the other on Bo. By the time we reached Interstate-5, he kept dozing off. Bo's head drooped up and down so frequently he looked like a bobble-head doll. Worried that his drowsiness was a danger sign, we stopped at an emergency room.

Stepping through a heavy set of double doors, I saw a lobby filled with people waiting to be seen. Then my eyes were drawn to a floor-to-ceiling window showcasing the Cascade Mountain Range. Set against a sapphire blue sky, a shimmering crescent-shaped moon hung between two peaks. At least we could enjoy a good view during our long wait.

We located the check-in desk and joined the line. Barely glancing up from her computer, the receptionist asked Bo the standard question, "What are you here for?" When he responded, "I passed out while driving 50 miles an hour down a highway," her eyes locked on his. Then she skittered into the back room. Within moments she was escorting him to an exam room.

In his efforts to uncover a medical cause for Bo passing out, the ER doctor gave him a physical exam, took an EKG, tested numerous vials of blood, and conducted phone consultations with other physicians. Hours later, he was still stumped. Finding no obvious explanation, he released Bo with instructions to see his family physician and gave him permission to sleep in the passenger seat on the drive home.

Postscript

Since that day, doctors tested Bo from stem to stern, from his brain to his heart, from blood work to sugar levels. After six months, they determined that he needed a pacemaker. Bo had the surgery and has now fully recovered.

One year after Bo's episode, he and I returned to the Milepost 100 rest stop. As we sat by the Skagit River, we gave thanks that his guardian angel was one hell of a good driver.

∽ Make it your story

Miracles happen all around us. They are not limited to supernatural or religious occurrences. A miracle can be big or small; spontaneous or worked for. We get to choose what constitutes a miracle in our lives.

If we take the time to think about it, many things we accept as commonplace are pretty miraculous: our hearts that continuously beat from before birth until our death; phone calls from people we were just thinking about; and finding something we thought was irrevocably lost. Extraordinary miracles make us catch our breath and mutter "Wow," but the daily ones are equally powerful.

What miracles have you or someone close to you experienced? Did those encounters with miracles provide comfort, induce fear, or both?

Write down a few situations you remember. Try to capture how you felt physically and mentally. Recording these memories can instill a sense of reverence for the spiritual forces that work outside the scope of day-to-day awareness.

Put on Hold

WAITING SUCKS. Whether I am stuck on hold listening to Muzak being piped into my ear, biding my time in an espresso line, or hanging out by the stove as my food heats, I hate wasting time waiting. Out of frustration, I've figured out ways to utilize the mandatory hiatuses such as lingering until the movie starts, the train passes, or the help desk can assist me.

Let's face it; there is no getting away from waiting. A Census Bureau report says America's population is expected to increase 50 percent by 2050. As our society becomes more crowded, we'll be biding our time even more. Our only line of defense is to figure out pleasant ways to cope.

It took determination, but over time I have found ways to turn waiting into a semi-positive experience. To help redirect anger and frustration generated by unwanted waits, I compiled a list of things that can be done during mandatory pauses.

✒ *Improve the flow*—If your workspace looks more like a parchment waterfall than a desk, take a moment to file or toss out some papers. According to the tenets of Feng Shui, clutter clogs the energy flow inside buildings, in yards, and on desks. The progress you make in clearing up your desk will improve the energy in your workspace and invigorate you.

✒ *Give it a break*—Take a stretching break. Standing up, walking, and stretching can all help improve your circulation, relieve tension, and enhance your energy level.

✒ *Zone out*—Unfocus your eyes and stare into space. Free-flowing thoughts or daydreams can lead to creative problem solving. Einstein believed that people could stimulate ingenious thought by allowing their imaginations to float freely, unrestrained by conventional inhibitions. His first crucial insight, which eventually led to his Special Theory of Relativity, came to him unexpectedly while he was daydreaming. Awaking from the daydream, he knew that he had to find a way to understand the scenes that had just played out in his mind. Einstein later said, "You could say, and I would say, that my entire scientific career has been a meditation on that dream."

✒ *Commune with a higher power*—More than 200 studies validate the effectiveness of prayer. Dr. Larry Dossey, author of *Prayer is Good Medicine*, recommends prayers of gratitude and openness, with no goal in mind. Instead of praying for a specific outcome, he suggests offering open-ended prayers, such as, "May the best thing happen," or "Thy will be done." According to Dr. Dossey, that attitude relieves us of the burden of "playing God."

✳ **Grab some air**—Take a few deep breaths. The increase in your oxygen level will reenergize you and help you think more clearly. One of the definitions of the word "inspire" is to draw in air by inhaling. By taking deep, conscious breaths, you may gain inspiration regarding a problem or project.

✳ **Hold a pose**—Doing mudras (also known as hand yoga) is a quick way to harmonize your body, mind and spirit. You probably have seen statues of holy deities holding their hands in mudra positions. One of the most common mudras is the prayer position. Simply place both hands together, leaving a small open space between the palms. This mudra creates a sense of peace and harmonizes both sides of the brain. One reason this mudra is so powerful is because there are 4,000 nerve endings in the tips of our fingers and this pose activates all of them.

✳ **Chortle, giggle, chuckle**—Whatever you call it, laughter is good medicine. Read online jokes, share a joke with a friend, or just start laughing. Forced laughter is just as effective as spontaneous laughter in reducing stress, strengthening the immune system, and releasing endorphins that improve one's mental disposition.

✳ **Indulge yourself**—Any excuse is a good reason to eat chocolate. And with the latest research, you can almost call it medicinal. Studies show that chocolate contains essential trace elements and nutrients such as iron, calcium, potassium, and vitamins A, B1, C, D, and E. According to a study conducted by Holland's National Institute of Public Health and Environment, "Chocolate contains up to four times the antioxidants found in tea." Just remember, not all chocolate is equal. The healthiest chocolates are plain dark products containing a minimum 70% or more cocoa solids, with low fat content and few additives.

✤ Make it your story

Turn the act of waiting into a mental recess. Try the techniques I suggested and you may discover that creativity is a byproduct of involuntary breaks. You might find that interruptions woven into your busy day nourish new ideas and give them time they need to germinate. Enrich your waits with silly ways to entertain yourself while you are waiting. If you want, you can keep a record of the techniques that are most helpful when you are temporarily put on hold.

Stepping Forward

Do you believe in paranormal phenomena?

According to a Gallup Poll, three out of four Americans believe in one or more of the following paranormal phenomena: extrasensory perception, haunted houses, ghosts, telepathy, clairvoyance, astrology, communicating with the dead, witches, reincarnation, and channeling spiritual entities.

Given the number of people who bet on lucky numbers or base decisions on their daily horoscopes, that statistic doesn't surprise me. What I find curious is people's reluctance to share personal paranormal experiences. Two concerns I hear most often are fears of not being believed or of being labeled crazy.

A less expressed explanation for why many of us refrain from sharing paranormal experiences is that we question the validity of our own experiences. In the book *Talking with Nature*, author Michael J. Roads describes his trepidations about exposing his ability to communicate with trees, water, rocks, and animals. When he first considered writing a book detailing his experiences, he felt fearful of being labeled weird and eccentric. He considered writing a fictional tale where he could hide his truths in a storyline, but dropped that idea. That's when he realized he was the one who had the most difficulty believing he could talk to nature and hear nature talk back to him.

Taking his problem out into nature, he sat by his favorite river and asked for help in finding a way to share his stories that people could easily understand and accept. Nature told him to write about his experience as it happened or forget the whole project. Eventually, Roads agreed to put aside his apprehensions and write his truth. His gamble paid off. When *Talking with Nature* was published, many people thanked him for sharing stories similar to what they had experienced but never dared to share.

Chances are high that the rest of us would gain the similar support if we opened up and spoke about our experiences with the paranormal. I know when I finally get up the nerve to share messages I have received through dreams and insights that have come to me in meditation, people usually can't wait to share similar tales from their lives.

My path to becoming a healing arts practitioner was paved with paranormal experiences. It began in 1999 when my father-in-law, John, a man whose many titles included healer, underwent open-heart surgery. During his recovery, the pain was so intense he pleaded with God to let him die. In response he heard God say, "No, you have more work to do."

When John told me that story, my inner voice said, "That's right. John needs to pass his healing gift to me." My initial response was shock. Where did that thought come from? I had no aspirations to become a healer; in fact, the very idea filled me with apprehension. I tried to banish the thought, but it kept looping through my mind like an unwelcome jingle.

Eventually I summoned up the courage to tell John. With great trepidation and knocking knees, I said, "Remember when you wanted to die but God told you that you had something to do first? Well, I heard an immediate response saying you need to pass on your healing gift to me."

John's eyes widened and he turned to look at his wife, Joy. As seconds passed, the silence grew louder and louder. Then he returned his gaze to me and with a broad smile said, "Joy and I thought the exact same thing."

Over the next three years, John taught me about his form of spiritual healing. Not long after he finished the lessons, he underwent back surgery. Complications arose during his recovery and John ended up in a coma. One night, as he lay in his hospital bed, I sat next to him and held his hand. After a few minutes, I felt an intense energy flowing from his hand into my body, like a supercharged electric current. Soon my whole body was physically vibrating. Knowing intuitively that John was transmitting his healing gift, I thanked him for honoring me. The next afternoon John died.

Thirteen days after John's death, a vision came to me during my morning meditation. A group of women healers formed a line, one behind the other. I was told each woman represented one of my past lives as a healer. Welcoming me back into the clan of healers, the women said they were glad to see me opening up to my healing skills and tapping into my many reincarnations as a healer.

A month later, I received another message about being a healer. One morning, after experiencing a fierce stomachache the night before, I sent healing energy through my chakras to clear away any energetic residue. When I reached the abdominal chakra, I felt a blockage. This was the same area that hurt the previous night, so I asked my spirit guides why that spot was causing me problems.

In response to my question, an internal dialogue began. A voice asked me who I thought I was to say I am a healer. "I am just me," I responded. The demand for my credentials continued. "What gives you the right to say you are a healer?" Immediately, my stomach started hurting. I could not think of an answer that would satisfy my interrogator. Then I heard myself say, "Nothing gives me the right. I open myself as a channel, a conduit for Spirit's healing energy. I do it to honor the healing energy that was gifted to me by my father-in-law, John. As he used to say, anyone can open themselves to these gifts. It is not that I am special; it is that I am channeling special energies."

It has been several years since John died, and he still comes to me in meditations. Occasionally he gifts me with a new level of healing energy and new insights into how I can best use my healing powers. In my mind's eye, I see his physical form, hear his voice, and feel his presence. He has told me his teachings are almost complete. Although I will be eternally thankful for all he shared, I will miss our visits.

While the visitations from the women healers and John helped me gather the courage to open my healing practice, I still feel leery about sharing this story. My inner critic is on red alert, sending out warnings about all the horrible things that will happen to me if I reveal this information. People will say I am full of myself, grandstanding, or unhinged. How my inner critic can divine other people's thoughts before they form, I don't know, but she assures me she has super powers.

After years of dealing with my inner critic in other areas of my life, I know nothing will appease her or make her go away. She is a permanent fixture in my life. The only thing I can control is my response to her. I believe the same is true for other people. Most of us can't stop our inner critics from haranguing us, nor can we know in advance how others will respond to our stories about paranormal experiences. The best we can do is speak our truths and not let the dire predictions of inner or outer critics stop us.

❧ Make it your story

Stepping forward and being true to yourself takes a leap of faith. For me it was stepping forward and being a healer. Your truth will be unique to you. Whatever your path, remember it is a life-long practice to accept who you are and be courageous enough to be that person. Being your true self, instead of who someone else wants you to be, requires commitment. On the plus side, the reward is often a new level of intimacy between friends, family, and community.

Ways to be true to yourself:

- *Remember by being yourself you are inspiring others to be themselves.*
- *Listen to your inner voice. It is good to get other people's input, but don't follow others' advice blindly or out of guilt. Use critical thinking and make up your own mind.*
- *Follow your inner compass. Be true to your values, even if your choice disappoints others.*
- *Appreciate your uniqueness. Develop your talents and gifts.*
- *Be honest with yourself. It is the first step in being honest with others.*

The Wisdom of Dreams

A dream which is not interpreted
is like a letter which is not read.
The Talmud

YEARS AGO, I HAD A NIGHTMARE about a fire that helped save my family's lives. During the dream, I figured out an escape plan that my family and I used the next night when a cheap extension cord combusted and actually set our house on fire.

A decade later, I heard about a bi-monthly dream group. Recalling my lifesaving fire dream, I decided to join and learn more about these nighttime dramas. Since then, I have learned how to use my dreams to help resolve numerous issues. For example, when I run into difficulty while writing an article, want help determining the best healing treatment for a client, or need assistance resolving a personal problem, I often review the situation just before going to bed and ask my dream maker for help. As I sleep, my dream mind takes over and I often wake up with a solution.

In my dream group, I have frequently seen dreams help members make positive changes in their lives. Shortly after a divorce, one woman began having a series of dreams focused on scaffoldings. First, the scaffoldings surrounded the outside of buildings. By working with that image, she realized she had the strength and support to safely begin rebuilding the everyday aspects of her waking life. Months later, the dream scaffoldings moved indoors, showing her it was time to begin working on her inner emotional wounds. A dream about trains showed another group member that his new business venture was on track. By continuing his efforts, he established a successful venture.

There are many schools of thought regarding dream interpretation. Two legendary ones are the teachings of Sigmund Freud and Carl Jung. My dream group follows the tenets of dream work teacher Jeremy Taylor, author of *Where People Fly* and *Water Runs Uphill*. According to Taylor's teachings, all dreams come in health and wholeness. That means even nightmares carry positive messages. Although we may wake up in fear with heart palpations, our subconscious mind believes we can benefit by facing the information being brought forward. For instance, by using the information in my house fire dream, I replaced the batteries in all the smoke detectors around my home and refined a fire escape route.

While my nightmare helped my family survive a house fire, some people reap financial gain from their nightmares. In her book, *Writers Dreaming*, Namoi Epel asked 26 writers how dreams had influenced their work. Sue Grafton, author of the Alphabet Mystery series, declared, "A frightening dream is wonderful for me because it recreates all the physiology that I need in describing my private-eye heroine, Kinsey Millhone, in a dangerous situation." Stephen King tells of the time he was writing his book *It* and the plotline got stuck. One night, after getting upset about the book's lack of direction, King called on his dream source for help. He fell asleep, and the solution came to him in the form of a nightmare. He awoke very frightened, but also very happy, because the dream gave him a plot direction. "I just took the dream as it was and put it in the book. Dropped it in. I didn't change a thing," he said.

Dreams are a form of communication between the body, mind, and spirit. As we sleep, our subconscious uses raw material from our emotions, thoughts, and actions to create mini screenplays. Dreams are also a way to get in touch with our inner wisdom or soul consciousness. By paying attention to dreams, we can learn a lot about ourselves.

Dreams are nighttime visions that influence our life the same way the moon influences tidal action—invisibly. We can watch high and low tides come and go without paying attention to the power the moon has over tidal action. Or we can be mindful and learn the pattern of the tides. Whether or not we see the connection between the moon and tidal action doesn't alter the reality of its existence. The same is true for our dream life. Whether we pay attention to dreams or not, they influence our lives consciously and unconsciously. By being mindful of them, we gain insights we can use in our waking life.

Each of us spends approximately eight hours, or a third of each day, sleeping. That equals 2,920 hours a year. If you are 25 years old, you have spent more than eight years of your life sleeping. If you are 50, you can double that number to 16. Before we die, most of us will have spent more than two decades asleep, so it makes sense to pay attention to the dream messages that percolate while we snooze.

Some people use dreams as a source of artistic inspiration. In an interview, musician Paul McCartney said he woke up one morning with the melody for the Beatles' hit song Yesterday playing in his head. All he had to do was add the words. Author Colleen J. McElroy, reports a similar experience. McElroy says that most of her writings are dictated to her while she sleeps. Her job is to write them down when she wakes up.

The Greek philosopher Aristotle thought that dreams could be indicators of conditions within the body. I found that to be true when, over a two-year period, I experienced extreme flu-like symptoms for one week out of every month. Doctors tested me at both ends and in the middle, but month after month the tests came back negative. Over time I noticed my doctors' concern fade. Their kindness became mere tolerance. I imagined my diagnosis changing from unknown to hypochondriac. In desperation, I begged my dreams to tell me what was happening. If I had been seeing ancient Egyptian physicians who instructed their patients to seek cures for their ailments in their dreams instead of a western-trained doctor, I might have shared the following dream with my doctors.

October 22

My stomach is hurting and something inside wants to push its way out. There is intense pressure against my stomach as it pushes and pushes. Then a long vine with one large leaf pops out of the right side of my stomach. (The location where I feel the pain in waking life).

I show it to the doctors with an attitude of "see I told you something was in there." They acknowledge I was right and cut the leaf off the vine. Then they go back to their business, as if that resolved everything.

Months later, an excruciating "flu" attack sent me fleeing to an emergency room. Within twenty-four hours I was on the operating table having my appendix removed. The surgeon later told me my inflamed appendix was severely scarred from repeated attacks. What I had thought was the flu turned out to be appendicitis.

After recovering from surgery, I looked up the appendix in my local library's medical dictionary. There I found a picture of a small, leaf-shaped organ hanging at the junction between the large and small intestines. My dream had correctly diagnosed my problem; I just did not have the knowledge to interpret it correctly.

After years of working with my dreams and reading numerous books about dreamwork, I have found certain techniques that help me remember and decipher my dreams.

First, I have a dream journal and pen next to my bed. (Some people use a tape recorder and later transcribe their dreams.) As I drift off to sleep, I tell myself that I want to remember at least one dream. If I have a specific question I want help answering, I repeat that question silently to myself as I fall asleep. Sometimes, I picture the situation I need help resolving. Upon awakening, I immediately write down my dreams in my bedside journal, even if my recollection is just a fragment, color or emotion. Any distraction can cause the dream to evaporate, so I have learned to jot down what I remember before I begin my daily routine. After recording a dream, I date it and give it a title. Once I have captured a dream or dream fragment, I then think about its possible meanings.

Because dreamtime messages are often presented in the form of symbols, I sometimes do research using the Internet or a dream dictionary to discover their archetypal or historic meanings. Because symbols mean different things to different people, I match dream dictionary definitions against my personal lexicon. For example, being adrift in the ocean might be a warning or distress call for someone who is aquaphobic, or instead a heartening, comforting image for a skilled swimmer.

One of the joys of working with dreams is deciphering puns or word play. Some are so silly, I groan when I figure them out. For example, a suitcase can mean being packed, as in being ready; making a pact or a deal; or emotional baggage. Images of mushrooms can be a dream pun on 'much room,' or a need to create distance from a particular situation. CD could signify 'seedy,' and celery may be dream language for 'salary.' Even names can become puns. Carmine might mean "car mine," a desire for a driver's license or a personal car. The name Frank could indicate it is time for an honest discussion with someone.

Through the years, I have noticed that the more I honor my dreams by paying attention and writing them down, the more they reveal. When my dream maker knows I am listening to its messages, I receive insights and premonitions that help me in my waking life.

⚜ Make it your story

Dreams are an excellent way to get in touch with your inner wisdom. Step one is to pay attention to your dream life. No one way is right for everyone, so experiment and see what works best for you. The key is to let your inner dream architect know you are curious and willing to learn how to better communicate with it. The more effort you put into remembering and working with your dreams, the more insights you will receive.

Here are some questions you can use to get started mining your dreams for meaning and significance:

- *What was the emotional tone of the dream? What was the primary emotion I felt when I awoke? Did I feel scared, happy, sad, or worried?*
- *Is there anything in my waking life that elicits a similar feeling? If so, what?*
- *Are the images in the dream primarily literal or symbolic?*
- *Can I identify parallels between images in my dream and what is happening in my waking life?*
- *Could the dream be foreshadowing a future event?*

525,000 and Change

"WHAT WOULD YOU DO if you had five hundred and twenty-five thousand and change that you could spend any way you wanted to?"

When I read that opening line in a recent email, my mind shot into overdrive and I began visualizing travel destinations. I pictured myself strolling across the lush Irish countryside and sipping a frothy cappuccino at a sidewalk café in France. Then I reached the second paragraph and reality wiped away my daydreams.

"If you live twelve more months, you are going to have 525,000 minutes to invest. Many of us have been trained to invest a great amount of that commodity in rehearsing our past, cursing a circumstance, nursing a problem, or fueling resentment. If we are not careful, we will spend our time doing just that."

The author of the inspirational email I was reading, speaker and writer Mary Manin Morrissey, wasn't talking about dollars. She was talking about how we use our time. Not the way we fill time with activities, but the time we waste on negative thinking instead of investing in uplifting thoughts.

I learned the downside of negative thinking when I worked as a special education teacher for an underfunded organization. After teaching all day, I brought my work problems home with me. During the evening, I mentally rehashed that day's crises and complained to everyone who would listen. By investing my off-work hours in fretting and fuming, I never enjoyed a respite from the stressful issues that filled my workdays. Sadly, all my mental storming never resolved a single issue.

Our minds work in mysterious ways. While it seems logical to assume the conscious part of our minds play the biggest role in creating our thought patterns and making decisions, research shows the opposite is true. Cognitive neuroscientists quoted in an article in US News & World Report said, "We are conscious of only about 5 percent of our cognitive activity . . . most of our decisions, actions, emotions, and behavior depends on the 95 percent of brain activity that goes beyond our conscious awareness."

According to Carl Jung, the mind is like an iceberg. The conscious mind (the tip of the iceberg) handles voluntary actions (moving our legs or scratching our nose), logic (figuring out our chances of getting a pay increase), and reasoning (calculating a server's tip). The largest portion of the iceberg, the piece lying deep beneath the water, symbolizes the unconscious. That section may be out of sight, but has a greater influence on our beliefs and actions than our conscious mind.

Alas, the unconscious does not always work in our favor. Let's say we consciously decide to take one action, such as signing up for a yoga class, and our unconscious sabotages our endeavor. We may "mistakenly" double book our schedule, forget the class' starting time, or convince ourselves that we'll never learn to cross our arms and balance on one foot, so why try.

Maybe we once saw yoga poses in a magazine and thought, "I could never be that flexible." Or we saw a slender woman in clingy yoga pants and imagined how our bulges would look sausaged into a polyester/spandex casing. Writings of psychologists, including Erik Erikson, suggest that the unconscious taps into those old stockpiled thought patterns about our flexibility and self-image and uses them to sabotage our goal of regularly attending yoga class.

If we really want to take that yoga class, we can stop our unconscious mind from sabotaging us by investing time in positive visualizations, affirmations, and positive thinking. The goal is to reprogram our minds with constructive thoughts and images so we can spend our time on this beloved earth joyously pursuing things that light us up.

Mary Oliver ends her poem, *The Summer Day*, with a wonderful life-affirming question, "Tell me, what is it you plan to do with your one wild and precious life?" While I love that line, sometimes looking at a birth-to-death plan can be overwhelming. What if we changed that sentence and asked ourselves, "What is it I plan to do with this one wild and precious day?" How are you going to spend your daily allotment of 1,440 minutes?

✌ Make it your story

Choose something you want to achieve, whether it is finding a new job or horseback riding. Then use the following techniques to quiet any inner critics and increase your chances of success:

Creative visualization is a process of imagining what you want to have happen. Another term for the process could be positive daydreaming. To change your unconscious view about learning yoga or any other activity you want to pursue, you need to create mental images of yourself doing the activity with ease and grace. Use multi-sensory imagery (seeing, hearing, sensing, smelling, tasting, as well as the feeling of moving). Throughout the day, employ all these senses to create images of yourself being competent in your chosen activity.

Utilize positive affirmations—short declarative statements—to target negative beliefs and replace them with constructive encouragement. Affirmations need to be positive, stated in the present tense, and focused on what you want rather than what you don't want. For instance, you could say, "As I practice yoga, I become more limber and graceful."

Negative thoughts are the insidious chatter that steals your joy, questions your commitment, and challenges your self-worth. To counter that type of thinking, you can add the phrase, "up until now." For example, the statement

"My balance is terrible" changes to "Up until now, my balance has been terrible." The inclusion of those three little words opens your mind to change and improvement.

Synchronicity

SOME PEOPLE ARE PLANNERS, while others drift through life letting fate determine their next move. I belong in the latter camp. For example, twenty-plus years ago, while staying home with my first baby, I realized I needed more mental stimulation than Mister Rogers or Sesame Street could offer. To reactivate my brain cells, I enrolled in a Japanese language class at a nearby community college. After years of studying Spanish and sign language, I wanted an entirely new challenge.

The first day of class I met a man named J.J., who worked as an interpreter for deaf people. During my two semesters of Japanese, J.J. became a family friend. When Bo was laid off from his job and began researching careers in computer technology, J.J. suggested a certification course in computer programming at an institute where he sometimes worked as an interpreter for deaf students. After evaluating the course, Bo signed up.

To supplement our income while Bo attended school, I started looking for a part-time job. J.J. again proposed a solution. He told me about a job opening with a community service center for the deaf and offered to be my reference. Within the month, I was hired and began working at that job.

That's how synchronicity can work. Taking the Japanese class introduced me to J.J., which in turn led to Bo's new career in computing and my employment at the community service center for the deaf. That series of events wouldn't have occurred if I hadn't signed up for that specific course at that precise time.

An interesting thing about synchronicities is that the more I notice them, the more they occur. It could be that a shift in my awareness allows me to see what was happening all along. Or it may be the universe is rewarding my attentiveness with more occurrences.

Whatever the reason, one of the things I love most about synchronicities is how they add a touch of mysticism to ordinary life. For instance, last week I told my son that my pen pal Bernie had not written for several months and I wondered if something was wrong. The next day when I checked my email, I found a letter from Bernie. Attached to her note was a copy of a prayer about love. One line, "Releasing all worries, all burdens and doubt, I bring light to the shadows of fear," seemed like the perfect words to read to my mother-in-law who was, coincidently, having surgery that day. After printing out the prayer, I stuck it in my purse and took the prayer to the hospital for my mother-in-law.

I believe synchronicities are more than fluke occurrences; they are providence, divine intervention. I sometimes imagine a universal force, be it God, Goddess, or Spirit, who watches the human drama play out.

With a God's eye view from the outer reaches of the stratosphere, one could see neighbors who pass each other's homes every day, but don't meet until they start working in the same office. Witness two people exercising side-by-side in the gym, but who don't notice each other until a mutual friend introduces them. Foresee a car accident that causes an injury so severe the driver loses his job, needs retraining, and, in the course of his studies, finds a passion for a subject that adds new meaning to his life.

I am not the only one I know who sees the magic in synchronicities. A shamanic healer, Sharlyn, recently told me about a synchronicity she experienced. After conducting a distance healing on her sister-in-law, who had cancer, Sharlyn turned on the television. There on the screen were the words "Cancer Free." She had inadvertently tuned into a program about a new cancer treatment.

Several days later, Sharlyn did a second distance healing session for her sister-in-law. At the conclusion of the treatment, Sharlyn again turned on the television and there on the screen were the exact same words "Cancer Free." Although it was a different day of the week and a different time of day, she had somehow tuned into the exact same program about a new cancer treatment. This time Sharlyn passed the information onto her sister-in-law.

Another friend, Anita, experienced a chain of synchronicities after deciding to change her negative work situation. One day she made a commitment to herself: within two months she'd leave her job, whether it meant transferring to another position or taking time off to search for a new job. The very day she made that decision, she got an unsolicited job offer from a different agency. The director personally asked Anita to apply for the position. Accepting the opportunity providence dropped into her lap, Anita submitted an application and was hired. Before the end of her two-month deadline, Anita was working at her new job.

Synchronicities can be big events or tiny everyday incidents with a magical spin. The key to getting the most out of these cosmic occurrences is to pay attention. You never know when something magical might happen or where it could lead you.

❧ Make it your story

Make a practice of looking for synchronicities in your life. Instead of taking it for granted when a friend calls at the exact moment you thought of her, or a check-out line opens up when you are running late to an important meeting, appreciate the synergistic magic in those situations.

Increase the possibility of synchronicities occurring in your life by asking God, Goddess, or Spirit to surprise and delight you with mind boggling coincidences. While synchronicity cannot be willed or forced, we can put out a request, and then make a commitment to being receptive to the answer.

A friend of mine always looks for a cosmic sign or synchronicity before moving homes or accepting a job offer. She consciously asks Spirit to give her a sign. Then she lets it go, relaxes, and waits to see what shows up.

Synchronicity can also show you things you did not even know you were looking for. Whether it is a clue about shifting your current goals or a coincidental meeting with a new love interest, synchronicity offers a momentary connection to the universal source of magic.

In-Between Spaces

We can find the space between sounds by finding our breath.
Thich Nhat Hanh

OUR DAILY LIVES ARE CHOCKFUL of goal-orientated activities. Whether it's moving from an apartment to a house or from school to a job, we tend to concentrate more on the completion of a task. The space between point A and point B gets less attention.

With our focus the finish line, we often miss the small moments that make up the marrow of our lives. How often are we preoccupied with work issues when a loved one talks to us? Or busy thinking about tomorrow as we drive through town. Because of our inattentiveness, we can miss hearing stories about our friends' or children's lives, or seeing sunsets with peach-colored clouds against a lapis blue sky.

It is natural for us to work towards physical, mental, and spiritual goals. What doesn't make sense is to jump from one task to another without taking time to savor the moments of stillness between our actions.

One way we can begin learning how to tune into the journey, instead of the goal, is by slowing down and paying attention to the pauses between our breaths, words, and steps.

Let's start with breathing. Each breath has two moments of stillness: between inhalation and exhalation and at the end of each exhalation, before our next inhalation. By focusing on these slivers of time, we can momentarily turn off our nonstop mental chatter and savor a brief respite. When our minds wander, we need only bring our focus back to the still point between breaths and into the present moment.

Written words and oral communication cannot exist without blank or silent spaces. Spaces are indispensable; without them, words lose their structure and their meaning. Writers use grammar to create pauses that emphasize specific words or phrases. Speakers employ pauses to build tension. We can create mini-breaks in our day by taking a moment to breathe between sentences while composing emails or verbally responding to questions. These momentary hiatuses clear our minds and help us form thoughtful responses.

When we walk, each step has brief spaces between the lifting, moving, and placement of our feet. We can use those spaces as a meditative tool by paying attention to each foot's alternating pattern of contact and release, how the foot rolls from the heel to the ball before lifting and starting the process again. Focusing on this repetitive pattern will shift our attention from our to-do lists to the now.

Another overlooked in-between space is the pause between a thought and an action, the gap between what is and what could be. We can learn to use these intervals to our benefit. Instead of giving in to knee-jerk reactions, we can teach ourselves to pause and choose how we want to react. The old adage "count to ten" gained popularity because of its effectiveness.

After you begin to savor the miniscule spaces in between your breaths, words, and steps, look for ways to expand those breaks.

Look for ways to create a few extra moments of stillness. Park a distance from your destination and walk, take the scenic route home, or schedule daily 10-minute mental health breaks. When you step back into your day-to-day activities, you might have a fresh perspective and see course adjustments you want to make.

Tuning in to the in-between spaces can give us time to catch our breath before we take on our next goal. This process doesn't take much time, can be done anywhere, any time and will make a difference in how we feel about the way we spend our time here on earth.

✃ Make It Your Story

Spend time noticing the space between your thoughts and actions. For example, watch for the sliver of time between locating your keys and picking them up, or recognizing you are thirsty and getting a drink. Once you recognize those gaps, begin paying attention to how you can use them to calm down, clarify a thought before speaking, or decide how you want to respond to a prickly situation.

When a freeway driver cuts you off, you encounter a rude person, or the waiter forgets your salad, take a moment to pause. Then take a long, deep breath (or two) and deliberately choose how you want to respond.

Look for ways to carve out a few extra moments of stillness during your day. Allow the phone to ring a few times before you pick it up, take a drink of water before you answer a question, or stand and stretch every 30 minutes.

After a while, you may discover new ways to incorporate pauses into your day.

Blind to Happiness

AT AGE TWENTY-FOUR I led a split life. My days were spent teaching handicapped infants aged birth to three. At night I wallowed in misery.

During work hours, I helped children develop critical self-help skills by concentrating on one minuscule step at a time. Progress was slow. But successes, like a two-year-old girl with cerebral palsy tremors learning to feed herself with a spoon and a three-year-old girl with blindness conquering zippers, were incredibly gratifying.

After eight hours spent helping my students face their ordeals, I went home to my own challenge. My live-in boyfriend, Jem, and I were breaking up. Months of disagreements interwoven with stony silences had taken their toll. My emotions were a scramble of sadness and exasperation; sadness over our failed relationship and exasperation with the process of untangling our lives. Until Jem saved up enough money to move, we were stuck sharing the same house. Progress was slow and not the tiniest bit rewarding.

Then, one day, a two-year-old named Rich toddled into my classroom. Sporting black curly hair and an elfin smile, he immediately won over my heart. From day one, his infectious laugh and silly antics were a balm for my tattered spirits. Born with all the advantages of a perfect birth, he lost his hearing after a bout of bacterial meningitis when he was eleven months old. Now he and his mother were relying on me to teach him the communication skills he needed to survive. But in order to teach Rich sign language, I first had to learn it myself.

Attending community college classes three nights a week, I studied sign language with the kind of diligence that comes easily to those who are trying to evade their personal lives. I quickly learned the hand positions for the manual alphabet and a smattering of sign language words. By the end of my first quarter, I was able to sign simple two-to-three-word sentences. An added bonus was time away from home.

Weeks rolled by, and still Jem hadn't moved out. Each time I asked him for a moving-out deadline, an argument ensued, leaving me so upset my heart felt black and blue. Since he was planning on moving out of town, my plan was to hold on to our modestly-priced rental. Until then, a constant twisting pain in my stomach underscored my need to minimize time around Jem.

A flyer posted at work offered a brief respite. A deaf-blind camp needed volunteer counselors. Although I had never worked with the deaf-blind before, I immediately signed up to attend the following weekend. While my motive might have looked altruistic, the overriding reason reeked of selfishness. I needed time away from the mess Jem and I had made of our relationship. The deaf-blind camp provided an opportunity to get away from my dismal home life and improve my sign language skills.

When the weekend rolled around, I packed my VW bug and drove down the congested freeway to the camp's country setting. From the on-ramp flanked by burger joints and gas stations to the camp's off-ramp surrounded by evergreen forest, I obsessed about my relationship with Jem. At exactly what point did our relationship start turning sour? I believed it was his fault. He thought it was my fault. Was he right? Could I be a Typhoid Mary of relationships and not know it? After all, I had been dating since I was fifteen without creating that "one perfect union."

By the time I arrived at the deaf-blind camp, I was swimming in self-absorption and despair. Fully convinced that my life was more wretched than anyone else's and that it always would be, I pulled into the dirt parking lot. When I stepped out of my car, I got a giant whiff of pine scent from the surrounding trees. I grabbed my suitcase from the car's trunk and looked around for the office.

As a noisy flock of crows flew overhead, I surveyed my surrounding. Three wooden structures, all painted barn red, formed a semicircle around the north end of the parking lot, with lush cedars, pines, and firs filling in the background. One building that resembled a bunkhouse, with a long rectangular shape and uniform string of windows, appeared to be the dorm. A large barn, complete with hayloft, had a group of adults out front mounting horses. The third building was a one-story wood structure. Several people dressed in faded blue jeans and T-shirts milled around out front. Guessing it was the office, I headed in that direction.

When I pushed open the door, I was struck by the silence. The only other organized camps I had attended were Girl Scout camps where I could hear girls hooting and laughing from yards away. Now I stood within feet of four people having an animated conversation and I heard nothing but silence. A second surprise was seeing two deaf-blind people using tactile communication. First, the listener put his hands over the speaker's hands in order to understand the message being signed. Then they reversed hand positions, so the other person could respond. Without crossing any marked borders, I suddenly had entered foreign territory.

When I approached the front desk clerk, I signed "Hello," then used the manual alphabet to form the hand positions for each letter in my name. Thankfully, the attendant understood my signing efforts and located my name on his sign-in sheet.

Once I made eye contact with the clerk, I signed "where's my," by first waving my index finger from side to side (where), then placing my right hand flat against my chest (my). Next I crossed my middle and index fingers on both hands, in order to sign the word "room" by placing my crossed fingers parallel in front of me, then side by side to form a box or room shape. Nodding his head in understanding, the clerk grabbed a packet of papers and a printed map with room locations. With a red marker, he circled my room number, then handed me the map and my room key.

I entered the dorm and found a dull institutional beige hallway teeming with a group of women, from teens to elderly, sharing silent conversations punctuated with guffaws of laughter. Shy about my beginner signing skills and unable to shake my depression, I made my way through the group without stopping to chat.

After unpacking, I pulled out the packet of papers and flipped to the schedule for the weekend. The first item on the agenda was horseback riding, which I had seen when I arrived. A game of football was about to begin on the back lawn, and a trip to a local shopping mall would depart in 20 minutes. I made a point to stay away from animals bigger than me. That eliminated horseback riding. Football was a sport I didn't watch or play. Even though I was not sure my limited signing skills were up to the task of escorting deaf-blind people, that left shopping.

After I pinned on my volunteer badge, I returned to the lobby just in time to see a large yellow school bus pull up outside. A tall woman sporting an official-looking blazer and a clipboard waved her hand in the air to get people's attention. Anyone interested in going to the shopping mall, she signed, needed to check in with her. A second woman, who appeared to be the co-leader, approached and asked if I was volunteering to help with the outing. Forming a fist with my right hand, I nodded it up and down to sign, "Yes." My lack of confidence became abundantly clear when my head simultaneously shook, "No."

She switched to spoken English and asked for my name and the extent of my experience with the deaf-blind community. I answered, "Colleen and none." Explaining my recent endeavor in learning sign language, I expressed doubts about my ability to interpret deaf-blind people's shopping requests accurately. The woman assured me there would be plenty of skilled signers who could help, as she walked me toward the bus. "Besides," she said, "if you don't go, one of the campers will have to stay behind. We need a one-on-one ratio for this trip."

The co-leader pointed out my bus seat and introduced me to Dorothy, the older deaf-blind woman I would be assisting. She looked to be about sixty, with long gray hair pulled back in a ponytail. Her stout figure was dressed in a loose-fitting brown dress. Her mouth had a slight downward turn, and there was no twinkle in her green eyes. I could only guess at the kind of life she had led. Was she deaf-blind from birth? Or had an illness robbed her of those two senses? Did she have a life partner or children?

Taking the lead, the co-leader spelled my first name into Dorothy's hand. Then it was my turn. Placing my hand in hers, I spelled out my last name. The physical contact required to communicate that information felt surprisingly intimate and awkward. That, plus my nervousness, kept me from initiating further conversation with Dorothy.

Silence filled the space between Dorothy and me as my mind wandered to my relationship (or non-relationship) with Jem. Within seconds, I recreated the despair that so frequently filled my free moments. I didn't want to stay with Jem, but how could I possibly go through the whole getting-to-know-you thing with another man? Hadn't I done it enough? I was sick to death of starting over. Mentally producing a futurist movie of my life, I saw myself as a relationship failure who spent her life in an eternal search for requited love.

Mentally jerking myself back into the present, I glanced around. A rainbow of people in colorful outfits filled the bus to capacity. Up and down the aisle there were animated conversations with fingers dancing in the air.

Waving a hand in my direction, Dorothy drew my attention back to her. "Can you hear?" she asked.

Placing my closed hand in hers I signed, "Yes."

"Can you see?"

"Yes."

"You must be very happy," she signed, using clipped, self-assured motions.

Momentary stunned by her declaration, I leaned back against the bus seat and looked out the window. A mixture of buildings and trees set against the glow of a setting sun streamed past me. Snatches of music from passing cars could be heard over the sound of wheels hitting the road. In that moment, I realized I had been focusing on what I didn't have (a loving relationship) and what I wanted (enough money to cover both halves of the rent). I had forgotten to stop and appreciate the many blessings in my life.

Turning back to Dorothy, I took her hand in mine. With gratitude, I formed a gentle fist and nodded it up and down. "Yes, yes, yes," I signed. I just needed to be reminded.

✂ Make it your story

Over the next few days, listen to your self-talk. Do you spend more time focusing on what you don't have, or being grateful for what you do have? Create a deliberate pity fest, where you write down every negative thing in your life. Now, turn the tables and list all your appreciations, including physical abilities, emotions, talents, and material objects. How did your energy level or emotions shift as you moved from one activity to the next? What changes occurred in your body or mind as you moved from pity to gratitude? Did you feel tension or tranquility?

If you are interested in generating a more positive mind set, try these exercises.

1. Before your next work meeting or social gathering, set a goal of finding X number of positive things that have happened. They may be very small things (liking the color of the walls) or large ones (meeting a new friend).

2. Keep a gratitude journal where you write down three positive things that happened each day.

3. Pay attention to your thoughts. Remember that your inner world (thoughts and beliefs) influences what you see in the outer world. What you believe about the world, you will see in the world. The more positive you are, the more positives you will see.

Doodles

HAVE YOU EVER NOTICED that your handouts from a meeting or class contain more doodles than notes? For some of us (me included) the combination of paper, pen, and someone lecturing creates an irresistible urge to doodle.

What exactly are doodles? First, they are not scribblings or hastily made marks on paper. Doodles are graphic expressions of what is stirring in our subconscious minds. We usually doodle when we are thinking about something else, attending a meeting, or talking on the phone. Doodling engages the attention of the linear, analytical left side of our brains with an activity so the holistic, intuitive right side can digest information on a multisensory level.

Some people equate doodling with boredom. One on-line business writer believes the duller the meeting, the more people doodle. He warns speakers not to have a "doodle meeting." I disagree with his assessment of doodling behavior. In fact, I go to the opposite extreme and often invite participants to doodle during workshops where I am a presenter. Before launching into the lecture portion of my presentation, I hand out drawing paper and boxes of freshly sharpened colored pencils. Past participants report that doodling improved their retention of the information presented.

A key to successful doodling is being nonjudgmental about the outcome. These are not works of art; they are a way to relax the taskmaster side of our brains so that we can absorb information while having fun. Sometimes we learn about the speaker's topic, other times we discover something about ourselves. One woman who attended my workshop about creativity and spirituality said she had an epiphany while doodling that changed her life. I don't take credit for her breakthrough. But I do believe that encouraging doodling helped create a situation where her insight could bubble up into her conscious mind.

In her book, *Spiritual Doodles and Mental Leapfrogs: Playbook for Unleashing Spiritual Self-expression*, author Katherine Q. Revoir supports my belief about the benefits of doodling. She says, "Doodling leads to creative ideas because the mind is lulled into a state of openness and is available for intuition to drop petals of creativity into your consciousness. Make no mistake about it: doodling is a powerful spiritual practice, especially if you give yourself the gift of not self-judging."

In some ways, doodles are similar to dreams; both are messengers from our subconscious and open to interpretation. While there are books and web sites where handwriting analysts attribute meanings to specific geometric shapes, symbols, and figures, I give their interpretation little credence. Yes, some symbols have universal meaning: circles are archetypal representations of the eternal whole, spirals are an ancient symbol of the goddess, snakes represent rebirth, triangles symbolize tirades, and the list goes on. But personal history and association with a particular shape also plays a role in establishing a doodle's meaning and significance. Just as dream dictionaries offer ideas for possible interpretations of symbols, predetermined meanings for specific shapes or drawings are just jumping-off points for understanding doodles. Because doodles reveal something about a person's mental state, only the doodler truly knows the meaning of a particular doodle.

High profile doodlers include former U.S. presidents. According to a book called *Presidential Doodles*, President John F. Kennedy was such a prolific doodler the archivists at the Kennedy Library have a large folder dedicated to his doodles. President Clinton was also known to doodle. Years ago, an article in *Atlantic Monthly* discussed a key event where Clinton used doodling while making a major decision. The article tells of a time in October 1993 when Clinton convened his national security team. Somali militiamen had just killed 18 U.S. soldiers. When the briefing concluded, Clinton stopped doodling, looked up, and said, "Okay, here's what we're going to do."

One of the joys of doodling is that anyone can do it. Even if you stopped drawing in elementary school, doodling is still fair game. So, the next time you have a pen in your hand, make a few doodles. Who knows, you might discover the process is a fun way to tap into your subconscious hopes or ambitions.

✃ Make It Your Story

Are you interested in moving beyond unconscious doodling? Here are two ways to expand your use of doodling:

1.) Think of a specific question you'd like answered. Once you have formed it in your mind, pick up a pencil or pen and doodle for three minutes. Create a judgment-free zone for your doodles and thoughts. Let your mind roam wherever it chooses. Stretch your thinking as your pencil forms shapes and figures. As thoughts bubble to the surface, jot them down next to your doodles. When the time is up, review your doodles and notes. Do they suggest new insights? Is there an answer to your question hidden in the shapes and spirals?

2.) Make a squiggle on a piece of paper. Now use that squiggle as a starting point for drawing a picture. When you are done, use the completed picture as inspiration for writing a poem. Use the doodle as an illustration for your finished product.

The Dash

IN A SHORT VIDEO CALLED *The Dash*, the speaker points out that the "dash" between our birth date and the date of our death represents the entirety of our time on earth. Against a background of heart-stirring music and a collage of stunning nature photographs, the story of a person speaking at a friend's funeral scrolls across the screen. The takeaway is to pay attention to how we spend our unique, personal dash.

In most obituaries, people's dash represents the big things they did in life, such as their accomplishments at work and what they contributed to their communities. But I believe the key elements that make up our final tombstone dash are an accumulation of the many little marks we make on life. If you look at life events using other punctuation marks, you'll find periods that mark endings in our lives; ellipses, a series of dots (typically three, such as "..."), indicate a pause in the flow of our life; and hyphens can be used to create compound words which explain the complexity of our lives. Only at the end of life, when these marks are viewed end-to-end, does the dash on our tombstones take form.

Funerals are one place we hear how people filled in the dash between birth and death. Many people have an aversion to these events. Not me. I don't mind attending them, even when I don't know the deceased. Unlike the characters in the movie *Harold and Maude*, who scouted out funerals of random strangers, I always have a link to the deceased, usually through a friend. While supporting my friends through those difficult occasions, I often hear inspiring comments at funerals. Later, I use those insights to rethink how I want to spend my dash.

At the memorial service of a friend's ex-husband, John, a man I had never met, people shared stories about their interactions with him. One recollection came from his bus driver. Standing to speak she said, "I took the day off work without pay to come praise John. He never used his blindness as a reason to be surly. Every day, no matter the weather or problems he was facing, John always had a smile and kind words to share. I learned a lot about the joy of living through John's optimism."

Leaving the service that day, I reflected on what constitutes a successful life. In my mind, John had achieved the pinnacle of success. He had touched the lives of people around him, not just friends and family, but also his bus driver. John's mark on the world did not come from being a high-powered executive or a globetrotting volunteer; the accolades he received were for being a positive, uplifting person. Since then, John's legacy has inspired me to be more mindful of my interactions with people I encounter in everyday life.

I found further insights during the service of an elderly friend named Maurine. At her memorial, her family told of the time she rode a bus across Washington State to visit friends confined at a World War II Japanese internment camp. When she arrived, the guard stationed at the front gate told her no one had ever come to visit. She responded, "Well, I have, and I am spending the weekend." And that is exactly what she did.

Maurine made her mark on life by standing up for her beliefs and standing by her friends. I use the story about Maurine to give me courage when I am going against the status quo.

Stories told at funerals remind me that it is how we treat people, and not our major accomplishments, that matter most. A friend once told me her goal in life was to be like a cool drink of water. I like that image so much I often claim it as my own. The idea of being remembered as a refreshing presence fills me with joy.

✣ Make It Your Story

The obituaries that appear in newspapers give us a brief glimpse into a deceased person's life.

When the time comes to summarize your life's dash, how do you want to be remembered? What would you want your obituary to say?

Take a moment and pretend you are looking back over your life from far in the future and write up an obituary for yourself. This is not a morbid activity; rather it is a useful way to decide what you want to accomplish and what really matters in your life. This exercise can help you set life goals.

Tombstone epitaphs highlight personality traits or life accomplishments. Some are serious and others are humorous. Write the one you would like to have on your gravestone. Here are a few examples of historical epitaphs:

Bette Davis (actor): "She did it the hard way."

Allan Pinkerton (private detective agency): "A friend to honesty and a foe to crime."

Winston Churchill (statesman): "I am ready to meet my Maker. Whether my Maker is prepared for the great ordeal of meeting me is another matter."

Margaret Daniels (occupation unknown): "She always said her feet were killing her, but nobody believed her."

Create an epitaph that you can spend the rest of your life living up to.

Grace

Songs to Live By

A RECENT EMAIL FROM A FRIEND ended with the tagline, "Maybe the Hokey Pokey is what life's all about." That sentence supports my belief that the truth about life—that evasive wisdom that people climb mountains, swim across oceans, and sit for days in cross-legged meditation to obtain—is right in front of us. It is in songs we have known most of our lives. Songs we have sung around the campfire. The first (or maybe the only) song we learned to play on an instrument. Songs that are so familiar, we stopped paying attention to the words.

Let's take a fresh look at three of these classics, beginning with the Hokey Pokey. Now there is a song that gets you out of your seat and moving. It is, by all definitions, a dancing song. You can't sit in your chair to sing this song. No siree. Only when everyone gets up and forms a circle can the Hokey Pokey begin.

The words are simple and to the point. "You put your right hand in, you put your right hand out, you put your right hand in, and you shake it all about. Do the hokey pokey and turn yourself around. That what it's all about." This routine continues with the left hand, right foot, left foot, head, bottom, and finally, the whole self.

What truths are hidden in the wiggles and the giggles that accompany this song?

First, lighten up. Don't take yourself or your situation too seriously. No matter how bad life gets (and we have all been through challenging times), a wiggle and a giggle will help you feel better.

Second, let's face it: life is full of mundane routines. Try singing these words to the tune of the Hokey Pokey and you'll see what I mean. "You leave your home for work, you leave your work for home, you buy yourself new stuff, and then you pay the bills. You do this every day, and never clown around, and that's what it's all about."

That's a sad snapshot of how many people squander their precious time on earth. Moving through life on automatic pilot, doing a bit of this and a bit of that without much thought or belief in alternative choices, can turn life into a series of boring routines instead of an ongoing marvelous adventure.

Use the Hokey Pokey's lesson to shake things up. Make some changes in your routine, starting with tiny modifications. Experiment eating with chopsticks, try a new route to work, or change the TV shows you watch. Then move up to something bigger. Maybe you could paint the walls in your living room a different color, commit to watching one comedy movie a month, or perhaps take a daily walk. Beware, there is often a domino effect; one shift in the status quo can lead to unexpected consequences. Change, movement, and laughter might help you see new options, reach for new vistas, and figure out what your life is all about.

Another song that holds keys to life's secrets is "All You Need is Love" by the Beatles. The refrain to the song is, "All you need is love, all you need is love, all you need is love, love, love is all you need."

It may be sound like a cliché, but love is more important than things. Yes, I know, that's a subversive thing to say in the land of mega malls and warehouse stores. But this bold belief is backed up by my encounters with people who have all of life's creature comforts, but very little happiness. One friend built a million-dollar house to her exact specifications. When it was complete, I asked her if the house brought her happiness. "No," she responded with a shake of her head. She then expounded on her next goal and how its completion would make her happy.

Things can be taken away, fortunes can be lost, but memories of loving and being loved last a lifetime. After all, when we are lying on our deathbeds, what will we treasure? Our silver gravy boat, a new stereo system, the balance in our bank account, or our relationships with the people we love? When life is boiled down to its essence, love is all we need; the rest is window dressing.

My final example of song-based wisdom comes from the old campfire favorite, "Row, Row, Row Your Boat," and its key phrase, "Life is but a dream."

Essentially, dreams are nighttime stories laced with symbols that are a blend of experiences from our waking life, including past, present, and possible futures. Dreams are the unconscious mind's way of saying it is time to pay attention to particular issues or situations. Contrary to the plethora of books claiming to interpret dream symbols, the true meaning of these symbols can only be deciphered by the dreamer. For example, one online dream dictionary says that seeing an alligator in one's dream, "symbolizes treachery, deceit, and hidden instincts." In my internal dream lexicon, alligators are symbols of gentle parenting or creating a space to birth new ideas. My positive image of alligators is based on a story I read about mother alligators carrying their tiny new babies in their mouths. Now when I dream about alligators, I look at ways I can nurture new, still-in-developmental-stage projects or ideas.

Like our nighttime dream landscape, our daytime lives are also made up of stories. And, although we all share a joint reality, how we personalize and interpret that reality is different. If two people look outside and see a rainstorm, they will both see water falling from the sky. But they will each have their own interpretation of what that means. One person might be happy he doesn't have to water his garden. The other might be upset because her camping trip got rained out. Each person's reaction is based on his or her personal experiences and outlook on life.

The refrain, "Life is but a dream," is a reminder that you and I and everyone alive chooses how we decipher our life stories and dreams. An event is just an event, until we give it significance. Whether it is a daytime event or nighttime dream, its importance is determined by the meaning we give it.

✂ Make it your story

Do not underestimate the power of music. Even silly songs can hold powerful messages. Think about songs you know by heart. Do they capture the memory of a special moment in your life or hidden song-based wisdom? What sage advice can you hear tucked in the lines or verses? Don't worry about the songwriter's meaning of a song. Think about what emotions and memories the song triggers for you.

After you have explored songs you know, break out of your comfort zone and listen to new genres of music and songs from different parts of the world. Notice if any insights or ideas arise as you explore new sounds.

Smiles for Grandma Foye

MY DAD'S MOM, GRANDMA FOYE, was a grouch. Or at least that is what I thought when I was a young child.

A tall, willowy woman who always dressed in a neatly pressed, calf-length floral dress and a gauzy hair net covering her tightly curled hair, Grandma didn't put up with any youthful nonsense. Her down-turned mouth and stern looks silently cramped my playful exuberance. During family visits, she told my four siblings and me, "Children should be seen, but not heard." According to my six-year-old reasoning, that meant "Stay away, I don't like kids." So I kept out of her way as much as possible. As a result, she and I never formed a bond. In theory, that 65-year-old woman was my grandma, but I never felt a grandmotherly love from or toward her.

Even her Christmas and birthday gifts rubbed me the wrong way. She gave utilitarian gifts like underwear and socks. Clothing with color, bows, or ruffles were rare enough to be considered an extravagance. Ever hopeful that I would find a new doll under the wrapping paper, I repeatedly experienced disappointment.

During the thirteen years I knew Grandma Foye, my knowledge about her early life was limited to a few facts: she was born in 1893 to German immigrant parents who immediately Americanized their family name, changing it from Muller to Miller. Although I mainly experienced her scowl, I saw and heard family stories about her softer side as a caregiver.

Three years before I was born, my Grandma was pulled back into her motherly caregiving role at age 55 when her daughter, my aunt Marguerite, contracted polio one month after giving birth to a baby girl. When Marguerite's husband abandoned her and their infant, Grandma stepped in to care for her daughter and granddaughter.

A decade later, after Marguerite had moved out and started a new life, my Grandpa Foye suffered a major stroke. In an instant, he lost his ability to walk or feed himself, and his speech became severely garbled. Following his two-week hospital stay, he came home in a wheelchair. Unable to return to work, he retired from his job at the Santa Fe Railroad. Until his death six years later, Grandma was his caregiver 24-7.

Each day, my rail thin, 60-plus year old grandma lifted my six-foot grandfather out of his wheelchair, washed him, dressed him, cooked his food, fed him, and washed the dishes. Since his garbled speech made it difficult to understand him, she had to intuit his needs and meet them.

As an adult reflecting on her life, I marvel at Grandma's ability to remain sane, much less smiling. Where I saw a stern German grandmother, there was also a loving wife and mother who went above the call of duty each and every day.

Several years after Grandma Foye's death, my dad sent me a faded, yellow newspaper clipping that showed me a completely different side of her life. It was titled *Miss Miller is successful. Smile is her rule for women.* In the space of a few paragraphs I learned about her personal philosophy regarding smiling and work.

The article described how my grandma had started the first temporary secretarial employment agency in the Los Angeles area. As a 23-year-old business owner, she located and placed stenographers for businesses, supervised her personal office staff, and proofread over a hundred letters each day.

When picking prospective employees for her businesses, she is quoted as saying, "I believe in smiling, in hard work, and in being kind. After all, success came to me just as much because I smiled as for any other reason."

"Why shouldn't we smile?" she went on to say. "If success is smiling at us, we can afford to, and if we are down on our luck, well why not smile so folks won't find it out? Show me a woman who smiles even though the clouds are dark and I'll show you a woman who will be successful when she finds the opportunity."

Marveling at my grouchy Grandma's philosophy on smiling, I continued reading. I soon learned she had worked ten-plus hours a day. "If I want something done well, I do it myself, and I am always absolutely certain that no work leaves my offices until it has my stamp of approval on it," she said. She kept up that schedule even after my dad was born in 1918. Grandma ran her secretarial business until 1922, the year her daughter Marguerite was born. Then she quit to care for her two children.

Putting down the article, I silently praised my grandma for being a forerunner for the women's movement. She broke new ground for women working outside the home. Then, when need arose, she took on the role of caregiver, caring first for her young children, then her adult daughter and granddaughter, and finally her invalid husband.

She may not have smiled much when I knew her, but I do. I smile with pride when I think of all of my Grandma Foye's accomplishments, and the important lesson she taught me long after her death. I have realized we only see a tiny piece of a person's total being, even when they are close family or friends. Beneath the surface, where we cannot see, there are many life experiences that influence how they behave.

✤ Make it your story

Have you ever made judgments about someone that you later regretted? Have others judged you wrongly? Examine those experiences. What did you learn from them?

Pay attention to how your judgments play a role in your communication. It is difficult to hear and understand what other people are saying when we are busy mentally judging them. Listen with an open mind and heart.

It takes effort, but it's possible to retrain your mind and reduce the number of automatic judgments you make. One way to do that is to work on creating a less critical mind. When a judgmental thought enters your mind, stop and examine it. Once you have identified a critical thought, challenge yourself to identify the assumptions you are making. Next, find ways to practice being more compassionate toward people you judge. Just because someone did one wrong thing, it does not necessarily make them a bad person.

For example, the mom you encounter with a screaming toddler and judge as a bad mom may be having an especially harried day at the grocery store. Instead of judging her, ask if you can help. She might want you to get the can of diced tomatoes she forgot, or help loading groceries into her car. If you don't want to actively help, you can smile and wish her a good day.

Cocooning

THE SKY IS A SOFT GRAY and the temperature is in the low 50s. A gentle breeze stirs the budding lilac bush outside my window. There are no threats of snowfall or downpours. Spring is opening up its box of paints and bringing color back to the Pacific Northwest. It is official—I survived another winter.

Yet, instead of delighting in the bright green shoots poking from the ground and flowers in a riot of pastel colors, I feel an urge to cocoon. Frolicking among the flowering fairy bells and larkspur does not appeal to me. I want to withdraw from the outside world and renew myself with some alone time.

One warning sign that tells me it's time to retreat and take what I call "comfort time," is that I feel disconnected from my core self. By that, I mean who I am when my roles as partner, mother, friend, and worker are stripped away.

Alone time is a rarity in my life, and sometimes I forget to tune into the still voice within urging me to focus on myself. Now that I stop and listen, I realize just how low my internal energy gauge is running. Long work hours, family crises, and the barrage of negative news from around the world leave me feeling depleted. It is time to slow down my level of activity and refill my internal reservoir.

Unfortunately, my growing awareness of the need to be alone coincides with a social gathering I had been looking forward to for weeks. It is a chance to catch up with friends and enjoy a gourmet potluck.

Because I enjoy these regular get-togethers, I initially ignore the inner voice that suggests I skip the gathering and instead claim time for myself. But over the course of a few hours, the urge for solitude increases. An internal argument rages about the pros and cons of attending the gather vs.

spending time alone. After all, my family and friends are expecting me to attend. How can I just skip it?

As the gathering's afternoon start time draws near, I implement my tried and true litmus test. First, I imagine attending the gathering and internally gauge how it would feel to attend. Then I picture myself staying home and tune into how that would feel. In my mind, I weigh the two experiences. When I picture myself being around people at the gathering, I feel a sense of discomfort and agitation in my gut. Imagining myself at home alone fills me with a sense of calm.

At that moment, I realize it is more important to get reacquainted with myself than gather with my friends and family. Staking my claim on quiet time, I explain to my family why I won't be joining them at the gathering. Thankfully, they support my decision.

Once the house is empty, I settle into my cocoon. When the phone rings, I let calls go straight through to voice mail. I ignore chores that need doing and emails waiting to be answered. I withdraw inward and focus on me.

Comfort time is an opportunity to spoil myself, to do exactly what I want to do, when I want to do it. I take pleasure in chanting the word "comfort." It sounds so restful. I have no idea how a dictionary would define it and I don't care.

I like to think of my hours of alone time as an adult version of a time out. I am temporarily removing myself from social interactions. The big difference is that instead of having the time out inflicted upon me by someone else, it is something I claim for myself.

I relish my cocooning time. After four hours of reconnecting with myself and enjoying my own company, I am refreshed and happy to see my family return from the gathering. Having satisfied my need to be alone, I am ready to hear stories about their outing and listen to tales from the outside world.

✻ Make it your story

In today's society, we have a vast number of ways to stay connected with family, friends and the world through the Internet, cell phones, and social media. Instead of searching for ways to engage with others, people now need to search for ways to be alone.

While introverts require alone time to recharge their internal batteries, it can benefit everyone. Solitude allows space for self-reflection, which is a key component in developing self-awareness. It also allows us time to reboot our minds and unwind.

Solitude allows us to learn what we think and how we want to spend our time when there is no input or pressure from other people. In conjunction with that, it allows people to see how their typical environment shapes their thoughts, actions, and behavior. Creating a temporary separation can also offer space for creative ideas and innovation. Sometimes the absence of other people's judgments and opinions allows for a more open exploration of new ideas.

Most people are more adapt at checking off accomplishments on their to-do lists than setting aside time to be alone. How do you rate your ability to find solitude? Claim some alone time to play hooky from your to-do list. Do something by yourself, for yourself, even if it's just for ten minutes.

A Miracle

IN NOVEMBER 2005, I had breakfast with a miracle. At a funky 50s-style diner near Los Angeles International Airport, I sat among massive ferns, apron-clad waiters, and the roar of city buses, listening to Christine Pechera tell me how she beat the odds to survive a very aggressive form of Non-Hodgkin's Lymphoma. Years before I was introduced to Christine through a mutual friend, the doctors gave Christine just one month to live. She chose to fight the disease—and won.

Looking across a grayish-blue Formica table at her cloud-busting smile, I marveled to think that this petite, 33-year-old Filipino woman with dark, shoulder length hair and brown eyes seemingly lit by an inner light found the fortitude to become a three-year survivor of a stem cell transplant, a type of bone marrow transplant which used her own stem cells instead of relying on a donor.

Most recipients know the survival rate statistics for bone marrow transplants are grim. At Christine's first support group meeting for bone marrow recipients, one woman looked around the room at her fellow recipients and said, "In two years, half of us will be dead." Not willing to let that negative statement hang in the air, Christine told me she immediately countered with an adamant, "No! We will all survive." Sadly, her prediction did not come true. Three years later, half the group had died.

Christine's odyssey into the world of hospitals, test results, excruciating pain, and isolation gave her a new outlook on life. She describes this transition exquisitely in this poem that she shared with me.

How Beautiful is this Life and How Blessed Am I.
by Christine A. Pechera

How Beautiful is this Life and how Blessed Am I
There was a time when I could smell the blossom of a Rose
When I could feel the warmth of the Sun on my skin
When I could hear the Laughter of children
But then one day my whole life collapsed underneath me
And I began to fall
It became dark. It became painful.
It became lonely.
I curled up into myself and cried and said:
"I just want to die"
My subconscious Mind heard me-
and my Body said:
"Okay"
And soon the illness came.
When the illness came, I feared it.
I didn't know it was to become my greatest Teacher
It showed me the Love of Family, Friends and Strangers-
That I couldn't see before
It revealed the Beauty and Presence of God-
Living and Vibrating all around Me
It gave me Gratitude for this so very brief Gift of Time on this Earth
And it taught me to say:
"Thank You, For I am Alive"
I thanked the illness for coming and teaching me these things-
It nodded.
And then-
Went away

So now, today-
I can see the Soul in the Blossom of a Rose
I can feel the Power of the Sun within Me
And I can Laugh like a Child again
The illness taught me how Precious is each Moment,
How Beautiful is this Life,
And how Blessed Am I.

As we sat eating a stack of buttermilk pancakes and drinking coffee so stale it required both cream and sugar, Christine shared her feelings of wonder towards everyday life. For her, the simple act of eating in a crowded restaurant and talking about frivolous topics, like her new boyfriend and movies, was a miraculous event. Just three years ago, when she underwent the stem cell transplant, Christine was given a near-fatal dose of chemotherapy and then brought back from the brink of death by a last-minute infusion of her own stem cells. After that, her body had to rebuild its entire immune system, literally from zero. Wracked with pain, suffering from throat and mouth ulcerations and gastrointestinal problems so severe that it was difficult, sometimes impossible, to chew and swallow food or drink, Christine was at risk of picking up infections and therefore had to live for weeks on the isolation ward at City of Hope, an innovative biomedical research, treatment, and educational institution in Los Angeles. That was followed by months of wearing a surgical mask and shunning public places.

"Sometimes when I am out in a restaurant, I stop and realize I am not talking about medical issues, test results, and bodily functions and break out in a smile," Christine explained. At these times, she said, she feels the presence of her fellow bone marrow transplant recipients who did not survive. "I can almost hear them saying, 'You're one of the privileged ones who gets to stay on earth. Savor those sweet syrupy pancakes and awful coffee for yourself and for all of us who passed over to the other side.'"

Bringing up the memories of her deceased friends sparked other reminiscences. Christine told me about her first New Year's Eve after leaving the hospital. For a graduate of the University of Southern California's Film School and a young filmmaker, she said she spent it in a "totally uncool" fashion. "I flew to New York to see my parents and we attended a dance sponsored by a local church." Although everyone there was over the age of 60 and married, Christine said it was the best New Year's Eve of her life. "I got to wear a pretty little dress. And I was surrounded by people who had been praying for me all year."

When midnight neared, the DJ put on Joe Cocker's famous 1975 song, "You Are So Beautiful." As Cocker cooed the main refrain, "You're everything I hoped for, you're everything I need, you are so beautiful, to me," Christine's dad took her hand. Describing that moment, Christine's eyes misted over. "We were both in tears before we even reached the middle of the dance floor." Out on the dance floor, her mom rushed to join them. "Slowly swaying in a three-person hug, cheeks touching, tears streaming, hearts bursting, we gently danced amongst the love stories of all the elderly couples around us."

Months later, when her 31st birthday approached, Christine said she surrendered to endless tears of gratitude and the laughter of celebration. She called it "the birthday that almost wasn't."

Christine also told me that during her long hospital stay, she would dream about a day when she could walk without exhaustion, pain, needles, or doctors. "That day came on my birthday. The sun tap-danced across my skin as my friend and I walked along Ocean Avenue in Santa Monica. The cool breeze whispered promises of continued health. Joy filled my heart and laughter filled my lungs."

At gatherings for bone marrow survivors, Christine often meets people who feel the need to use their "second chance" to change the world or effect a large-scale change in society by getting involved with environmental issues or politics. She, on the other hand, believes that by talking to people and sharing her story, she can create change one person at a time. "If I could tell people just one thing I learned from my illness, it would be that you have no idea how many people love you."

After sharing breakfast with her, I had faith that Christine could indeed change the world one person at a time. I knew for certain she had changed my attitude about my flight back home to Seattle.

As I prepared to leave her company and head to the airport, I thought about my usual mind-set regarding the long lines at check-in, security screening, and the boring hour-plus spent waiting for the plane. Instead of indulging in self-pity, I thanked Christine for sharing her positive outlook on life. Riding in the van from the rental car agency, I told myself, "Today I am going to appreciate the fact that I am healthy enough to be around crowds, I have the prosperity to fly, and when I arrive home, I get to hug my family. I will focus on my blessings, which far outweigh the hassles." Once more, I gave thanks for the gift I received by being in Christine's presence.

Make it your story

Acknowledging the good that you already have in your life is the foundation for all abundance.
Eckhart Tolle

People generally take good health for granted. It is treated like a baseline state, how we expect to feel. Most of us only notice our health when something is amiss. Otherwise, we walk from the car to a store and take trash cans to the curb with little or no thought of the intricate body mechanics necessary to complete those simple tasks.

We forget that in a split second everything can change. Instantaneous shifts have happened to me through a car accident, a bulging disc, and a case of shingles. In a flash, I lost my mobility. It has also occurred more slowly with the onset of colds, coughs, and flus. Nothing refocuses my attention on the benefits of good health better then when I lose it.

One way to appreciate our complex bodies, even in times of good health, is mindfulness. This practice brings awareness to the intricacies of our bodies as they diligently work day in and day out. Plus, mindfulness, and the positive feelings it promotes, have been proven to help maintain good health by reducing emotional stress, lowering blood pressure, and increasing immune function. In essence, you can help maintain your good health by being consciously thankful for your good health.

Some people say mindfulness is the art of paying attention on purpose. You can increase your mindfulness (and health) by taking time throughout your day to:

- *Notice your surroundings—Use as many senses as possible to observe the world around you. For example, instead of just looking at a tree, feel the texture of its leaves and smell the tree's scent.*
- *Pause and focus on your breath—Consciously exhale. Then count to three and inhale. Repeat three times.*
- *Write out three gratitudes—List things from today or general things you appreciate.*

Luck vs. Attitude

FOR YEARS, I BELIEVED a canyon-wide schism existed between fortuity and misfortune. But I've changed my mind.

The subject of luck came up after a wild two-day, 125-mile excursion my two kids and I took from Seattle, Washington, to Vancouver, in beautiful British Columbia, Canada. Our mission was to scope out children's activities for a travel article assignment.

The moment we hit Interstate-5 heading north, it began raining. Not a typical Pacific Northwest drizzle. This was a windshield-wipers-on-high-and-I-still-can't-see-the-road downpour. The driving rain continued for our entire trip, washing out the hiking trails and closing the attractions I had planned to write about. Before heading home, we rewarded ourselves for putting up with two days of frustration by stopping at an indoor science center.

We spent the afternoon testing our mental strength against brain-teasing puzzles, experiencing a computerized geological expedition, and enjoying our dry surroundings. Sprinting back to our car through a torrential rainstorm, we found a smashed window, water streaming onto the driver's seat, and our suitcases gone. Before anger could take hold, I realized my kids and I were lucky. If we'd stumbled onto the scene while the burglary was in progress we might have been physically assaulted or worse. Besides, our monetary losses were minor. We had one broken window and the loss of a few clothes.

After we arrived home, I told a friend about our adventure. She said the trip was full of bad luck. I disagreed. Sloshing through two days of rain-drenched outings, my kids and I joked about our misadventures. As the absurdity of being foiled by closure after closure grew, so did our laughter. Talking about the theft, we imagined the thieves' faces when they found out they risked a jail sentence for a bunch of dirty clothes and snickered, "They were the ones with the bad luck."

Of course, our situation only involved the loss of physical possessions and the repair of a car window. The question of luck becomes more complicated when life-and-death issues are at stake.

While at her doctor's office, my friend T.J. noticed numerous signs touting the importance of regular mammograms. Even though she wasn't scheduled to endure the torturous breast clamp for another year, she had one done. The exam resulted in the discovery of cancer in one breast, and soon thereafter a partial mastectomy.

"Your guardian angel must have been watching over you," I told T.J. "I've never heard of anyone volunteering for an extra mammogram."

But, if T.J. was lucky, where was her guardian angel while the cancer was taking root? Was it luck to find the cancer while it was still treatable? Or unlucky to be diagnosed with cancer and undergo months of chemotherapy and radiation?

T.J.'s story grows more complicated when her ten-year-old son Rick's ordeal is thrown into the mix. Three days before T.J.'s scheduled mastectomy, she and her sister Jan planned a 24-hour beach vacation. With their swim-suits packed and the car loaded, they were just about ready to head out the door. Suddenly, Rick burst from his bedroom crying. Holding his neck, he wailed, "It hurts!" Jan, a registered nurse, immediately suspected meningitis.

They whisked Rick to the local hospital, where doctors confirmed Jan's suspicion. The question was what kind of meningitis? Days passed before they would learn if he had viral meningitis or the deadly bacterial meningitis.

Were Rick and his family lucky Jan was visiting and Rick received immediate medical attention? Or unlucky that a few days later, T.J. was on the eighth floor of a hospital recovering from a mastectomy while Rick was on the sixth floor of the same hospital still awaiting test results?

As I pondered T.J. and Rick's plight, I started reassessing my ideas about good luck and bad luck. I concluded that the terms good luck and bad luck are just labels. The critical issue is how one responds to life's events. Everyone living on this giant blue-green marble will experience good times, middle-of-the-road events, and a splattering of hellish times during their lives. Crossed fingers and rabbit foot charms can't change those facts.

Our power lies not in luck, but in how we react to life's changing cir-cumstances. For me, that means attitude. Every situation can be viewed from a variety of perspectives. My kids and I could have arrived home from Vancouver raging mad. But by laughing at two days of straight rain and the thieves who stole our smelly socks, we pulled into the driveway smiling, with a story we enjoy retelling.

Recently, I heard a saying that sums up the change in my philosophy about fortuity and misfortune: "Attitude is more important than fact." Rick came down with viral meningitis. That is a fact. But he recovered within a week and was soon back to shooting paintballs at his older brother. T.J. underwent months of cancer treatments. But she remained optimistic about her future and thankful for her excellent medical care. She might not have been able to control the winds of fate, but she trimmed her sails with a positive attitude.

All of this has lead me to the inescapable conclusion that Martha Washington was right: "The greatest part of our happiness depends on our dispositions, not our circumstances."

✂ Make it your story

Don't underestimate the power of a positive attitude. Instead of being locked into a reactive mindset, practice new ways of regarding life's surprises. With an upbeat attitude, you can turn unexpected events into adventures, disappointments into discoveries, and fears into innovations.

Most of our attitudes bubble to the surface without our awareness. We tend to automatically react without taking the time to consciously think about how we want to respond. It pays dividends to pause a moment, pay attention to our thoughts, and make a deliberate choice to be positive.

When you notice a negative knee-jerk thought or reaction to a situation, try these ideas:

• Look for something positive in the situation, even if it is tiny.

Finding something positive can help elevate your mood. It doesn't need to be anything major; it can be as small as liking the color of someone's eyes or enjoying a breeze on your face.

• Find humor in what is happening.

My kids and I love reminiscing about the mishaps from our trip to Vancouver. We break into laughter every time we retell our tale. Try it out yourself and see if it helps you navigate tough times.

• Mine the situation for a lesson you can use in the future.

Finding a nugget of useful information helps mitigate the sad and remorseful feeling that can accompany a negative situation.

• Turn negative self-talk into positive comments.

Most people talk to themselves in ways that they would never talk to another human being. If you hear yourself saying hurtful things to yourself, stop. Give yourself the same respect you would give someone else.

• Write down your feelings or find someone to talk with.

Expressing yourself in writing or verbally can help reduce the intensity of what you are feeling.

Making these changes takes practice. Persistence is the key to changing your automatic responses from negative to positive. With conscious repetition, you will succeed.

Animal Wisdom

LAST MONTH A TURTLE WINKED AT ME. Honestly. I even have a witness.

A friend and I were visiting Lake Shrine, a spiritual sanctuary built by Paramahansa Yogananda, founder of the Self-Realization Foundation and author of *Autobiography of a Yogi*. Located in Southern California, a few blocks from the Pacific Ocean, this ten-acre oasis offers a respite from Los Angeles' frenetic energy. As I stepped inside the gates of this serene haven, I could feel the stress drop off my shoulders. Bird songs mingled with muted traffic sounds as we strolled around a natural spring-fed lake. Lush gardens with flora from six continents bordered the lake, creating a bouquet of scents that changed every few steps.

As I rested on a bench that overlooked the emerald green lake, I saw a pair of turtles, with dark green shells and red stripes behind their eyes, sunning on a rock. As someone who talks to everything from her car to her cat to her houseplants, I greeted the turtles and told them that turtles were one of my totem animals. In response, the turtle on the right stuck out his neck as far as it would go and turned around to look at me. Encouraged by his attention, I told him I appreciated having turtle medicine in my life. That's when the turtle gave me a one-eyed wink. Before I could utter a word, my friend exclaimed, "That turtle just winked at you."

In Native American lore, it is believed that communication between humans and animals often comes in the form of a totem animal. These are birds, reptiles, insects or other animals that come to people in meditations, visions, or dreams. Each animal holds symbolic significance and lessons that the person needs to learn. The totem animals embody attributes or characteristics the person needs at a specific time in his or her life. For instance, bee represents fertility, a good totem for someone wanting to conceive; fox symbolizes cleverness, a helpful attribute for person working on a business deal; and dolphin represents intuition, a useful trait for a healer.

A person can have several totem animals throughout his or her life. Sometimes a totem animal stays for a short period of time. Then, depending on a person's life journey, it might be replaced by another totem animal. Other times, a totem animal stays with someone for a long time.

I first learned about totem animals in 1979. On our first date, Bo invited me to attend a guided meditation led by Sun Bear, a Chippewa medicine man who founded the Bear Tribe. During that meditation, a turtle appeared to me and gave me an eight-word message. "Move to an island and start a family." Those words turned out to be a blueprint for the next two years of my life. Within the next 24 months, my boyfriend and I moved from Seattle to Orcas Island, married, and, within a year, started a family.

My interaction with the turtle at Lake Shrine helped me remember that turtle medicine teaches flexibility and the ability to find harmony within one's environment. Frequently, when I travel to Los Angeles to visit family, the frantic pace of life seeps into my consciousness and I become agitated. After my encounter with the turtle, I slowed down, meditated in various locations around the grounds, and tapped into a quiet tranquility deep inside myself. Even when I left Lake Shrine and returned to the world of freeway mazes and crowds of people, I was able to remain centered.

Though the turtle totem has been a part of my life for more than twenty years, I have also been blessed by the presence of other totem animals. In fact, I could fill a couple of totem poles with all the animals that have shared their wisdom with me. Some came to me through guided meditations, others in dreams, and some in waking life.

When I see the same animal several times within a short period of time or see an animal outside its normal habitat, I take note and look up their attributes in Ted Andrews' book, *Animal Speak: The Spiritual & Magical Powers of Creatures Great & Small,* a dictionary of animal totems that describes their attributes. For example, this past spring, a pair of ducks flew into my yard. Although I live near a pond, this was the first (and only) time ducks had ever landed in my yard. Later that week, while out walking, I saw a pair of ducks walking down a street—across a busy intersection and two blocks away from the pond. Because I was seeing ducks outside their natural habitat, I looked up their symbolism in *Animal Speak*. There I learned that a duck totem can help one clearly see and deal with emotions. Soon after my encounter with the ducks, a close friend went into the hospital for a series of medical procedures. Keeping the duck totem in mind, I paid extra attention to my emotional state of mind during that difficult time. During my frequent visits to the hospital, I honored my needs as well as those of my friend. I took breaks to eat, walked around the neighborhood, and treated myself with more compassion than I might have if the ducks had not shown up in my life.

⤋ Make it your story

If you want to discover your totem animals, ask yourself the following questions:

What animals are you currently interested in learning about?

What is your favorite animal? It could be a mammal, bird, reptile, insect, fish, or another creature.

When you are out in nature, whether it is a city park or a forest, what animal do you notice most frequently?

When you go to the zoo, what is the first animal you want to visit?

What animal scares you?

What animal fascinates you?

Which animals frequent your dreams?

Review your answers and choose a totem animal. Don't worry about choosing the wrong animal, only you can know for sure what totem animal is right for your life journey.

Once you have decided on a specific totem, bring pictures or statues of that animal into your home. Read about your totem and learn about its qualities and characteristics. This will let your totem animal know that you are open to receiving information and learning from it. Once the animal understands that you are open to hearing its wisdom, it may bring you messages through dreams or in your waking life. Use your journal to record your process of identifying and working with your totem animal.

Choosing Life

FOR MUCH OF MY ADULT LIFE, I viewed suicide as my ace in the hole. Anytime there was a crisis, whether it was a breakup with a boyfriend or a dispute at work, I automatically thought, "If this doesn't work out, I can always kill myself."

That attitude may sound flippant, but those were not trivial thoughts. I often spent hours figuring out quick, effective ways to kill myself. Looking back, the pleasure I experienced knowing I could choose death at any moment seems disturbingly macabre.

Back then, suicide felt like my only way out of difficult situations. I did not realize that if I was miserable, I had the power to change the situation, my attitude, or both.

I came closest to committing suicide during a time of deep despair while attending college. Filled with feelings of profound hopelessness that I thought would last forever, I was consumed by negative thoughts. Thankfully, my friend Diane dropped by unexpectedly. She talked me through my despondency and helped me regain a healthier perspective on life.

Although I narrowly escaped paying the ultimate price, this episode did not put an end to my suicidal thoughts. I continued planning ways to end my life.

Then one day while meditating, I had a revelation so powerful that I wrote down the date in my journal—March 11, 2000. That morning I realized that by focusing on suicide, I was not fully living. In that instant, I saw my life divided into two parts. Half my attention was turned toward life-affirming actions, the other half searching for the best suicide plan.

From that revelation, a question arose. What if I lived my life without an exit plan? I tried to imagine how my life would change if suicide wasn't an option. What would be different if I had to make this life work until my natural death? My answer was I would be more engaged with life.

Over the next few days, I mulled over my revelation and resolved to shift my focus from dying to living. To help me make this transition, I applied a principle I had successfully used to make other changes in my life—redirecting my attention. My subconscious mind had shown me it supported change by bringing the issue to my attention during meditation. Now I needed to work with my conscious thoughts.

Refocusing my thinking required considerable effort. Each time I heard the familiar refrain, "If this problem doesn't work out, I'll just kill myself," I replaced it with the question, "Since suicide is no longer an option, what will you do to resolve this problem?" With unwavering conviction, I stopped looking for a way out and instead focused on resolving my problems.

As I released self-hating thoughts and embraced my right to change situations that were not working, I began appreciating life more. Nature's palette of colors came into sharper focus. Food tasted more delectable. I became more engaged with my work, the people in my life, and my dreams for the future. By replacing my old suicide refrain with the axiom, "This, too, shall pass," I slowly learned to release sorrows more easily and allow joy in more fully.

Since firmly rejecting suicide's allure, I have met individuals whose relatives and friends killed themselves. Seeing the anguish survivors suffer showed me the terrible legacy suicide leaves behind. I now know that no matter how bad I felt, it paled in comparison to the ongoing grief I would have caused others had I killed myself.

Today I realize that each person is born for a reason. Yes, there are times of hopelessness, when it is hard to understand one's purpose. Yet everyone has value and something unique to give the world. And suicide deprives everyone of that special gift.

✧ Make It Your Story

This is one time I hope you cannot relate to my story. However, if you are depressed or suicidal, reach out for help. Call a trusted friend, therapist, crisis clinic, or the national suicide prevention number: 800-273-8255 (text 741741). Although you may feel embarrassed to share your deep feelings or think you are exposing a weakness, people you connect with will be glad you called them instead of trying to handle the situation by yourself. Tell the person about the thoughts going through your mind. If you have a suicide plan, tell them what it is.

Give yourself 48 hours before implementing any life-ending plans. Emotions are not fixed. From your vantage point it may look like there is no hope, but it is impossible to know how things will change unless you postpone your decision. You may feel completely different within 48 hours.

Avoid all alcohol and drugs. These substances make it harder to think clearly.

Make your home safe. Put away all pills, knives, razors, or firearms. If you can't do that, find somewhere safe to stay or someone to stay with you.

If you are feeling down, but not suicidal, try shifting your perspective. Spin your mental wheels in the opposite direction and transform your litany of complaints into a list of blessings. Think of it as a game. The more positive thoughts you generate, the better chance you have for a bliss-filled day.

Here are a few examples of how to turn negatives into positives: I have to go to work—I will be able to pay my rent this month; I did a terrible job—I learned from the experience and can do better next time; I am exhausted—I am doing the best I can. It is important to believe (even if only a little bit) the positive statement you choose.

Staying in Shape

A WHILE AGO, I WAS ASKED why I maintain a daily meditation practice. Why don't I reserve meditation for stressful times when I need to calm down? I explained that meditation provides me with a slice of quiet time each day when I can withdraw from all the "have-tos" and focus inward. Later, when I had time to reflect on the question, I realized my reasons are more complex.

In many ways, daily meditation is similar to working out in a gym. For both activities to have an optimal effect on my health and well-being, I need to do them regularly.

A big reason I exercise regularly is to retain my strength and agility, two attributes that need to be built up and maintained over time. If I want to put out the extra physical effort required to lift a 40-pound bag of cat litter into my shopping cart or to dance past midnight, I need to exercise regularly.

Meditation imparts different, yet equally important qualities. Since I began meditating, I have found a place of stillness inside myself. Now, when I notice I am in a stressful situation, whether it is a conflict with a person or dealing with a computer problem, I can tap into that source of stillness and, in a short time, feel more at peace with the world around me and with myself. Meditation also clears my mind and allows me to work more efficiently. But, there is one requisite: I have to meditate regularly in order to draw on these benefits at a moment's notice.

I remember years ago, when I was just out of college and looking for a new job in a new town. With each passing week, my savings shrank while my sense of hopelessness rose. Looking back on that time, I can see that my despondency worked against me. Instead of presenting myself as a self-assured professional, my legitimate yet overt fear of not being hired gave me an air of neediness and desperation—the exact opposite of what an employer wants in an employee.

If I had meditated during that period of my life, I could have drawn on my ability to stay calm in times of stress. A regular mediation routine would have allowed me to take several deep breaths and recreate the sense of peace before I entered my interviews.

My awareness of the wonderful outcomes gained from regular exercise and meditation doesn't make it any easier to maintain these habits. Being disciplined remains challenging. Some days I would rather do anything—clean the toilet or pick splinters out of my finger—than trudge to the gym. Those days require a set of mental calisthenics to prod me into going to the gym. The same holds true for meditation. I frequently experience internal battles with myself about time spent sitting still when I "should be" doing other things.

I blame these struggles on an inner gremlin that regularly urges me skip a day or two or three of meditation and exercise. It has taken many years for me to realize that my inner gremlin does not have my best interests at heart. When I recognize her voice, I patiently listen to her suggestions that I skip the gym or meditation. I do not argue with her or disagree with her opinions. That would be an exercise in futility. She always wants the last word. Instead, I thank her for her viewpoint, then pack up my gym bag, and head out the door or sit down and meditate.

Because it is impossible to know in advance when I am going to need to draw on the physical strength I gain from regular workouts at the gym or the inner sense of tranquility I develop through daily meditation, I maintain my regular routines. Then, when unexpected situations arise, I am ready.

⤖ Make it Your Story

What task do you want to practice regularly? Is it a new language or musical instrument? Or are you looking for ways to incorporate more movement into your life?

Try different methods for motivating yourself. Here are five ideas to get you started:

- *Break the task down into small segments.*
- *Make it fun.*
- *Remind yourself why you want to regularly do this task.*
- *Set up an accountability system with a friend.*
- *Set up a reward for when you accomplish the task.*

The Silver Birch

One could do worse than be a swinger of birches.
Birches by Robert Frost

SAD NEWS ACCOMPANIED the introduction to my new neighbor.

After introducing himself, he announced his plan to cut down the silver birch tree standing at the north corner of my garage, just inside his property line. When I moved into the neighborhood, 17 years ago, the tree was just a scrawny sapling. Over the years, I watched it grow into a towering, 30-foot giant. Like a perpetual teenager, the silver birch's annual growth spurts, sometimes as much as two feet in one year, stretched its silvery-white bark. Every spring I observed a new crop of small diamond shaped leaves adorn the branches. A hint of a breeze was occasion enough for the bright green leaves to twirl and dance. Dazzling sunshine and warm winds worked together during the summer months to transform the birch leaves into tiny mirrors. Then, as summer folded into fall, a snap of cold weather transformed the leaves into a yellow blaze. Gradually the leaves browned and autumn rainstorms drove them down by the bucket load.

And that is what my new neighbor objected to—fall leaves that would soon fill his driveway.

When he called in the tree cutter, my neighbor probably didn't know that birch trees colonized North America after the last Ice Age approximately 13,000 years ago. Nor would he have known that the birch tree, which may look fragile, often finds a foothold in regions of the Arctic tundra where other trees are unable to grow. His focus was on the boat he parked in his front yard. If he did not take action soon, the birch tree's falling bounty would turn his uncovered boat into a leaf-catcher.

I developed my deep appreciation for birch trees one summer when a herniated disc in my neck left me writhing in pain, unable to walk, drive, hold a book, write, or do anything productive. The only semi-comfortable position I found was lying down. Quickly tiring of lying on the couch watching television, I spent hours outside reclining in a lounge chair and watching leaves swing and sway in a giant, 50-foot silver birch that grew on the south side of my yard. Gazing at the birch tree, my body and mind briefly escaped the around-the-clock pain that otherwise consumed my consciousness. In an inexplicable way, I felt the tree was saving my sanity and my life. The moments of peace and renewal I gained from our afternoons together gave me the strength to endure the unceasing pain.

After a month of misery, my slow recovery advanced to a point where I was able to walk a few blocks to a nearby park. There, on the banks of a small pond, stood a stately silver birch with branches stretching up to the sky and out over the water. In a crook of the tree's trunk was a perfect, naturally formed seat, flat and broad. Many afternoons I stopped, sat in the tree, and swung my feet over the water. The tree nurtured me by providing me with a destination and a place to rest.

Along the way, I learned that in Celtic mythology the birch tree is known as the bringer of strength and for offering protection in times of adversity. Its wood is believed to ward off evil. Since it appears delicate, while in fact it is extremely strong, the birch teaches that strength can often be found in apparent fragility. The birch's mystical attributes matched the gifts I had received from the birch trees in my backyard and neighborhood park during the summer of my recuperation.

That is why, when I learned about the planned demise of my neighbor's silver birch, it touched my core. While that specific birch tree had not played a role in helping me survive the summer of pain, its relations were my saviors. I wanted to help the tree, but didn't know what to do. No matter how sad I felt about losing the birch, I knew the tree belonged to my neighbor and he had every right to cut it down.

My strong feelings surprised me. Whole forests go up in flames every year during wildfire season and I don't mourn, so why did I care so much about this one tree? It was because of the birch trees that had helped me convalesce. I felt I could give back to this species of tree by helping my neighbor's tree.

Talking to a friend about my conundrum, she suggested I tell the tree what was going to happen so that it could release its spirit before the tree-cutter arrived.

"Where would its spirit go?" I asked.

"I don't know," answered my friend. "But the tree will know what to do."

I was intrigued with the idea of helping the tree release its spirit. Although I had long believed that everything had a life force, be it an animal, stone, or tree, I had never pondered what happens to a tree's spirit when it is cut down.

The next afternoon, when no one else was around, I went outside and began a one-sided conversation with the birch tree. Before revealing what I knew about its demise, I tried to soften the blow by telling it how much I had loved watching it grow up. I mentioned each season, and the many ways it brought beauty to the neighborhood. When I delivered the bad news, I didn't notice any reaction. The birch tree's white trunk did not bend in sorrow and its leaves didn't tremble in fear. To be honest, I wasn't sure it understood me.

So, I began talking to my two birch heroes, the trees that had helped me survive that long ago summer when I was convalescencing. I told them about the birch that was going to be cut down, its location, and the scheduled date of its demise. I asked them to warn the birch and request that its spirit flee before the physical tree was chopped into firewood.

I added the neighbor's tree to my prayer list. Along with praying for friends and relatives who were undergoing hard times, I began praying for the release of the silver birch's spirit.

Too soon, the dreaded day came. The tree-cutter was scheduled to arrive at noon. As luck would have it, my neighbor had to run an errand and asked Bo to take charge of getting the tree cut down. Then Bo was called away unexpectedly. That left me. If the tree-cutter arrived before the neighbor got home, I was supposed to point out the tree to be cut. I felt like Judas. After all the loving attention I had given the tree, how could I pronounce its death sentence? I played with the idea of telling the tree-cutter there had been a change in plans, that no tree was coming down. Thankfully, I was spared the need to test my resolve when my neighbor returned home ahead of schedule and reclaimed his responsibility.

Throughout that morning, I made several trips to the backyard to tell the tree it was time for its spirit to leave. Time was ticking; the truck carrying the tree-cutter was on its way. As noon approached, a growing sense of panic rose within me. Then I heard the deep rumble of a truck turning onto our street. I ran outside to tell the birch tree to release its spirit. The tree looked the same. Its silver-white bark created the perfect canvas for its cheerful yellow leaves. As I started to plead with it one last time, I felt a palpable difference, a void I could feel in my chest.

In an instant, I saw myself back in a hospital room, standing beside my mother-in-law's bed as she slipped from a coma into death. Then I flashed forward a few years to my father-in-law's passing, as he inhaled a breath that was never released. I remembered how, in a split second, my in-laws' presence had changed. Their bodies looked the same, but their life force was gone. That invisible spirit that animated them, that made them into the people I knew and loved, had vanished. Looking at the silver birch, I recognized that same absence of life force. I knew without a doubt that the cosmic dance of life and death, that unexplainable thread that separates the living from the dead, is similar for humans and trees.

Fully aware that the tree's spirit had escaped, I retreated back inside, hoping to avoid the traumatic event. But the sounds of the tree being ground into wood chips pierced the house walls. When the noise stopped, I reluctantly stepped outside to survey the damage. The void left behind startled me. Where the birch's leaves had once twirled and danced on gentle breezes, there was now nothing but empty space. Like a recently departed friend, the tree's absence felt larger than its presence.

✧ Make it your story

Our lives are intricately intertwined with the world of nature. Although our relationship with trees often goes unnoticed, trees and people both rely on sunlight and water for nourishment.

The presence of trees benefits humans in a number of ways. Trees clean our air, produce the oxygen we need to breathe, provide shade that keeps city streets cooler, fight soil erosion, and provide us with fruit.

See if you can find other connections between trees and people by developing a relationship with a tree. Walk by a variety of trees and notice if any particular one calls to you. This process is similar to finding a human friend. We are naturally drawn to some people more than others. Look for a tree that seems interesting, either in the way it looks or how you feel when you are in its proximity.

Once you identify your tree, visit it on a regular basis. Begin by allowing yourself to feel any discomfort that arises from trying something new. When you communicate with your tree, you can do it silently or out loud. Start by introducing yourself. Tell the tree what you appreciate about it. Does it provide shade or shelter for birds and squirrels? Is it fruit bearing? Spend a few moments in silent contact. Touch its trunk and try to sense the life force going through the tree. You may even feel energy pulsating through the tree, similar to a heartbeat.

Play the "what if" game and write down your musings. What if the tree could talk? What stories could it tell you? What if the tree could move? Where would it go?

Conscious Living

The Power of Joy

ONE EARLY SPRING MORNING, I received a phone call from my friend Jackie. "I have an extra ticket to His Holiness the Dalai Lama's talk at the University of Washington. If you can be ready and at my house in fifteen minutes, it's yours."

His Holiness the 14th Dalai Lama was in Seattle to participate in a five-day event sponsored by Seeds of Compassion. Although I had seen him three days earlier, along with 50,000 other people at a Seattle stadium, I leapt at the chance to see him speaking with Anglican Archbishop Desmond Tutu. Sitting at the kitchen table in my pajamas, I eagerly said, "I'll be there." Within minutes, I cleared my calendar, dressed, and hopped in my car. The clock was ticking.

Although Jackie lives within seven miles of my home, my efforts to reach her house were thwarted by red lights and slow drivers. I chanted "change, change, change" to signals and "move, move, move" to drivers. But as the minutes ticked by on the dashboard clock, my agitation grew into a ball of tension in my stomach.

Then I remembered a concept I heard the Dalai Lama speak about several years earlier in Portland, Oregon. He said that if we wanted peace in the world, we needed to bring the essence of peace into our daily interactions with others. The Dalai Lama called it "personal disarmament." He said it is not enough to work toward world disarmament, we also must focus on our personal behavior. Through thoughts and actions, we need to make our slice of the world a more peaceful place. Putting world peace bumper stickers on our cars, then raging at red lights and slow drivers, is not the answer.

Taking a deep breath, I realized the absurdity of getting frustrated by other drivers while on my way to see a man whose life goal is to spread peace. Ironically, right after I shifted my attitude, I got a series of green lights and made it to Jackie's place just a couple of minutes late.

The talk at the University of Washington included speakers from a variety of religious traditions. But my focus was on the Dalai Lama and Archbishop Tutu.

We sat in the bleachers, across a basketball court but directly in front of the Dalai Lama and Archbishop Tutu. The Dalai Lama wore crimson and saffron robes; Archbishop Tutu sported a hot pink zuchetto on his head and a matching floor-length vestment. Their vibrant attire lit up the stage.

Sitting side-by-side, these two holy men brought a mischievous element to their serious discussion about caring for the children of the world and global peace. The importance and weight of the day's topics didn't stop them from kidding each other and sharing gales of laughter.

As I witnessed them joking around, I thought, if anyone had just cause to lose themselves to despair, it was these two holy men. The Dalai Lama has lived in exile from his homeland of Tibet since 1959. After he escaped the country, China's Red Guard destroyed most of Tibet's temples and persecuted many lamas and nuns. In South Africa, Archbishop Tutu lived through the atrocities perpetrated during apartheid, and now chairs the Truth and Reconciliation Commission, a court-like body where victims of violent repression relate their experiences.

Yet, these two men, who have witnessed people behaving at their worst, acted like two young kids, poking and teasing each other. Instead of focusing on the negative, the Dalai Lama and Archbishop Tutu manifested the best qualities of humanity: forgiveness, compassion, and happiness. The joy that bubbled up from within them was palpable.

Since seeing these two holy men speak, I have been working to bring their peace and joy into my life. When I read tragic newspaper articles, sit in traffic, or hear stories about how the current economy is affecting people around the world, I picture both of them on stage in front of thousands of people, laughing and enjoying the moment. As I do this, my sense of hopelessness evaporates and I find myself smiling.

❧ Make it your story

Begin your quest for personal disarmament by befriending yourself—a task that is easier to think about than to implement. As Phillip C. McGraw (a.k.a. Dr. Phil) once said, "At this very moment, you may be saying to yourself that you have any number of admirable qualities. You are a loyal friend, a caring person, someone who is smart, dependable, and fun to be around. That's wonderful, and I'm happy for you, but let me ask you this: are you being any of those things to yourself?"

One way to practice compassion and kindness with yourself is to pay attention to the monologue playing inside your head. When you observe negative statements about yourself swirling around your mind, convert them into positive or neutral thoughts.

With loving compassion (the kind you usually reserve for family and friends), refocus your attention on gratitude, change the wording from an attack on yourself into an affirmative declaration, or shift your attention to something pleasing in your environment (such as a hot vanilla latte or golden fall leaves).

The more you engage in the process of personal disarmament, the easier it becomes to practice self-compassion.

Bus Life

MY LIFE AS A BUS RIDER DIDN'T BEGIN with a noble decision to reduce my carbon footprint or to save money. It was jump-started when my car died.

On a starless night in March, I was on my way home from visiting family about two hours south of Seattle. With no warning, my car went from a smooth-riding 60 mph to zero. There was no shaking or sputtering before it abruptly broke down on Interstate 5.

Sitting in my car on the side of the road, I remembered the mysterious message I heard in meditation that day. "You will make it down south, but you won't make it back." Although I did not understand it at the time, now the meaning was clear.

Sitting in the stillness, I felt simultaneously lucky and completely freaked out. My good fortune was not breaking down in the fast lane and causing a major traffic jam or an accident. The panic came from being alone on a dark freeway with cars zooming past me. Every time a car flew by, it sent a tiny earthquake through me and my car. My insides quivered and my heart pounded.

After taking several slow deep breaths, I calmed down enough to call a tow truck service. It happened to be a busy night for tow truck drivers, and my wait time was set at three hours.

The arrival of the tow truck driver and the long 95-mile tow home unfolded without incident. The next bombshell didn't come until the following morning, when the auto repair shop declared my car beyond resuscitation.

I briefly shopped for a replacement car, before hearing my inner voice suggest bus life. Initially, I pooh-poohed the idea of going without a car. I had learned to drive on the Los Angeles freeways, and, up until then, considered owning my own car a necessity. The idea of being carless challenged the core image of myself as independent and able to get anywhere by myself. My ultimate decision to go carless mystifies my family and friends almost as much as it bewilders me.

For some people, it is a privilege to own and drive a car. For me it is a privilege to ride the bus. Not everyone can afford a car, and not everyone can afford the time it takes to ride the bus. Currently, I am a time-rich bus rider; my schedule allows me to live at a slower pace.

I often hear people lamenting their fast-paced lives. They bemoan constantly being on the go, navigating traffic and racing from one errand to another. I understand their dilemma. When I had a car, I too lived a fast-paced life. In addition to the usual trips for work and shopping, I was a volunteer-aholic. If someone had a need, I felt obliged to fill it. I required an extra-large calendar to fit my long daily to-do lists.

Being a bus rider, I can only go as fast as the buses allow. Between the walking (bus riding requires a lot of walking), waiting for buses, missing buses, and watching overfull buses pass me by, I cannot race anywhere. Getting two or three errands done per day is my maximum. A quick trip to the store that used to take me twenty minutes, now takes over an hour. My life went from supercharged to a snail pace. And, surprisingly, I like it.

Instead of keeping an eye on traffic, I sit on the bus and rubberneck to my heart's content. This allows me to people watch, notice the changing seasons, and check out new housing developments in ways I never could when driving. As a recovering volunteer-aholic with codependent tendencies, I have curbed my inclination to over-volunteer. By prioritizing my artwork, I devote more time for creative projects like collaging, storytelling, and writing.

Yes, there are numerous hassles involved with bus riding. Because I don't like standing on busy street corners at night, I go out less in the evening. When it rains, I get wet. During summer heat waves, I swelter in the sun. On any given day, a bus trip that was supposed to take half an hour can take twice as long due to mechanical problems or long stops to accommodate the loading of wheelchairs and strollers. Even with those hassles, the benefits currently outweigh the negatives.

Another plus is the people I meet on the bus. Although most people are plugged into their phones, a few folks are still open to talking. On a bus ride home from Tacoma, I met a 92-year-old World War II veteran. He was heading home after changing theater tickets to accommodate his new girl-friend's early bedtime. He and I talked nonstop for 45 minutes. I learned about his career as a Yosemite National Park tour bus driver, how he grew up speaking Italian, and that he did not believe in emailing someone when a pen and paper did the job just fine.

One day a woman locked step with me as I disembarked the bus and complimented me on my smile. As I turned to thank her, I saw a woman in her mid-thirties wearing a wool cap. She was rail-thin and appeared to be bald beneath the cap. As we crossed a busy intersection, she told me she had terminal cancer and, for a myriad of reasons, would soon be homeless. We walked together for two blocks as she told me all the bad things happening in her life. Instead of problem-solving, I focused my attention on witnessing her story. Her demeanor, words, and facial expressions all conveyed extreme sadness, until she shared her life passion. The woman's whole being lit up when she spoke about her spiritual pursuits. I cherish those few minutes that bus riding allowed me to spend with her.

Bus life puts me in contact with a wide swath of humanity. At a few of my regular bus stops there is a parade of scantily dressed prostitutes and people tweaked out on drugs. I have seen bus drivers cuss and scream at other drivers and college students diligently studying while the person next to them converses with a wilting flower. In some ways, buses are an equalizing zone. Homeless people catching a few winks sit side by side with young professionals heading off to their jobs at Google and Amazon. Mormon missionaries and con artists strike up conversations, weaving around their unspoken motives, spinning stories and offering miracles.

Speaking of miracles, since becoming a bus rider, my aggravation level has plummeted. When I drove, I was frequently agitated or angry at traffic and other drivers. Now I can make it through several days without feeling vexed.

Being carless has also meant getting rides in other people's cars to or from weekly and monthly events. The regularly shared time has transformed acquaintances into friends. Catching rides home from parties and events has allowed me to get to know people I never would have spent time with if I were driving my own car. Spending these intimate moments with other people has given me peeks into their lives, and in the process enriched my own life.

I don't image I will stay carless forever, but right now the lifestyle suits me.

✂ Make it your story

"I feel I change my mind all the time. And I sort of feel that's your responsibility as a person, as a human being—to constantly be updating your positions on as many things as possible. And if you don't contradict yourself on a regular basis, then you're not thinking."
Malcolm Gladwell

I once read a story about an elderly man who went to church during a torrential downpour. When asked why he decided to come out in the pouring rain, he responded, "I didn't decide to come out in today's storm. At age 20 I made a commitment to go to church every week."

Some people may find that commitment admirable. I don't. I believe decisions need to be reviewed. Something that was true for me as a teenager does not necessarily fit my life now. The world is constantly changing, and so am I. Why should I remain locked into a decision? I admire the courage it takes to revisit a settled question, reexamine it, and possibly discover a different answer.

One way to rethink a decision is to use the "five whys" technique. This technique was originally developed by Toyota Industries to help the company with problem solving. Begin with the decision, problem, or issue you want to review. Then ask your first "why" question. Use each subsequent answer as a jumping off place for the next question. Move quickly from one question to the next to avoid jumping to a conclusion before you have a full picture.

Here is an example: I decided when I got this job to stay until retirement. Now I am reevaluating that decision.

Why?—There is no chance for promotion.

Why?—I don't have the necessary educational degree to qualify for advancement.

Why?—I can't afford to pursue a higher degree.

Why?—My job doesn't give paid time off for schooling or help pay tuition.

Why?—The administration expects short-term results and frequent staff turnovers.

My new decision: to find a new job with education benefits that will allow me to pursue an advanced degree.

What's that Tune?

EVERY DAY, I FIND MYSELF UNCONSCIOUSLY humming or singing various songs. I call the source of these tunes my subconscious jukebox. My "mental singing" can usually be heard only inside my head. People around me don't know that I am singing while standing at the ATM or in the checkout line at the grocery store, unless they happen to notice a slight sway in my hips or a tapping foot. Sometimes, however, snatches of songs burst from my mouth surprising me, as well as people nearby.

My subconscious jukebox has a broad array of melodies and an uncanny ability to select just the right song for any situation. Because of this accuracy, I have gotten into the habit of deliberately going over the lyrics to see if the song ties into current life issues. Usually, I find a connection.

Once, I found myself slipping into a blue mood while participating in a dolphin swim in Hawaii. I had waited a lifetime to swim with wild dolphins and I expected everything to be perfect. When reality fell short of my high expectations, I got depressed.

For that situation, my subconscious jukebox played "Fun, Fun, Fun" by the Beach Boys. The words, "And we'll have fun, fun, fun," kept repeating ad nauseam. After hearing those words loop through my mind for hours while swimming, taking a shower, and dining, the message finally sank in: stop being so serious and have fun. It was November, the rainy season in Seattle, and I was in sunny Hawaii. Instead of struggling to get reality to match my preconceived ideas and dreams, I focused on the joy of being in the warm ocean water with wild dolphins.

Another time, while doing multiple loads of laundry, I heard the lyrics from "Sixteen Tons," a 1940s folk song written by Merle Travis. The verse that caught my attention was, "You load sixteen tons and what do you get? Another day older and deeper in debt; Saint Peter don't you call me 'cause I can't go; I owe my soul to the company store." Since I was working as a free-lance writer, I didn't think the lyrics were referring to my work life. Giving the verse some thought, I realized I was feeling overwhelmed by never-ending household chores. While I did not "owe my soul to the company store," I was taking on an elephant's share of family duties. The song served as a divining rod, locating a potential trouble spot before I became consciously aware of it. This insight allowed me to talk with family members and read-just our respective workloads before resentments rooted and grew.

Before my dad passed away after a long bout with Alzheimer's and Parkinson's disease, songs from 1950s musicals worked like a mental alarm clock, reminding me to call him and check in. Songs can also serve as a warning system. If I am talking to a stranger and I hear Simon and Garfunkel's song, "Fifty Ways to Leave Your Lover," I know to exit the situa-tion as soon as possible. The words, "You just slip out the back, Jack, make a new plan, Stan, you don't need to be coy, Roy, just get yourself free," call attention to potential dangers I may be overlooking. The song also reminds me that I do not need to be polite when exiting. I can just hop on the bus and get myself free.

Sometimes I sing or chant at the beginning of my morning meditation. As I close my eyes and settle in, my subconscious jukebox chooses a song. Often, the song establishes the theme for that meditation. After singing for a few minutes, I ride the current of the words into a meditative state.

✥ Make it your story

Do the songs you sing hold messages for you? Pay attention to the lyrics and you might receive clarification or solutions to a pestering problem. If you don't have a subconscious jukebox, pay attention to connections between songs you hear on the radio and your thoughts. Whether the song comes from an internal or external source, the lyrics can provide "aha" moments that help your decision-making process, offer a warning, or serve as a reminder to smile and not take life too seriously.

When lyrics get caught in a loop and keep playing repeatedly in your mind, write them down. Underneath the lyrics, do a "quick writing" session. Write non-stop for ten minutes. If you become stuck, write out "I am stuck" until inspiration strikes. When you are finished, read what you have written. Notice if there are clues that can help you in your life.

Take the High Road

OUT OF THE CORNER OF MY EYE, I see a flash of red. Instantly my foot hits the brakes before my brain registers what is happening: a sports car pulled out of its parking spot, swerved in front of me, and cut me off. Under my breath I mutter, "What are you thinking?"

It happens all the time. Drivers do squirrelly things, dangerous antics that could cause a wreck. When I am on the receiving end and feeling Zen-like, I wish the driver a safe journey. Otherwise, I fling a few choice words at the driver as he zooms past.

Occasionally, we all do stupid things while driving. I know I do them. Not intentionally, but it happens. And when it does, I usually have a rational explanation to account for my reckless behavior. I'll bet you do, too. In fact, I would wager most people could justify their risky behavior behind the wheel. That's why I propose we cut each other a bit of slack.

The truth is, we will never know why a driver cuts us off, drives over or under the speed limit, or runs a red light. While tailgating drivers who have angered us or screaming obscenities might make us momentarily feel better, neither behavior makes the situation any better. If you look at the situation from a karmic point of view, any negative energy or action you toss out into the world will boomerang back at you.

What if we turn things around and assume other drivers have reasons for their misbehavior? Those reasons may not be valid, or even legal, but if you stopped offenders in mid-act, they could tell you what prompted their transgression.

If you enjoy making up stories about people's behaviors, then think up good reasons for their gaffes instead of bad ones. Here are a few situations with plausible explanations.

A guy cuts you off on your way to work. Until he hears the squeal of your brakes, you and your car are not even on his mental screen. He just got laid off and has no idea how he'll pay his mortgage. Not only is he unaware he came within three inches of being slammed in the rear end, he is so preoccupied with his worries that he barely knows he is behind the wheel of a two-ton sedan barreling down the freeway at 65 miles per hour.

Should he be on the road? Probably not. But sending him on his way with a negative gesture will not improve his day or yours.

Then there is the slow-mo who goes five miles under the 25-miles-an-hour speed limit through your residential neighborhood. Most drivers are aching to go faster, but not this driver, who is recovering from a stroke. This is his first post-stroke outing behind the wheel. He is testing his ability to drive. He'll only drive a couple of miles from home and then reverse his route. Unfortunately, you're the one behind him until he turns around.

What about the driver who ran the signal two full seconds after it turned red? She just learned her son was in a serious car accident and is speeding to the hospital emergency room.

Does everyone who drives erratically have a reason? If you count "because I wanted to" as a reason, the answer is probably yes.

The point is that cutting people slack actually benefits you more than the other driver. Getting in a stew and fuming about someone who cut you off can ruin your day. Tailgating can cause a wreck. Gesturing at other drivers has the potential of leading to a physical altercation or worse. Nothing is gained by any of those reactions.

Instead of getting steamed by others' foolhardy driving, try taking a few deep breaths and chanting, "This too shall pass." If you are feeling especially virtuous, send them a prayer for protected travel. Otherwise, know that you are doing all the drivers on the road a favor by not exacerbating the situation and putting more people in danger.

And, if you follow the principles of karma, by cutting other drivers some slack, people may do the same for you. Of course, it might not happen in this lifetime. But that's another story.

✃ Make it your story

Try switching up your reactions to other people's behavior. For half a day, forgive others for their mistakes and wish them a safe journey. If you get cut off while driving, avoid cursing and send the driver a silent prayer for protection. During the second half of the day, express your righteous indignation when someone does something you perceive as stupid or reckless. If someone takes a parking space you were eyeing, curse under your breath or stomp your feet (but avoid any actions that might create conflict between you and the other person). At the conclusion of each incident, review your reaction. Which response gave you a sense of peace and satisfaction?

No Horse Sense

HIGH ON GUSTO, BUT LOW on common sense, I was about to embark on a two-day horse packing trip. Envy was to blame for my predicament. Every year, my college roommate, Lisa Jones, and her family galloped off on a five-day horse packing trip. Year after year, I heard detailed accounts of stars so bright she didn't need a flashlight and silence so intense it could almost be felt.

Although I had avoided horses since I was a kid, over the years Lisa's stories spun a magic spell. Finally, I'd had enough. "It's my turn," I declared, calling Lisa on the phone. I talked her into flying out from New Mexico for a weekend horse packing trip outside Cle Elum in Washington state. Caught up in the dreaminess of the Jones family's stories, I whitewashed the key element—riding a horse.

Under a gray sky, ripe with the threat of rain, Lisa and I drove up to the horse ranch. Getting out of the car, the smell of wet hay and horses permeated my senses.

Inside the corral, our trail guide, Debby, a solidly built blonde, picked out horses for the group of six riders based on our equestrian skills. "I am giving the faster horses to experienced riders," she said. "Newer riders will get the less spirited horses." Lisa got one of the best horses, while I, with little experience and zero skill, got Bowzer. A horse named after a dog.

Stepping up next to my 1,400-pound horse, my heart did the conga. I clutched my water bottle to my chest, and I remembered why I had stayed away from horses for so long—they scare me. They are big and powerful, but, unlike a car, can't be shut off with the turn of a key.

Bowzer was chestnut brown, with a shiny black mane and a white splotch over his left eye. Smaller white marks dripped down his face to his snout, as if he'd been splattered with a cream pie by a previous rider. Staring into his haughty brown eyes, I felt a sense of foreboding as I realized how unprepared I was for this trip. I did not go on any practice rides before heading out on this weekend adventure. In fact, I hadn't been on a horse in over a decade.

A glitch in my thinking process must have caused my native intelligence to go offline when I made these plans. My skewed interpretation of Lisa's adventures had left out a few vital elements: she raised and trained horses, while I had spent half a lifetime shunning them. Near panic, I dredged up my worst horse experience, the day a horse bit me.

Thirty years earlier, my Girl Scout troop had done volunteer work at a horse ranch and my job was grooming the horses. While I brushed a towering black horse, he bent his head down, bared mammoth teeth, and bit my shoulder. Scared more than hurt, I stifled my tears. The scout leader added insult to injury by jokingly blaming the furry jacket I wore for attracting the horse's bite.

Standing next to Bowzer, I took several deep breaths and weighed my choices. Leave and lose my non-refundable trip fee and tell Lisa she'd have to go on the trip by herself. Or stay and gain control over my fear.

I decided to stay and prepared to mount Bowzer. Even with a step stool, it was quite a climb onto his back. With the guide's help, I managed to straddle my wobbly legs across my 15-hand horse. As I adjusted my body in the hard saddle, Debby gave me a few riding instructions. Then, in a single fluid movement, she mounted her horse and took the lead. Lisa, the other riders, and I followed in single file. The camp wrangler and cook packed our personal gear on a separate string of well-muscled horses and took a steeper, faster trail, to prepare camp for our arrival.

As we ascended the first hill, frustration welled up inside me. Being an inexperienced rider, I was put in the middle of the string of horses. Lisa, one of the best riders, brought up the end, thus preventing any chance of conversation between us.

With no one to distract me, I rehashed my childhood adventures with horses. My girlfriends used to coax me into short trail rides on rented horses. They invariably picked fast horses for themselves and the slowest horse—seemingly one step away from retirement—for me. I remember cajoling every horse I ever rode just to keep it moving along the trail. Instead of brains, my horses seemed to have magnets that drew them back towards the barn. All these years later, the same pattern was playing out again. Lisa got the good horse and I got the slow-mo horse. Having a slower horse than Lisa was okay. But Bowzer ignored my nudges and verbal commands.

Jarring bounces on the saddle jerked me back to the present. The key point of Debby's riding instructions, "Put the balls of your feet on the stirrups and stand when trotting," struck home. Only a few hours into the ride and it was a toss-up as to which was worse, my sore behind or the ache of my leg muscles from following Debby's advice and standing while trotting.

Sitting high above the ground, I pulled myself out of my tirade of mental grumbling and looked around at the beauty of my surroundings. With a deep inhale, I filled my city lungs with clean mountain air. We passed emerald green valleys juxtaposed against volcanic-gray outcroppings just as streaks of cobalt blue sky broke through the clouds.

Our surefooted horses kept to the path as we wound our way up a steep rocky trail. As the sun emerged from behind a bank of clouds, my pre-trip images of lazily daydreaming as my horse did the work evaporated. Without constant vigilance, Bowzer led me under low branches, sideswiped my leg against tree trunks, and abruptly stopped for impromptu snacks of prickly, purple-flowered thistles and tall, tender stalks of grass.

With scraped arms and legs, I was seething inside. Cursing to myself, I damned my horse and the whole blasted adventure. What possessed me to put myself in a situation where I was dependent on a giant beast I feared?

Just then, Lisa rode up alongside me. Sensing my anger, she said, "Horses are sensitive creatures. Bowzer knows you are mad at him. If you want to avoid more scrapes and bruises, start exuding confidence. Or try singing. Life always seems better when it's put to song."

Instead of following her advice, I continued to silently fume as the dense, pine-scented forest opened up into a view of Gallagher Head Lake. We had reached our picnic area for lunch.

I gingerly dismounted and tied Bowzer's reins to a nearby tree. Lisa and I grabbed a couple of five-layer sandwiches and headed off away from the group. Munching on lunch, I expounded on my thoughts about the term "tenderfoot." "My feet are doing fine," I said. "It's another part of my anatomy that feels tender." This anatomical bend in the conversation was cut short when Bowzer performed his Houdini imitation, effortlessly untying himself from the tree and wandering over to an irresistible patch of thistles. Although he didn't get far, it was one more annoyance on a growing list.

A blustery breeze picked up as we remounted and rode through a meadow filled with a rainbow of wildflowers: red cyclamen, snow white daisies, scarlet Indian paintbrush, violet asters, lemon-colored yarrow, and purple monk's hood. Breathing in their blended perfume, I experienced a moment of peace.

As we entered an area with thick underbrush, a circle of pesky bugs gathered around Bowzer's ankles. He started doing an erratic two-step, causing me to grip the reins tighter. Then he bucked and I lost my balance. Realizing I didn't have a prayer of staying in the saddle, I ever so slowly started sliding off. Like a practiced stuntwoman, I gently rolled down Bowzer's side and off away from his hooves.

Lisa started to dismount, but before she could get off her horse, I was back on Bowzer. People rushed to my side to ask about what had happened and to see if I was okay. I was thankful Lisa could verify the cause of my fall. It wasn't lack of skill that landed me on my derriere; Bowzer bucked me off.

Brushing off everyone's concern with forced cheer, I sat high in the saddle, stroking Bowzer's coarse mane, strokes intended to calm me more than him. Maybe it was fool's pride, but I didn't want anyone to know how shaken I felt. As their attention refocused on the trail, my body turned to Jell-O. I held my knees into Bowzer's sides and hung onto the reins as a physical quake shook my body.

Once my heartbeat returned to normal, I took a mental survey of the pluses and minuses of my adventure. I was cold and sore, but I had ridden 12 miles and narrowly escaped being kicked in the head by Bowzer. This adventure had tested me. But I rose to the challenge and found personal, if not physical, satisfaction riding in the saddle.

By dusk, the wind was whipping at 40 miles an hour and packed a cold wallop. When we stopped to put on hats and gloves and extra layers of clothing, we looked down a hillside and saw smoke coming from our camp. The cook and wrangler had prepared a welcoming campfire. Trailing down the hill, we entered camp, where the enticing smell of hot coffee drew us to the kitchen tent.

I was ecstatic to be on solid ground and out from under Bowzer's control. I may have physically been the one on top, but he was bigger, stronger, and the dominant player. For the rest of the night, Bowzer was the wrangler's responsibility. I was off duty.

Tuning my attention to the surroundings, I noticed that the quiet was so intense I could almost feel it. Lisa was right on that score. Turning 360 degrees, I saw miles of old-growth trees, patches of native grass, and snow-covered mountain peaks. Atop a nearby hill, I caught a distant glimpse of a large herd of elk. I had to go through hell to get here, but it was worth it. There was an emptiness, almost a sacred void to this wilderness.

That evening, Lisa and I sat around the campfire getting to know our fellow riders. We sang old campfire songs while the cook played guitar. Later, a short, dark, and handsome wrangler taught us rope tricks and how to lasso a tree stump.

The night sky was just as I had imagined. A kaleidoscope of brilliant stars lit the way to my dome tent. I drifted off to sleep listening to the horses whinny and the wind howl.

The next morning, we awoke to the smell of homemade biscuits and hot coffee; a stark contrast to the horse smells that permeated everything, including my hat. When I stretched my stiff muscles, my body sounded like a bowl of Rice Crispies after the milk is poured. Sitting down to a gourmet breakfast of sausage and bell pepper quiche, I watched as the wrangler reloaded our gear on the pack horses. Off to the side of the cook tent, a cluster of tiny violet butterflies fluttered in the sky.

Before we mounted for our second and final day, Lisa gave me some words of advice. "If you don't want a repeat of your first day, you'll need to declare a détente with Bowzer. He has lots of experience intimidating riders. You need to firmly, but lovingly, let him know you're in charge."

I remounted my horse feeling more confident than the day before. With nothing to lose, I laid down the law to Bowzer. I explained that I was in charge and if he wanted to stop for a thistle or two, he would have to stop bumping me into trees. After we'd ridden a few miles through the forest without any scrapes against hard surfaces, I knew we'd reached a mutual understanding. Maybe he respected my new confidence, or maybe he knew these were our last hours together and soon he would be rid of me. Either way, we rode peacefully to a glacier-blue waterfall.

After tying up Bowzer so he could munch on his beloved thistles, Lisa and I took off our shoes and dipped our feet in the icy cold water. We leaned against a large boulder marbled with brown moss and white lichen and we marveled at the past 36 hours. I had overcome my knee-knocking fear of Bowzer and enjoyed some exceptional wilderness moments. But more importantly, I learned a valuable lesson; to swear off all attempts at keeping up with the Joneses. Henceforth, I would practice "farginen," a Yiddish word which means to respect a friend's success, attainments, and possessions. Instead of begrudging Lisa's and the rest of the Jones family's annual horse packing trip, I would send them silent blessings for a happy and safe adventure.

As for our future adventures, Lisa and I promised to limit our transportation to wheeled vehicles instead of hooves.

⤷ Make it your story

Before you go out and buy the same car as your neighbor or sign up for the same baseball team as your co-worker, stop for a moment. First, ask yourself why. Is there a deeper reason behind your desire? Could it be associated with low self-esteem, frustrations at work, or past failures? Clarify your desires. Do you really want to drive that exact car or be the best pitcher in your district?

Imagine how your life would look if you were on par with your version of the Joneses. In your fantasy, does it feel stressful or invigorating? Do you want to jump back into your old life, or are you happy with your new circumstances? Using your active imagination, conjure up as many details as possible. How does it feel in your body? What thoughts are going through your mind?

If you determine the things you crave are genuinely what you want, set realistic goals to achieve your objectives. If you realize your yearnings are just knee jerk reactions and you really don't want what the Joneses have, make a list of what would make you happy. Then set about fulfilling your dream life.

Unconscious Bias

GIVEN MY UPBRINGING in a small California beach town where the only dark-skinned people were surfers with tans, flunking a test about racial biases should not have surprised me. But it did. If asked, I would have confidently declared myself unbiased. The results told a different story.

I first learned about the Race Implicit Association Test (Race IAT) in Malcolm Gladwell's book, *Blink*. In essence, this computerized tool measures one's attitude or preference towards black or white people. A remarkable aspect of the test is how it measures unconscious preferences or implicit reactions that, if formulated as direct questions and presented to a participant, would be consciously denied. The test results can, as Gladwell so aptly puts it, "hit you over the head with its conclusions." The one factor that made my failure more palatable was the fact that I was in good company; Gladwell also flunked. The automatic preference range in the Race IAT runs from slight, moderate, or strong preference, to little or no preference for either white or black people. Both he and I scored "moderate automatic preference for whites" the first time each of us took the test. The fact that he is half black and still scored at that level relieved my mortification a teensy bit.

My small beach community in Southern California was so white, rumor had it that the police stopped people of color if they drove through town. The unspoken assumption was that the only reason for them to be in town was to cause trouble. While I have no proof that such conduct ever happened, I knew adults with overt racial prejudices who would have supported that kind of police response.

Though my early childhood lacked encounters with minorities, I later attended a Catholic high school in downtown Los Angeles with a healthy mix of races, if not religions. It was the late sixties, a time of social and political upheaval. But I was culturally ignorant and took little notice of what went on around me, whether it was newspaper headlines broadcasting stories about Black Power, or the race riots in Watts, just 15 miles from my home. Even though I had friends from different ethnic groups, in my youthful naiveté, I failed to register the full extent of the cultural diversity in surrounding towns or even those clothed in identical navy blue school uniforms at my high school.

Following my college graduation, I traveled throughout most of Europe and the United States. At one point, during a six-month stopover in Atlanta, Georgia, I worked as one of two token whites at a state institution for severely handicapped infants. A move to Washington State landed me a series of teaching jobs where I taught children from multiple racial backgrounds. But it was not until I began work as a writing tutor in a university's Minority Affairs Instructional Center in 2003 that I came face to face with my dormant biases and cultural ignorance. There, my consciousness became saturated in a sea of ethnic diversity as I edited college papers of students from around the world.

Gladwell believes we have control over our conscious attitudes, but not our unconscious attitudes. The results that come out in the Race IAT are churned out by the giant internal computer we call our unconscious. He says the attitudes that show up in the scores can differ from our stated beliefs because our internal computer "crunches all the data it can from the experiences we've had, the people we've met, the lessons we've learned, the books we've read, the movies we've watched, and so on, and it forms an opinion." Our unconscious takes all those odds and ends and comes to a conclusion. Because our thoughts are rooted in group consciousness and not solely based on our individual experiences, the test results may reflect attitudes learned from being part of a culture that regards one race more highly than another. A glance at history's numerous examples of prejudices held by people around the world validates that belief. However, since leaving home, I made a deliberate effort to change the unconscious programming I received as child. By becoming more familiar with diversity, I worked to expunge many of my knee-jerk assumptions.

Although I did not take the racial test before I started working at the Instructional Center, I have a sneaking suspicion that, had I done so, I might have garnered a worse score. At the Instructional Center, constant exposure to a broad variety of cultural beliefs and political viewpoints broadened my core opinions about and experiences with minorities.

Initially, there were times when I wondered about my ability to help people with backgrounds so different from mine. And sometimes I felt intimidated by a few students with sneers and "I dare you to help me" attitudes. It would have been easy to wait for someone else to assist them, but my work ethic wouldn't let me. Offering my help, I watched students from Africa, Korea, Russia, and other countries around the world settle into chairs beside me and pull out their class papers. In the course of a single day, I might edit students' interpretations of poetry, biology reports, term papers, personal essays, and more. It was gratifying, when, by the end of the sessions, the sneers turned into smiles.

During my first quarter, it became apparent that my beliefs about world events were going to get a good shaking at least once a day. Instead of reading newspaper reports about genocide in Sudan or people who had emigrated from Vietnam, I was sitting across the table from people who had experienced those events first hand. One rail-thin man with ebony skin told me he had witnessed hundreds of horrific killings in his native Sudan. A Vietnamese immigrant labeled the pirates that robbed her family at high sea as "good" because they did not kill or rape anyone. "They only took our food and valuables," she said. One African American student brought in a paper about Mr. Lynch, a white man who wrote a book outlining the most effective tortures for keeping black slaves in line. Reading the essay, I was appalled to learn that one of his methods—hanging one slave to serve as an example to the others—eventually took on his name and became known as "lynching."

The students' personal statements, which highlighted hardships or triumphs, quickly became my favorites. They reinforced my belief that everyone has a powerful tale to tell. In the process of editing papers, I read about students crossing mountains through a spray of gunfire in an attempt to escape from their native countries and the pain of leaving behind all they loved, not out of choice, but survival. In timid voices, students described overcoming cultural barriers, surviving crippling illnesses (their own and family members'), and spending their childhoods in unimaginable poverty.

Reading snippets of these lives humbled me and inspired me to make a more gallant effort to look beyond people's outward appearances and focus on our common humanity. Now, when I come into contact with someone who I would have previously considered intimidating, I deliberately smile and search for common ground. My goal is to emulate an approach His Holiness the Dalai Lama described in his book *A Human Approach to World Peace*. "Whenever I meet even a 'foreigner,' I have always the same feeling," he writes. "I am meeting another member of the human family. This attitude has deepened my affection and respect for all beings."

In *Blink*, Gladwell mentions that he and a number of friends took the Race ITA test several times with no change in their scores. Only one man, a track-and-field athlete, was able to alter his score. After taking the test every day with no change, he suddenly jumped from having a positive association for whites to having a positive association with blacks. The new result, he realized, came about because he had spent the morning watching black athletes compete in the Olympics. From that incident, Gladwell extrapolated that looking at positive images or reading positive stories about black (or white) people might change one's scores. In conjunction with his premise, I would add a desire to release one's vise-like grip on biases.

Inspired by the idea that change was possible, I decided to test Gladwell's thesis. I had first taken the test over a weekend. What if I took it again at work? Would my interactions with minorities affect my score? The next day I waited until I had met with several students. Then I sat down at the computer and took the test. The results showed my automatic preference had changed from "moderate automatic preference for whites" to "little to no preference for white Americans relative to black Americans." Yippee! My unconscious was now in sync with my conscious mind.

Working at the Instructional Center helped me stop seeing the difference between people and instead focus on commonalities. Add in the scientific evidence from the United States government's Genome project website, which states that any two people are 99.9 percent identical at the genetic level, and it is ridiculous not to see the similarities I share with the person sitting across the table from me, regardless of his or her cultural background.

In the end, how I treat people during everyday encounters is more important than my results on the Race Implicit Association Test. Will my score remain in the "no preference" category when I no longer work at a Minority Affairs Instructional Center? I don't know. The only certainty is my determination to use what I have learned during my job and consciously eliminate prejudicial thoughts and actions. I just hope my unconscious mind keeps up.

⤜ Make it your story

Prejudice knows no limits. Body size, mental or physical illnesses, ethnicity, and financial status can all provoke prejudice. Some people have strong biases against the thin, smart, rich, and famous.

It is interesting to think about where our prejudices originate. A song from the 1958 movie South Pacific, *"You've Got to Be Carefully Taught," talks about the process of being taught prejudices. Here is the first stanza of this musical number, written by Rodgers and Hammerstein:*

> *You've got to be taught*
> *To hate and fear,*
> *You've got to be taught*
> *From year to year,*
> *It's got to be drummed*
> *In your dear little ear*
> *You've got to be carefully taught.*

Think about your opinions regarding prejudices. Have you experienced discrimination? If so, how? What images stand out in your memory? Are you prejudiced against other people's politics, race, or religion? Where do your prejudices show up?

If you want to become more tolerant, try becoming a good listener. Instead of planning what you're going to say next, pay full attention to the speaker. To do this, you need to be open to differing points of view. Otherwise, your mental blinders will prevent you from listening openly to what other people are saying.

Avoid black-and-white thinking and instead strive to see the middle ground. Prejudice breeds prejudice. Perpetrators feel more empowered and victims feel demoralized. The cycle of bigotry, stereotyping, and stigmatizing will shift with personal reflection and change. Check for any hidden agendas before expressing your viewpoint. Are you dehumanizing someone or belittling another person's opinion? It is fine to disagree with a person's opinion, but not to attack them verbally or physically. Keep the disagreement focused on content and not personality.

Normally You

I JUST LEARNED THERE IS ANOTHER WOMAN in my partner Bo's life. Unfortunately, she is neither demure nor happy to exist on the sidelines, accepting crumbs of his time. This intruder dominates Bo's mind. I guess, deep down, I knew there was someone else. After all, I couldn't be with him for more than 25 years and not notice these things.

The conversation that revealed her identity began simply enough as we drove through Seattle on Interstate-5. After weeks of cool and drizzly Seattle weather, a gloriously sunny day exposed city vistas washed clean by the rain. Snowcapped mountain ranges on both sides of the freeway glistened in the sunshine. As we pulled onto the off-ramp, I rolled down the window and remarked, "I want to turn off the air conditioning and enjoy this moment of warm summer heat." Without hesitation, Bo responded with, "Normally you want to be cool."

I was momentarily stymied, unsure how to respond to his blanket statement. Then I recalled him making the same remark several times in the past. With that recollection, I became miffed. Bo was comparing my desire for a warm summer breeze blowing across my face with the wishes of a woman called Normally You. "I am not talking about Normally You, whoever she is," I said. "I am talking about what I want in this moment."

As you can probably guess, Normally You is not a person in the physical sense. But that doesn't mean she isn't interfering in the relationship between my partner and me. In fact, her absence of a body makes her more dangerous. Bo can be with her anytime, anywhere. Even when we are dining alone, she can pop up and monopolize his thoughts. I might be blithely munching on my salad, totally unaware of her presence, when he mistakes me for her. Instead of asking what I believe, feel, think, or desire, Bo digs into his recollections of what Normally You has believed, felt, thought, or desired in the past. Proud that he knows what I want, he then acts accordingly. Unfortunately for me, my current desires don't always match his assumptions.

Once my intruder antenna was activated, I noticed yet another presence in the car with us. It was You Never, an entity whose desires and opinions are the antithesis of flexibility. After hearing her views on a subject, Bo believed there was no reason to revisit the subject. For example, except for rare occasions when it is extremely hot outside, I have an aversion to iced drinks. Therefore, at summer picnics when glasses of blissfully cool iced tea are being passed out, Bo remembers what You Never wants and gives me the only glass of tepid tea.

At this point, our sedan was getting pretty crowded, and I was feeling frustrated with Bo's preconceived ideas about my wants and desires. Just as I opened my mouth to denounce Bo's harem of Normally You and You Never, I noticed the presence of still more intruders. There, sitting alongside Bo's twosome, were male versions with the same names that I'd conjured up as stand-ins for Bo. Instead of asking his opinion, I, too, reached into my store-house of memories to answer questions about his wants and needs. Instead of asking if Bo wanted to see the latest science fiction movie, I'd automatically buy tickets prior to the film's release date. After all, he would normally want to be first in line on opening day.

I recognized that Bo and I had a problem. Relying on these intruders' opinions robbed us of authentic communication with each other. Their lack of depth and flexibility, plus their adherence to static preferences spelled doom. How could we change and grow if we based today's decisions on yesterday's information? It was time to label these intruding thoughts for what they were—assumptions and old stories we kept alive past their prime.

After dinner, I sat down next to Bo and raised the issue about our not-so-dear friends, Normally You and You Never. Sweetening our conversation with two bowls of chocolate thunder ice cream, I laid out the epiphany I'd had during our car ride.

I concluded by saying, "Those intruders are coming between us and we need to stop them." Bo immediately recognized the culprits and agreed with my conclusion. Together, we brainstormed ways to counter these saboteurs. "Maybe we can stop taking each other's likes and dislikes for granted," I suggested. "After all, if you base my dessert preference on Normally You's opinions, I will only get chocolate, never anything with pralines or caramel. And the same goes for you. You'll always get chocolate ice cream and never raspberry sherbet."

Bo added his suggestion, saying, "We can expose these saboteurs' wily ways by questioning their proclamations and suggestions. Even when we think we know what the other person wants, let's start double-checking to make sure we are right."

A couple of days later we were back in the car again, heading down Interstate-5. Turning toward me with a smile, Bo said, "Let's stop for dinner at that Mexican restaurant You Always like."

"That would be great," I said. "Then we can take in a walk. You Never miss your evening walk."

"Yeah," he added with a laugh, "And afterwards we can stop for a chocolate sundae. Normally You want chocolate after dinner."

Our new techniques and a healthy dose of humor were helping us defuse the intruders' power and encouraging us to have better person-to-person communication. As an added bonus, we were creating more room in our relationship to be ourselves.

Make it your story

Has automatic communication infiltrated your relationships with friends or family members? Do you have intruders, similar to "Normally You" and "You Never" wreaking havoc with your cherished relationships? What are your intruders' names? Do you parrot their views, or double-check your assumptions just in case a loved one's preferences or outlooks have changed?

Mindful communication is a key ingredient for maintaining strong relationships. But it takes works. Most of us have quirky communication habits that interfere with our ability to connect with others. As you go through your day, practice these keys to mindful communication:

1. Listen without interrupting or mentally planning your response. Focus your attention on what your loved one is saying.

2. Allow others to express negative emotions, such as anger or frustration, without trying to fix them or running away. As you are listening, remember not to take everything they say personally. Sometimes people just need to vent. In addition, you are not responsible for resolving issues that arise. Being present and allowing a loved one to express bottled-up feelings is the gift you are giving.

3. Set aside time for a daily check-in with a loved one. Ask these three questions: What worked; what didn't work; what are you most grateful for today?

A Graceful Stumble

I AM A PROPONENT OF STUMBLING. Not in the sense of falling or tripping over your feet. The stumbling I refer to involves careening off one's life path and into new, unexpected directions.

Instead of following a preset route and checking off life's milestones (school, work, and family), cultivating the ability to stumble gracefully enables us to respond to those times when we are derailed by unanticipated events. The key to successful stumbling is the ability to navigate a shift off course and find positive aspects in the changing situation.

Let me give you an example of how stumbling reshaped my life. Years ago, I drove across country, from Georgia to Seattle, intending to spend Christmas with my sister and her family. I recently had graduated from college with a degree in education and had spent time traveling and working in Europe. My plan involved several more months of touring of North America before I settled down and looked for a teaching job.

Everything was going swimmingly until my van broke down three days after Christmas. Having been on the road for months, I did not have the financial resources to fix my van and continue traveling. So I stayed in Seattle and started looking for a way to earn money.

Unfortunately, my arrival coincided with Seattle's slow recovery from one of the city's biggest economic downturns. A few years before my arrival, there had been a billboard at the edge of town boldly saying, "Would the last one to leave Seattle please turn off the lights."

After job searching for several weeks, I felt lucky to find a waitress job at a dive in the Capitol Hill neighborhood. The restaurant was dumpy and full of belligerent patrons. We made daily calls to 911 for assistance with drunk and unruly patrons. The health department would have closed the place if they caught the cook taking his daily sponge bath in the kitchen sink.

Working that job motivated me to alter my plan and put my yet-to-be-used teaching certificate to work. My quest began with volunteer work at a nonprofit school for preschool children with disabilities and ended six months later when I landed a job at the same school.

Although my original plan did not involve putting down roots in Seattle, I made the most of my situation. By the time Christmas rolled around again, I was doing what I had dreamt about since third grade—teaching. The broken van and dreadful job were not events I consciously would have chosen as part of my life journey, but I used them as an impetus to fulfill my vision of teaching.

We all have had moments when our lives are moving forward according to our plans, when—wham—we hit a major rut in the road and our game markers are knocked off the board. In an instant, our hopes and dreams are derailed. Sure, we can get back on the board, but not in the same place. Change is mandatory.

Those are the times when the art of graceful stumbling comes in handy. To stumble productively, we need certain traits, each of which can be represented by the letters in "stumble."

Strength—having the inner resources to trust that things will work out.

Truth—being honest with others and ourselves as we negotiate this new situation.

Understanding—knowing that there will be good days and bad days.

Movement—taking positive steps toward our next goal.

Balance—maintaining our equilibrium with work/play and action/ relaxation.

Love—treating ourselves and our loved ones with tenderness.

Effort—realizing this new path will only work if we put our energy into making things happen.

Most career books say nothing about stumbling. But it is a worthy skill to develop. I stumbled into Seattle and created a new life for myself. Years later, I stumbled into a writers' meeting and ended up becoming a professional writer. Who knows where my next stumble will lead me.

✂ Make it your story

Think about times when you thought you had everything worked out and then you stumbled or were bumped off course. Where did those diversions lead you? Did you handle them with grace or fight the change?

Flexibility is a key ingredient in setting goals. Having a rigid hold on a particular idea or goal can block your ability to see or accept alternative approaches. And, it doesn't allow for creative stumbles.

In employment and relationships, you may learn new information that changes how you want to move forward. It is helpful to periodically stop, look at your original goal, and reevaluate your plans. You may choose to stay the *course, or decide that your original goal no longer serves you. It is important to leave wiggle room when making major plans.*

If you get stuck, think of someone you respect, maybe a leader in your field or a teacher. Try putting yourself in their shoes and think of ways they would approach or resolve your situation.

Brain Lapse

AFTER 200 HOURS OF MIND-NUMBING SILENCE, my brain felt discombobulated. It was day nine of a ten-day silent meditation. Situated on 50 acres of lush farmland, the retreat center was located outside a small town in Washington State with a booming population of fewer than a thousand. There were no city noises, such as traffic or sirens. During the duration of the retreat, there were few ambient noises around the center. All radios, cell phones, TVs, and conversations were verboten. We ate in silence, walked in silence, meditated in silence, and performed our daily ablutions in silence.

Having never experienced ten days of silence, I had no idea how torturous it could be. The droning of my internal voice was grating on my nerves like fingernails on a chalkboard. Although I am usually drawn to the introvert side of the social scale, every cell in my body craved conversation.

The retreat's daily schedule was almost as tedious as my inner dialogue. Every day, the same thing happened at the same time. By day three I had memorized the schedule, from early morning rising at 4 AM to bedtime at 10 PM. Each day included hours of meditation, broken up by meal times and brief stretching breaks. In the evening, there were periods of meditation and a videotaped instructional talk. We listened, the presenter talked. The one area of flexibility was an optional question and answer period with our meditation teacher, after the final meditation, and right before bedtime. That slim slice of time was our only opportunity to flex our vocal cords.

On the ninth evening, my mind fixated on the upcoming Q and A session. Lofty spiritual thoughts were pushed aside by fantasies of listening to the sweet sound of people talking.

The evening began just like the others, with an hour of meditation, then the instructional talk. During the break after the talk, I eagerly awaited the

Q and A period. As I watched several people leave the meditation hall, I wondered how they could pass up the chance to break the silence. Then, a few minutes later they all returned. "Well," I thought, "they can't resist the opportunity to exercise their vocal cords."

I sat up straighter; excited that so many people would be attending the session. Surely we would get a good dialogue going. Then I waited. And waited. But no one raised their hand with a question.

Puzzled, I glanced around the hall. Everyone else was sitting calmly in meditative poses with their eyes closed. Even the teacher was sitting in a meditative pose, apparently unconcerned that he was keeping us all waiting. Was I the only one disturbed by the long wait? Too anxious to meditate, I kept fidgeting, swinging my arms and stretching my legs.

Looking up, I witnessed the teacher rising out of his lotus position and leaving the room. I was shocked. How could he get up and leave while we were all waiting for the question and answer period to begin? Well, I reasoned, he must really need to relieve himself. After several minutes, when he did not return, I worried that something had happened to him. Looking around to see if others were concerned, I noted they were still sitting patiently in contemplative postures.

At last, the teacher returned. One of the students made a move to stand. "Ah," I thought, "time for questions." Then the student sat back down; apparently he had just been rearranging his sitting position.

With disappointment, I saw the teacher return to his lotus pose. His behavior was astounding. Why wasn't he starting the evening talk? And how could everyone else be so patient?

As time crept by, I grew more and more agitated. Finally, I stood up and stormed out into the foyer for a drink of water. One of the retreat helpers followed me and asked if I was OK. "I am fine," I said. "But when do the questions begin?" She told me in five minutes. "Man," I thought, "why are they making us wait five more minutes?"

At 9 PM, many of the people who seemed to have waited so patiently left. I could not fathom why they waited so long, then left just as the questions were about to begin.

Not until after the Q and A session, when I was back at the dorm, did I realize what had happened. There was no waiting period between the instruction talk and question session. It was the regularly scheduled

45-minute meditation that always followed the instruction period. My tunnel vision focus had created a mental blackout. As a result, I completely forgot about that scheduled meditation.

The evidence—the teacher and students all sitting in meditative poses—was not enough to clue me in on what was really happening. All the information was right there in front of me. But because I was holding onto what I believed, that it was question and answer time, I could not see the truth. I had previously heard about mental lapses, but had never experienced anything quite like that before. All input that contradicted my reality was disregarded. I had to be right, no matter what the facts were.

The next day, driving home from the retreat, I was still mulling over the incident. I marveled at my ability to completely block out information that contradicted my mindset. Right then, I made a promise to myself. When I get headstrong or perturbed about a situation that isn't bothering anyone else who is equally affected, I will stop, open the iron lock on my brain, and see if any facts need to be reviewed. Then, I will use those clues to reevaluate my stance. I may choose to stand tough, but at least I will have reached my decision with an open mind.

⚘ Make it your story

Our minds are masters of trickery. We imagine scenarios and then we act as if they are true. No matter how much evidence there is to the contrary, we continue to hold onto our viewpoints. It is as if we create mental or emotional blinders to keep out the truth.

Mental blinders allow us to hold tight to our preconceived ideas. These blinders skew reality and prevent us from paying attention to factual information about people and situations. In the story, I decided it was time for the Q and A session even though there was ample proof to the contrary. My mental blinders blocked out any data that would counter my belief.

Emotional blinders allow us to look sympathetic when someone shares personal information, without us needing to feel empathy. We respond with simple platitudes, such as "sorry for your loss," and move on to another topic. With emotional blinders, we avoid being emotionally vulnerable and really listening to and connecting with what the other person is going through. We also miss the connections that are formed through heartfelt sharing.

What kinds of blinders do you use? Think about ways you can avoid blinders that keep you from fully engaging with people and events. Although it did not help me at the meditation center, the first step, in most situations is to turn off all electronic devices and focus solely on the person or situation in front of you. Removing distractions helps to release any preconceived ideas and be open to what transpires. Experiment with different ways to put aside your blinders.

Introspection

Planting Good Seeds

THE LAW OF KARMA is a fundamental doctrine in Eastern religions. But what does it mean? Simply put, it means what goes around comes around; similar actions will lead to similar results. In other words, if we perform a good deed, someday we will receive a good deed. Bad actions garner negative consequences.

Karma is not innately good or bad. The quality of the karma we collect is determined by intentional actions we perform. Each of these actions plants karmic seeds. This refers to conscious actions done with our body, speech, and thoughts, not "mindless" actions such as walking, sitting, or sleeping. Our attitudes or thoughts while performing deeds help determine what kinds of karmic seeds get planted.

For example, if I help my neighbor move furniture with kindness in my heart, my action plants positive seeds. Suppose I do the same action, but this time I mentally begrudge the loss of my free time. That deed plants negative seeds.

Karmic seeds germinate over time. Unlike our western adage about money, "You can't take it with you," a key element of karmic seeds is that they are carried over from lifetime to lifetime. Actions from past lifetimes (seeds planted) can affect your current life. Seeds planted in this lifetime may come to fruition in another lifetime. Although many Christians do not believe in karma, the basic idea behind karmic seeds is similar to the belief stated in Galatians 6:7-10: "...whatsoever a man soweth, that shall he also reap."

Now for the good news: if you are worried about negative seeds you might have planted, here are four steps for rectifying mistakes or pulling up bad karmic seeds. These actions are valuable because the process of undoing damage in this lifetime helps prevent future suffering.

1. *Generate compassion*—Practice thinking compassionate thoughts about others. If you catch yourself having negative thoughts about someone, consciously redirect your thoughts towards that person's positive attributes (even if the characteristic is as small as the person's nice smile or pleasant speaking voice).

2. *Be repentant*—Be truly sorry for your actions or thoughts.

3. *Resolve not to repeat the deed*—Promise yourself that you will not do the action again. It is important to be honest about your intention to change your ways. If you aren't sincere, don't make the promise. Deliberating lying to yourself or others plants more bad seeds.

4. *Develop a remedial practice*—Resolve to behave better in the future. Create a practice that will create good karma. This can be prayer, meditation, chanting, reading sacred texts, or reciting mantras. Or, it can be simply behaving differently if a similar situation arises.

We have all participated in numerous negative actions, and can't expect to counteract or pull all the bad seeds at once. Therefore, it is important to repeat these four steps regularly. In addition, developing a firm resolve to not repeat a negative action generates powerful purification.

✂ Make it your story

It is never too late to start generating good karma by cultivating healthy seeds. Choose a past event you would like to correct. Review the four steps for rectifying mistakes or pulling bad karmic seeds:

• *Generate compassion for yourself.*

Remind yourself of your good qualities. Look beyond your negative behavior or angry words to see the whole person. Instead of focusing on what you find to be off-putting, think about your positive traits. These can be global attributes, such as the desire to know happiness and avoid suffering, or more personal ones, like being respectful or socially minded.

- *Be repentant.*

The first step is to recognize you have done something wrong, either through your actions or thoughts. Once you are aware of what you have done, make amends. If you cannot fix the problem, ask for forgiveness and look for ways to demonstrate your intention to change.

- *Resolve not to repeat the deed.*

To err is human. But once a mistake is recognized, it is important to not repeat it. Make a commitment to yourself not to repeat the action, behavior, thought, or words.

- *Develop a remedial practice.*

Write out an action plan for how you can pull the bad seed and plant good a one in its place. Then begin implementing your plan.

Driving Down the Freeway of Life

IMAGINE THIS SCENE.

You have spent the last few weeks preparing for an important meeting. Today is the day and everything is ready. Your research is complete. The action plan is written. The only thing left is to drive ten miles to your destination and present your ideas.

Pulling out of the driveway, you praise yourself for leaving ten minutes early. You reach over to give your briefcase a reassuring pat, but it is not there. It's in the house, sitting on the table next to the door.

Slamming the car into park, you race back inside. You grab your briefcase, take one last swig of what is now lukewarm coffee, and bolt out the door. You tell yourself everything will be okay. You are still eight minutes ahead of schedule.

Back behind the wheel, it takes inordinate self-control to stay at the legal speed limit. As you turn the corner, you find a yellow school bus stopped up ahead. You drum your fingers impatiently on the steering wheel while you watch as a line of kids s-l-o-w-l-y board the bus. Finally, the bus driver folds in the red stop sign and inches forward. You feel a sense of hope. Thanks to your early departure, you are still five minutes ahead of schedule.

When you reach the freeway onramp, you check the traffic flow. All lanes are moving smoothly. The traffic gods are on your side today. You breathe a sigh of relief as you whiz into the left lane. Relaxing your grip on the steering wheel, you begin mentally reviewing your presentation.

Suddenly, the soft whine of a siren floats into your consciousness. Looking around, you try to establish where the sound is coming from. The volume builds. In the rearview mirror, you see an aid car heading toward your rear bumper. Without much thought, you move to the right and let it pass.

Then you see a flood of red taillights up ahead. Traffic slows down. Keeping panic at bay, you tell yourself it is a temporary slowdown. You will be through it in no time.

But the situation worsens. Now traffic is stopped across all four lanes. Another aid car zooms up the shoulder of the freeway, followed by a fire truck and a police car. There is obviously a major injury accident up ahead. You will be late for your meeting.

What is your response? If you are like many people in this situation, you bang the steering wheel and start cussing. While it initially feels good to let off steam, you notice the more you yell, the more frustrated you feel. Maybe your blood pressure even rises a few points. An inner voice tells you that if you enter the meeting in that state of mind, you will fail to achieve your goal.

So, you stop swearing, take a deep breath, and decide to try an alternative response. You contact the people at your destination and let them know what is happening. Then you send good wishes to all people involved in the accident and the workers helping them. After all, the injured people in the collision blocking your progress and the aid workers could use a dose of goodwill.

As your car idles, you give thanks for your functioning car, the gas in your tank, the clothes on your back, and your home to return to at the end of the day. Ticking off your list of good fortunes, you feel your body relax.

Finally, traffic starts flowing. The drive is slow, but you reach your destination. Stopping just outside the door, you realize your positive mind-set is going to set an upbeat tone for the meeting. Success feels like a certainty.

⤴ Make it your story

There are an increasing number of cars on the road. This increases the odds of you encountering bad drivers, slowdowns, and accidents. Here are some tips for staying calm.

- *Don't start out anxious. Leave your house or office on time. Give yourself plenty of time to get where you are going.*
- *Focus on gratitude in your life. It can be something as small as enjoying the song playing on the radio.*
- *Don't expect other drivers to be courteous. By deleting this expectation, you avoid being disappointed every time someone cuts you off or won't let you into the line of traffic.*
- *Don't take other drivers' behavior personally. You did not cause their bad driving and you cannot change it.*

If you are on the road and you recognize your anger rising:

- *Do deep breathing exercises. Inhale for the count of ten. Hold your breath for five seconds and then slowly exhale.*
- *Chant a calming sentence such as, "I am peaceful."*
- *Pull off the road and calm down.*

Silence

THE CLANG OF A BRASS GONG woke me at dawn. Rolling out of bed, I slipped on my green crocs and then headed outside. A light morning mist filled an expanse of open land behind my bunkhouse at a retreat center southeast of Olympia, Washington. In the distance, an owl hooted. And, although I could not see them, I sensed the presence of the three deer I had seen the previous evening.

Overhead, a sliver of the crescent-shaped moon and the morning star sparkled against a cobalt blue sky. Aside from birds playing call and response from the nearby trees, a palpable silence surrounded me. Taking a deep breath, I breathed in thick, cool air, and then released another level of stress I had brought with me from my workaday world.

It was day three of a three-day silent meditation. Sixty-eight hours of glorious silence, almost half that time spent in meditation.

In a world of 24/7 noise and distractions, where some people are uncomfortable walking without a cell phone or iPod attached to their ear, I relish quiet. Instead of being distracted by what is happening around me, I have time to consider what is going on inside me. Extended periods of silent mediation allow me time to check in with myself and explore my unconscious thoughts.

During this particular retreat, the key insight that surfaced was my inability to keep my thoughts focused on the present moment. Instead of paying attention to what I was doing, I observed myself looking ahead to the next activity. In the quiet of the meditation hall, part of my mind planned what I would eat for breakfast. Sitting at the breakfast table, I thought about the hot shower that I was going to take after I finished eating my oatmeal. Later, as hot water cascaded down my back, I began yearning for a walk around the grounds. I daydreamed about a nap as I walked the grassy meadow paths. My mind wandered everywhere except into the present moment.

The concept of being in the now is both ancient and new. It is one of the foundations of Buddhism, and a tenet of the New Age philosophy. Like many people, I often get so lost in my thoughts—fantasizing about the past or the future—that I miss what is going on around me. When I can be in the now, I become mindful of the present moment, and experience what is actually occurring in my life.

During the retreat, when my mind wandered, I repeated the mantra, "focus on the now." It was like trying to rein in a wild horse. But, instead of using sugar cubes to coax my mind to stay in the present moment, I repeated the four-word mantra and used other techniques to gently nudge my thoughts each time they began to roam. I told myself to feel my breath, the way cool air entered my nostrils and left with a hint of warmness; to taste how the nuts and raisins contrasted with the soft mushiness of the oatmeal; to be aware of the relaxing effect hot water had on my shoulder muscles; to smell the flowers along the walkway, and to notice the variety of leaves on the trees. With repeated prodding, my focus returned to the present.

Slowly, as the hours passed, I began to experience periods of stillness, being in the present moment with no yearnings and no expectations. In meditation, I relaxed into the waves of breath moving through my body.

Following this flow, my mind and body entered the still point, that place that brings quiet to the heart.

T. S. Eliot offers a succinct description of the still point in his poem, *Burnt Norton*: "Where the past and future are gathered. Neither movement from nor towards, neither ascent nor decline. Except for the point, the still point."

After the retreat, I continued observing my thoughts. To my surprise and delight, I found I could frequently focus on one task without yearning for the next activity on my list. Spending those three days in silence, diligently working on bringing my focus to the present, helped me break the pattern of wandering. I did not eliminate the issue entirely, but I made progress toward staying in the present moment.

❧ Make it your story

Most of our time is spent dwelling on the past or future tripping about what is to come instead paying attention to the present moment. Learning how to be in the present moment takes practice.

One tool for practicing how to be in the moment is eliminating distractions. Experiment with mini-periods of quiet time—five to ten minutes—to connect with your inner self. You can do this by simply turning off outside distractions such as music, television, and other electronic devices. Sit or stand quietly and notice how it feels to be still. Do you feel jittery or uncomfortable? Do you feel a sense of peace?

Another technique is to focus your attention on doing one activity. Notice all aspects of what you're doing—how your body feels, sensory input, and your thoughts. As you do this, you will probably observe your thoughts jumping from one topic to another. That's normal. Mentally note when your mind wanders and bring it back to the task at hand. Don't worry about how many times you have to rein in your mind. Just continue to refocus it on the single activity.

January Shade

ONE DAY IN MID-JANUARY, I was out walking and thinking about my life. I had reached a point where I needed to make some changes. There were no doubts about what I needed to do, only my reluctance to let go of what was comfortable and familiar. Part of my reluctance came from not knowing what my life would look like if I released the old.

As I mulled over my dilemma, I noticed a maple tree that was still holding on to its leaves from the previous spring. I immediately recognized the similarity between the tree and myself. When I arrived back home, I wrote this poem:

Mid-January
and a maple tree stubbornly holds onto its leaves.

They linger, green and attached.
Refusing to change color,
the leaves quietly boycotted fall.
Now they snub winter.
Stepping into the tree's shade, I plead,
"Drop your old leaves. Holding on could kill you.
Make room for new growth."

Then the words turn on me.
I realize the tree and I are the same.
For new to enter, I must let go of the old.

In my work, personal, and spiritual life
I must let go of the old,
allow fallow time,
leafless time,
naked time.

Beneath the surface,
in the darkness,
out of sight,
Change takes hold.

As spring bulbs are nourished in darkness,
my soul is nurtured by introspection.

Like the maple,
I must release the old,
stand naked,
open to growth.

⤴ Make it your story

Letting go of the old makes room for the new. Choose one thing you want to release. It could be a possession, memory, or habit.

Before you jump into action, practice the art of letting go as you exhale. Focus on letting all the air out of your lungs. Even do a few extra puffs to make sure you released every drop of air. Then slowly count to ten before you inhale. How does that feel? Are you comfortable with the void between breaths? Or do you feel panicky? Does your experience with your breath match the way you feel letting go of things or habits?

Pull out some paper and write down ideas of what you could let go.

- *Do you have things around your house that you have not used in the past six months or year and no longer need?*
- *Does your job still give you satisfaction? Is there still room for growth and new opportunities? Or is it time to start planning a change in employment?*
- *Are there people in your life who no longer share your interests, people whom you hold onto out of habit or guilt?*
- *Do you have unhealthy habits or negative thoughts you would like to release?*

Write down what your life would look like if you let go of that which no longer serves you. Describe how you feel when you imagine letting go. Then reframe it and write about what your life might look like if you hold on.

If you are inclined, follow your contemplation time with action, and let go something that no longer serves you.

Dealing with Difficult People

MOST OF US HAVE MET PEOPLE who are difficult to get along with. Sometimes these challenging people are family members, other times friends or co-workers. No matter the relationship, difficult people can be, well, difficult.

Chances are you've met the human version of Eeyore, the melancholy donkey in *Winnie the Pooh*. If it is raining, he complains about getting wet. When the sun shines, he grumbles about being too hot. Eeyore even pointed out the downside of a celebration in his honor by saying, "After all, what are birthdays? Here today and gone tomorrow."

Eeyore's traits apply equally to males and females. I remember an encounter I had with a woman who had spent several hours and many dollars on a complete makeover. When I complimented her on how great she looked, she scowled and said, "Are you saying I used to look awful?"

Any list of stereotypical difficult people also includes Nasty Ned, who enjoys making himself look good at the expense of other people, and Deceitful Doris, who lies even when it would be just as easy to tell the truth. Each of these personalities creates challenges for those who interact with them.

My personal challenge is a difficult person I will call Hatty. She took the traits of the previously mentioned types, added backstabbing, and wrapped them all together with an air of icy, artificial politeness. The worst part of having Hatty in my life is that, while I can limit my interactions with her, I cannot eliminate them.

Stories about Hatty's nasty behavior run the gamut from deceitfulness to emotional abuse. An incident that captures Hatty's character is when she moved her elderly husband of twenty-five years out of their multi-million-dollar home and into assisted living. She furnished his room with a decades-old card table, one folding metal chair, a second-hand twin bed, and a threadbare armchair.

One day, after enduring an abusive telephone conversation with Hatty, I talked to a friend who recommended I read Pema Chodron's book, *The Places That Scare You*. In Chodron's book, she suggests using interactions with difficult people as a spiritual practice. "Because they challenge us to the limits of our open-mindedness, difficult relationships are in many ways the most valuable for practice. The people who irritate us are the ones who inevitably blow our cover . . . if we want to practice patience and unconditional loving-kindness and an enemy arrives, we are in luck," wrote Chodron.

Taking this advice to heart, I began developing a strategy for dealing with Hatty. As I worked on my plan, I found an added bonus—it also works with other difficult people I encounter.

I wish I could say the result was a miraculous transformation in how I felt about Hatty—that I became Christlike, learned to recognize the suffering and pain behind Hatty's infuriating behavior, and showered her with compassion. Unfortunately, I didn't. My goal was more self-centered. I wanted to find a way to detach myself from Hatty's antics and stop allowing her to steal my peace of mind.

The first part of my strategy was developing a response to Hatty's negativity. Instead of seething inside when she started an argument, I silently chanted mantras or did deep breathing to keep myself calm. Even these simple actions were difficult. On many occasions, it took all the self-control I could muster not to squabble with her. I had to remind myself that responding to her behavior with hostility would leave a nasty residue inside of me, without resolving anything.

In the process of practicing calmness, I learned silence can be a powerful force. A long pause before responding allowed Hatty's venomous words to hang in the air and gave me thinking space before I responded. Using that moment, I would reaffirm that I couldn't change her, I could only change how I reacted to her.

I am embarrassed to tell you that, even today, if given the opportunity to dip Hattie into a pool of loving kindness, I would be tempted to hold her under just a little bit longer than necessary. However, I have achieved two successes. I pray for Hatty every day, and I stopped taking her behavior personally. I even feel twinges of sympathy when I realize her meanness has more to do with who she is than anything I did or said.

❧ Make it Your Story

The truth is, you can't change other people. Trying to change them only creates a power struggle, raises their defenses, and makes things worse. And, it can turn you into a person even you don't want to be around. All you can do is change yourself.

The Serenity Prayer is a well-recognized part of all 12-step programs. Below is a version an ingenious person adapted to focus on accepting people instead of things and situations.

God grant me the serenity;
To accept the people I cannot change;

Courage to change the one I can;
And wisdom to know that person is me.

Brainstorm alternative ways to respond to troublesome people's antics. Are there ways you can reclaim your power by drawing boundaries around the kind of behavior you will or won't accept?

Most people are not totally bad. Even those you have constant conflict with probably have a few positive traits. Make a list of your difficult person's positive characteristics. It can be as small as the color of their eyes. This doesn't mean you are pretending that person's negative traits don't exist. You are just spending a few minutes focusing on the positive.

What effect does this exercise have on your interactions? Can you talk with the other person about things you admire about them?

Difficult people who show up in your life as relatives, co-workers, neighbors, bosses, or clerks provide an opportunity to put your spiritual beliefs into action. More than one author has called them teachers, brought into our lives to deliver a divine kick in the butt. Explore new ways you can deal with difficult people. In addition to setting boundaries, you can take deep breaths, count to ten before speaking, or call a friend for moral support.

The Power of Words

DURING COLLEGE, MY FRIEND LISA introduced me to a surefire way to ease whatever bothered me: talk about it. Whether Lisa had a cold, a bad hair day, or a broken heart, her friends knew about it. Her philosophy was simple: if you share your physical or emotional pain with others, you lighten your burden and don't have to carry it around by yourself. Lisa was a firm believer in the adage "a problem shared is a problem halved."

It turns out Lisa was right. Researchers at the University of California in Los Angeles recently discovered that verbalizing or writing about feelings decreases grief, anger, and pain, thus promoting better health.

Matthew D. Lieberman, PhD, and a team of researchers conducted a brain imaging study at UCLA. They began by flashing photographs of faces expressing strong emotions, such as fury, sadness, or fear, at study participants. Researchers found that the images, flashed so quickly they only registered subliminally, were enough to trigger a part of the participants' brains called the amygdala. This section of the brain serves as an "alarm" to protect the body in times of danger.

Once participants' emotional warning systems were activated, researchers asked them to label the emotion expressed by each face. According to an article in the journal Psychological Science, the act of attaching the correct label to each face reduced the activity in participants' "alarm centers." In addition to lessening the response in that area of the brain, putting feelings into words activated another region of the brain associated with thinking in words about emotional experiences. While research is not conclusive, that particular area of the brain is believed to function as a shut-off switch for the amygdala's alarm system.

Lieberman explained his theory in a news release. "When you put feelings into words, you're activating this prefrontal region and seeing a reduced response in the amygdala," he said. "In the same way you hit the brake when you're driving when you see a yellow light, when you put feelings into words, you seem to be hitting the brakes on your emotional responses."

These research results can be implemented with a single action: expressing your emotions with words.

✂ Make it Your Story

The next time you feel despondent or physically ill, test out Lieberman's ideas by putting a label on the emotion you are experiencing. Say the label aloud to yourself or use a friend as your sounding board. Notice if there is a shift in how you feel physically or emotionally.

Another strategy is to write out your feelings. Sharing your writings is always optional. After you are done writing, re-examine how you feel. If you detect changes, write down your observations.

Switch between verbalizing and writing out your feelings to determine which works best for you. You may have a strong preference for one technique, or find your choice is situational. If the latter is true, your favored process will depend on what you are experiencing. Either way, you will lighten your physical or emotional pain and, as Lisa often said, not have to carry the burden around by yourself.

A Journey to Forgiveness

"We can never obtain peace in the outer world
until we make peace with ourselves."
His Holiness the Dalai Lama

DO YOU SPEND TIME REPLAYING incidents where someone wronged you? If you do, you're not alone. Many of us allow people who've mistreated us to dominate our thoughts. Unfortunately, the perpetrators usually remain unaffected by our mental tirades.

During ten-plus years of research, two psychology professors at Seattle University, Jan O. Rowe and Steen Halling, learned that forgiveness is more than the acceptance of an apology—it is a journey. According to their research, the event that creates a need for forgiveness causes a tearing in the fabric of one's life, one's world. A person's sense of self is violated, and "the future, as it was anticipated before the event, is irrevocably changed."

Initially, many of us are unable to forgive, even if the offender apologizes. First, we need to experience shock, anger, fear, hurt, and grief. During this stage, a trusted therapist, friend, or family member can be extremely helpful. An empathic person provides a sounding board, allowing us to face our hurt, recover our emotional equilibrium, and move from blame to healing.

After a period of time (this varies from person to person), we begin to realize that dwelling on our anger and resentment is hurting us physically and emotionally. According to Dr. Everett L. Worthington, Jr., Executive Director of A Campaign for Forgiveness, "Forgiveness is both a decision and a real change in emotional experience. That change in emotion is related to better mental and physical health." To support this proposition, Dr. Worthington's organization has funded 46 research projects on the effects of forgiveness. Studies investigating the physical effects of forgiveness show that people who choose to forgive have reduced rates of stress and better cardiovascular health.

One myth that prevents us from letting go of our hurt, anger, and recriminations is the belief that forgiving an offense means we condone it, or that forgiveness is a sign of weakness. Neither belief is true. Forgiveness is a courageous act that liberates us from our role as victim. By refusing to allow another person's callous behavior to govern our health and happiness, we take back our power. Forgiveness aids our own well-being.

In the book *Building Your Field of Dreams* by Mary Manin Morrissey, a man named Al uses prayer to facilitate forgiveness toward his double-crossing friend, Bruce. After being told he can start the prayer any way he wants, Al makes up this prayer: "If a truck doesn't run him down first, God, let Bruce be happy and do well." Over time, Al let go of his anger and dropped the section about the truck.

In an interview, Ishmael Beah, author of *A Long Way Gone: Memoirs of a Boy Soldier*, was asked for his opinion of forgiveness. After fleeing attacking rebels at age 12, Beah fought in the Sierra Leona civil war for five years. From his experience, Beah learned that, "A lot of people, when they say, 'forgive and forget,' they think you completely wash your brain out and forget everything. That is not the concept. What I think is you forgive and you forget so you can transform your experiences, not necessarily forget them, but transform them so that they don't haunt you or handicap you or kill you."

Unfortunately, we often believe forgiveness is only possible if our perpetrator shows remorse. In actuality, we can help ourselves by changing the way we think about them, even when they remain locked in the role of villain. Taking away their "monster" status and seeing them as human beings reduces their influence.

The act of forgiveness helps restore our sense of worthiness and allows us to be more compassionate towards others. Rowe and Halling found that forgiving another person transcends our relationship with that person and opens us to the world and ourselves in new ways. "It is more than letting go; it is also a new beginning." At its best, this vision of newness is so compelling it feels like a gift of grace.

⚘ Make it your story

Think about times when you have forgiven or been forgiven. Did you forgive immediately or did you first need time to sort through your feelings? How did it feel to be forgiven? Is it easier to forgive others than to forgive yourself?

Look at the flip side of forgiveness. Recall a time when you held onto a grievance. How did your unwillingness to forgive affect your life?

Here are two forgiveness exercises you can try:

1. Write a letter to the person who "wronged" you. This letter is for your eyes only, not to share. The purpose is to express your feelings about the situation needing forgiveness, and how you feel about the person. The act of writing will help you process your thoughts and release some of your feelings.

2. Make a list of the benefits of letting go of resentment. This could include: more time focused on creativity or positive thoughts; improved physical and mental health; releasing victimhood and embracing serenity.

Morning Rituals

MOST OF US ENGAGE in some kind of morning ritual. Whether it is hitting the snooze button three times or walking the dog while in your bathrobe, these everyday routines help us transition from a sleepy dream world to our active on-the-go-lives. In addition to the usual routine of showering, eating, and dressing, many of us create sacred rituals to add a spiritual tenor to our day.

After musing about the spiritual rituals I use to start my day (recording my dreams and meditating), I asked some friends how they incorporated spiritual practices into their morning rituals. Here is a sampling of their responses.

When Karen realized she seldom woke up with a feeling of joy or gratitude for the day ahead, she decided to begin each morning on a positive note. She now chants several mantras before she gets out of bed, gives thanks for the gift of another day, and closes with this loving-kindness mantra:

May I be at peace.
May I be free of suffering and the root of all suffering.
May I remember the beauty, the joy, the strength of my own true nature.
May I live my life with ease.

"This little ritual has made a big difference in how I start my day. I get up feeling at peace, grounded, and connected to my deeper self," Karen explains.

Some people adapt programs that have been practiced for decades. Bill bases his morning prayer-meditation-journaling exercise on Alcoholics Anonymous' 12-Step Program. "I start by asking Spirit/God/Nameless-One/

Higher Power to guide my thinking, so that it will be free from self-pity, dishonesty, and selfishness. 'Thy Will, not mine, be done.' Then I think through the events of the day ahead and write a brief timeline of the upcoming day," he says. Bill's next two steps are meditation and a closing prayer.

A cup of java plays a central role in several of the rituals people shared with me. Carole uses the time it takes to brew her coffee to balance her energy and activate her chakras, a practice that aligns her energy physically, mentally, emotionally, and spiritually. Another woman, Julie, enjoys sipping a cup of coffee by herself before she begins interacting with her family or the outside world.

Maxie begins her day outside with morning prayers under the evergreens. First, she gives thanks for the new day and sends blessings to the spirit keepers of the four directions. Then, she expresses gratitude for her abundance, and shares her bounty with nature by feeding the birds and squirrels that gather in her yard. She ends her morning ritual with this prayer: "May everything I do, everything I think, everything I say today be done in perfect ways, with harm to none, in pure love."

Birds aren't the only ones singing at the break of day. Every morning, no matter how she feels, Ginger sings the same prayer song. "My little prayer offering is like a touchstone for my day. It is my 'good morning' to the universe and begins my day with love," says Ginger.

Cathy starts her day by listening to a CD, *Songs of the Spirit III* by Karen Drucker. She especially treasures these verses from the song "I Start My Day with Love:" "I start my day with love . . . I start my day with peace . . . I start my day with joy." This music provides Cathy with a gentle way to wake up and helps her set clear intentions for her day.

Many people told me about their meditation practices. For one woman, meditation comes before any other activity. Otherwise, she says, she gets caught up in the distractions of life. She insists that if she wipes down even one kitchen counter en route from her bed to her meditation cushion, her rhythm is thrown off and she'll fritter away the time she set aside for meditation.

Two friends invite movement into their meditations. One does a daily walking meditation around her neighborhood. The other performs her morning ablutions with spiritual mindfulness. This requires her to put aside work concerns and concentrate on every action involved in her routine.

Dreamwork is another popular ritual. Several people said they write down their dreams when they first wake up. Some use dreams as a jumping off place for journaling. Others mull over their dreams throughout the morning, mining them for insights into their lives.

✂ Make it your story

Morning rituals can increase your productivity, enhance your connection to the universal source, and create a calm and centering start to your day. Here is a recap of some things people I spoke to include in their morning rituals:

- *Meditation*
- *Prayer*
- *Writing down last night's dreams*
- *Clearing chakras*
- *Stepping out into nature*
- *Listening to music*

If you haven't established a morning ritual, start by composing a list of things that bring you pleasure. Do you love singing, walking in nature, eating a favorite food, or practicing yoga? Design a morning ritual that incorporates one or two activities. The key is to design a morning ritual that lifts your spirits and gives you a positive beginning to your day.

Life Purpose

THE MONTH OF FEBRUARY is an interesting combination of winter and emerging spring. As the cold winds blow across steel gray skies, signs of the coming spring begin to pop up in the Pacific Northwest. Even though the ground is frozen in the grasp of winter, glorious bright daffodils begin to push their way up through the rock-hard soil and display their spectacular yellow blooms.

In March, the tulips take their turn, turning plots of brown earth into vibrant patchwork quilts. By May, the irises and lilies provide us with bright palates of color.

Each flower bulb is destined to become a specific flower. There is no threat of a daffodil bulb becoming a lily, or an anemone bulb turning into a gladiolus. The scientific name for this goal-directed energy contained in each bulb is entelechy (en tel i k). Essentially, this hundred-dollar word means the actualization of potentiality, or fulfilling one's life purpose.

Bringing one's destiny to fruition is not limited to flowers. The potential to do so exists in each of us. In her book, *The Hero and the Goddess*, writer-philosopher Jean Houston says we have a need to "tap into a symbolic or archetypal expression of the entelechy principle operating in our lives. Entelechy is all about the possibilities encoded in each of us." We all know an acorn is programmed to be an oak tree and a butterfly lives inside the caterpillar, but what about us? Do we know what our entelechy, or soul purpose, is?

Unlike flower bulbs, our life purpose does not emerge spontaneously when we mature. In fact, there are so many people searching for their "true calling," a cottage industry has sprung up around the topic. Shelves of books and dozens of workshops offer suggestions and road maps to finding one's life purpose.

In his book Callings: *Finding and Following an Authentic Life*, Greg Levoy says fear is a major obstacle for people trying to find their life purpose. Often, this fear manifests as a fear of failure. Some people deal with this fear by believing that if they don't try, they can't fail. Levoy says he gave up that line of thinking after being told that if he was not failing regularly, he was living so far below his potential that he was failing anyway.

For me, writing has been my teacher regarding the fear of failure. It is a simple fact: if I don't submit my work and face the possibility of rejection, I can't get published. Repeatedly facing the fear of failure in my writing life has thickened my skin and given me the gumption to try other endeavors.

As Sue Monk Kidd says in her book *The Dance of the Dissident Daughter*, entelechy "pulses inside us, trying to complete who we are uniquely meant to be." We can fight against it, but in the end trying and failing is better than not trying at all.

✂ Make it your story

If you are searching for your life purpose, try using these four questions to examine your inner landscape:

1. *What makes you happy? List people, activities, hobbies, and social causes.*

2. Are you ever engaged in a project and lose track of time? If so, what are you doing when that happens?

3. When do you feel the best about yourself? What are you doing?

4. If you knew your life was about to end, what would you most regret not having done?

People's life purpose is often connected with something they feel passionate about or something that makes them happy. With that in mind, review your answers. Do you see areas of your life that might lead you toward your life purpose?

The point of this exercise is not to find your one true calling. It is to begin the journey. When you have an idea, follow it. Then periodically look around and see if you are happy with the direction you are taking. If you are, continue moving forward. Otherwise, it is time to revamp your plan.

Noise Pollution: Breaking the Cycle

AS A SOCIETY, WE HAVE BECOME CONDITIONED to constant input. One gas station near my home even has a tiny TV screen that activates when the pump is switched on. As my gas tank is filling, my mind is being filled with new information.

Over the years, I have seen more and more people walking down the street with cell phones glued to their ears or ear buds blocking out their surroundings. Some folks rush from one meeting to another trying to sandwich in a few minutes of phone business or checking Facebook instead of taking a mini-break to gather their thoughts. Constant input from the outside may keep us entertained, but it also prevents us from staying in touch with our own thoughts. These trends make me wonder— are people developing a fear of being alone with their own thoughts?

An acquaintance named Susan declares one day a month a "Sacred Day." On that day, she avoids all forms of news (TV, radio, and newspapers) and refrains from driving or buying anything. Susan spends her quiet day at home meditating, listening to music, and reading. After diving deeply into the silence of her own mind, she returns to her everyday life calmer and happier.

✂ Make it your story

If a 24-hour "Sacred Day" break is out of reach, try a brief ten-minute quiet break once a day for a week. Turn off your music, television, cell phone, computer, and all other noise-making devices. Drive with the radio turned off, exercise without your iPod, or spend time at home without the television turned on. Allow your mind to wander. Follow your thoughts as they skip-jump over and in between seemingly different topics. Pay attention to the topics you think about, and then try to retrace how you got to a particular thought.

How did you feel about taking a break from outside input and allowing time for introspection? Were you comfortable or uneasy? Did you gain clarity about any issues in your life?

Decision Making

*Eeny, meeny, miny, moe
Catch a tiger by the toe
If he hollers let him go,
Eeny, meeny, miny, moe.*
Nursery Rhyme

SOMETIMES LIFE FEELS like an unending series of decisions which gobble up valuable time. From morning to night, we are choosing between options—from which outfit to wear to what to fix for dinner. Consider the time it takes to decide which can of tomatoes to buy. After choosing between whole, crushed, diced, or fire-roasted tomatoes, you still need to make up your mind about organic, non-organic, low-sodium, or added spices. If you stop to read the ingredient labels, add more time. This vast array of choices is a blessing and a curse. If you aren't immobilized by the choices, you can buy exactly what you want.

Is there anything we can do to make decision making easier? According to a study done by lead researcher Ap Dijksterhuis and his colleagues at the University of Amsterdam in the Netherlands, it depends of the type of decision you are making. If you are making a simple decision, such as purchasing an inexpensive item or picking out a restaurant, it is best to clarify what you want, gather all relevant facts, spend time consciously thinking about your options, then make a decision.

Complex decisions, which involve the purchase of expensive items or life-changing decisions such as choosing a place to live, deciding to marry, or picking a career path, require a different process. For these decisions, Dijksterhuis suggests that you make a list of your requirements, research all relevant facts, then put your choices aside. Instead of consciously thinking about your choices, let your subconscious take over. Get mentally involved in another activity. In a few hours, or preferably a day, come back to your choices, and, without deliberating, make a decision.

Drawing on information gathered through experiments in laboratories with volunteer students and with real-life shoppers, the researchers found reasons why conscious deliberation doesn't work when making major decisions. When we are engaged in conscious deliberation, our brains automatically limit the amount of information being processed. Instead of looking at the whole picture, we consider only a fraction of the relevant information. To complicate matters even more, the conscious mind can exaggerate the importance of some aspects at the expense of others.

In contrast, unconscious thought allows people to process large amounts of pertinent information without prioritizing or deleting any relevant facts. While we are sleeping, daydreaming, or occupied with other unrelated activities, our brains can work with the volume of information involved in making a complex decision and pick the best option. The old adage "sleep on it" turns out to be good advice.

One disconcerting scenario the study leaves out is when you wake up and, instead of having clarity, you hear multiple answers. What can you do then?

If you are feeling confused, the best thing to do is to stop, take a few deep breaths, quiet your mind, then reconsider your options. Be patient. If you are mentally thrashing around you won't hear a clear answer. You need to be calm and receptive. Try this technique and the most appropriate course of action should become obvious.

However, if you are still uncertain, look for the solution that has the most magnetism. Picture yourself choosing one option, then image making a different choice. How does your body respond? Do any of the choices elicit positive or negative physical sensations in your body or your thinking? Take the course of action that feels most trustworthy.

᠅ Make it your story

Practice these two decision-making processes. First, work with the one for making minor decisions, such as which movie to see or deodorant to buy. For the next week or two, think about the outcome of minor decisions you have made. Are you pleased with your decisions, or do you wish you had chosen different options? If you are generally happy with the outcomes of your minor decisions, try the process designed for making major decisions. Once you have fine-tuned processes that work for you, decision making will be easier and the results more satisfying.

Divine Lessons

Breathing with Helen

MY FRIEND HELEN FLEW TO CANADA for a week's vacation with her sister and never returned. A neatly dressed 60-year-old woman with Helen's slim figure, silver-gray curls, and radiant smile came back, but it wasn't the Helen I knew. The woman who got off the plane was dazed and confused. It was hard to imagine how she negotiated the plane transfer required to get to the Seattle airport.

In an effort to find out the reason for her confusion, Helen's neighbor and I took her to several doctors' appointments. Using a signature that resembled chicken scratch more than her usually precise penmanship, she signed numerous forms authorizing a series of tests and giving her doctors permission to tell her neighbor and me the results.

I remember the June morning when I learned the test results. The doctor called while I was alone with Helen at her condo. The tests were conclusive. Helen had an inoperable brain tumor located in the center of her frontal lobe. The tumor's placement made it impossible to treat with surgery and it would not respond to chemotherapy. The doctor suggested radiation treatments to shrink Helen's cranial swelling and reduce the severity of her frequent headaches. Helen's best hope was that the radiation treatments might add a month to her life. With or without treatments, Helen had only three or four months to live.

By early September, any hope for a miraculous cure had died. Now bed-ridden, Helen's king size bed dwarfed her rail-thin body. The figure in the bed barely resembled the woman I'd known for seven years. The elegant Helen who always dressed with care and entered rooms with a ready smile was gone.

As she lay in her bed, covered up to her chin with a white eyelet bed-spread trimmed with lace, I could see only the face of my dear friend. Her once carefully coiffured hair hung limply around her emaciated face. The bright, smiling eyes that encouraged me through a dozen drafts of my first book were dull and vacant. No longer physically able to eat or drink, her bodily functions were shutting down. And, although she could have been fed intravenously, one had to ask why. It would only prolong the inevitable. With no food or water, Helen would be dead within a few days.

One afternoon, I had the opportunity to sit alone with Helen in her bedroom. She floated in and out of consciousness as I sat on her bed and talked about things I remembered from when she was healthy. Although she could only flutter her eyelids in response, I hoped she could feel the love behind my words. I recalled the numerous times she boosted the morale of friends and acquaintances by listening with genuine interest to the stories of their lives. Helen always encouraged members of our writers' club to pursue their writing dreams. Mentally replaying some of her pep talks, I wondered if she had kept enough of her confidence-building elixir for herself. Over the past year, she and I had talked about her struggles to become more assertive. Instead of giving her time away to everyone who asked for help, she was learning how to say that magical two-letter word, "no," and to focus on her own needs and writing aspirations. But at her core, Helen remained a giver. She had been making great strides to combat her tendency to give too much when her brain tumor threw up an impen-etrable roadblock. In an instant, her life as a world traveler, published writer, and first-rate friend collapsed.

Sitting beside her, I told Helen how her death was transforming my spiritual beliefs. I had begun the summer with my aversion to anything religious fully intact. Then, slowly, my door of resistance cracked open. Helen's condo became a laboratory where spiritual practices were put to the test. I knew she'd get a kick out of hearing about me praying, chanting, and using touch healing. Although Helen was never pushy about her religious beliefs, she always let me know how important spirituality was to her well-being.

After about fifteen minutes, I grew tired of hearing myself talk. Over the past three months, I coped best when I could help Helen with her physical needs—cooking food, running errands, and helping her dress. Now she was beyond those necessities, and I didn't know what to do.

I stood up, moved to the window, and watched sunlight dance across Puget Sound. A group of gulls circled overhead as a ferry prepared to land at the Edmonds dock. As I turned back, I caught a glimpse of my dear friend in the mirror over her dresser. Seeing her as a stranger might, my heart sank and I slumped to the floor. With my back against the cool outside wall, I watched the erratic rise and fall of her chest. Soon I found myself trying to match my breath with hers, but the irregular rhythm made it difficult for me to stay in synch.

Hearing Helen draw in a raspy breath, I matched her shallow intake. Seconds passed. My lungs were about to explode when I finally heard her exhale. Whew! Then I waited, literally breathless, for her next intake. There was no pattern, no rhythm. The irregularity of her breaths reminded me of the Energizer Bunny winding down its drumming. Beat, beat-beat, half-beat, beat.

Within a few minutes, my lungs begged for more oxygen. Taking in half a dozen lung-filling deep breaths, I could almost hear my body say, "Ah, that feels better." Then I returned to my breath-matching challenge with Helen. Sharing the room's air with my dying friend felt sacred because I knew it was the last thing she and I could share together.

A week later, Helen died. As I looked back on our last afternoon together, I could almost feel the strain my lungs felt when I matched her ragged breaths. Having felt Helen's laborious breathing within my own body helped me release my earthly ties with her and better accept her death.

⚘ Make it your story

Many people have contradictory attitudes towards death. On the one hand, they are fascinated by celebrity deaths, regularly read obituaries in the newspa-

per, and track disasters where people die in tragic circumstances. Yet they try to avoid thinking about their own deaths.

Whether you think about it or plan for it or ignore it, death is guaranteed. You received a round trip ticket when you were born. The only aspect you can partially control is the in-between space. What will you do between now and when you die?

A 2007 movie call The Bucket List *popularized the notion of writing down a list of things you want to do before you die (or "kick the bucket"). The premise of the movie is that two terminally ill men (Jack Nicholson and Morgan Freeman) meet in a hospital and go on a road trip to fulfill a wish list of things they want to do before they die.*

On your laptop or paper, create your own bucket list with things you most want to experience before you die. In order to make your list doable, list easy-to-accomplish items as well as challenges. You can list places you want to see, activities you want to experience, or skills you want to achieve. The only limit is your imagination.

Here are a few ideas to get you started:

- *Attend a live concert*
- *Eat crepes in Paris*
- *Take an improv class*
- *Go on a blind date*
- *Attend a Native American pow wow*
- *Sing karaoke in public*
- *Learn to play poker*
- *Write a poem*
- *Drive across the United States*
- *Grow a plant from seed*
- *Order room service*

What If

"I WAS JUST ROBBED AT GUNPOINT." The words exploded out of my son, Spence, and stopped my heart as assuredly as a bullet could have stopped his. Thankfully, he immediately followed up his gut-wrenching announcement by assuring me that he was okay.

The robbery took place one month into Spence's five-month study abroad program in Quito, Ecuador. He and a friend were walking along a main road during a rainstorm. As dusk wrestled with the final rays of sunlight, three men rushed toward them, one pointing a gun. "Give us your wallet and cell phone," the gunman demanded, aiming his weapon at my son's head. Spence and his friend immediately complied. Spence turned over his wallet containing five dollars, a credit card, and his Washington state driver's license, along with his cell phone. The thieves then took his friend's backpack, which contained a laptop and an iPod.

During my conversation with Spence, I made triple sure he was physically unharmed, and then I offered up a deep prayer of thanks to Divine Spirit for my son's safety. My heart almost glowed with love and appreciation as I reveled in the positive aspect of the story: Spence was alive and unharmed.

In the next moment, raw fear slammed gratitude aside, and I slipped into the world of "what ifs."

What if Spence had challenged the thieves, or they had decided to eliminate all witnesses? Panic rose to my throat as I realized I could just as easily have gotten a call from the Ecuadorian police telling me my son was dead.

The expansive appreciation and elation I had felt seconds before melted away. I could feel my cells contracting with bone-chilling terror. In my imagination, I reached across the 5,000 miles that separated me from my son and teleported him back into to the safety of our home.

Just before I fully succumbed to my fears, a tiny space arose between my thoughts of thankfulness and the negative emotions that threatened my mental health. In that tiny buffer zone, I realized I had a choice. I could focus on the "what ifs," or be thankful for the reality of what was. Where I put my thoughts would determine how I felt. The "what if" road led to anguishing scenarios of what it would feel like to lose my son. Focusing on what really happened, Spence being physically fine, filled me with joy.

I felt pulled between the two forces. As Spence's mother, wasn't it my job to panic? Could I listen to my son's encounter with a loaded gun and see only the positive? Didn't I have a responsibility to rage against the thieves and conjure up disastrous scenarios of what could have happened? Somehow it seemed wrong not to go to pieces.

I recalled other situations in which I had wandered down the "what if" trail and didn't pay attention to what had actually occurred. Replaying those scenarios, I could almost feel a tarry blackness begin to spread its tentacles of doom inside my mind.

Standing at the junction between gratitude and despair, I knew I had to make my choice quickly. If the new theories about quantum physics were right and the way I thought would directly influence my body chemistry and physiology, my decision could impact my overall health. Reminding myself that getting depressed would not help Spence, I chose to focus on the good news. There were enough scary aspects of Spence's story without manufacturing a list of "what ifs."

⤲ Make it Your Story

One way to avoid detours into the land of "what ifs" is by practicing mindfulness. Simply put, mindfulness is the ability to be present to what you are experiencing from moment to moment, without drifting into thoughts about the past or concerns about the future.

Being able to shift into mindfulness requires ongoing practice. Begin by taking a few moments every day to bring your full attention to the activity with which you are engaged. Tune into your senses and mentally describe your experience to yourself. Pick out the colors or textures in your surroundings. Listen to ambient sounds. What can you identify? Observe your thoughts and emotions and how they affect your body. Can you feel your heart beating or your internal temperature changing? Pay attention to your breathing. Are you taking shallow or deep breaths?

As you practice this awareness, realize that mindfulness is a way to break your mind's old habit of darting between thoughts of the past, present, and future. The goal is not to be in the moment a hundred percent of the time. Rather, the objective is to develop the ability to shift into focused awareness when you want or need to.

Allowing

JUST BEFORE THE CRISPNESS OF FALL pushed summer out of reach, I took a solo two-hour drive northeast from Seattle to the Cascade foothills. Parking along the side of the road outside Granite Falls on the Mountain Loop Highway, I shut off my car's motor. In the quiet that followed, I felt embraced by the sounds of birds calling out from atop tall cedars and alder leaves rustling in the wind.

Looking around the forest of cedars, Douglas firs, western hemlocks, vine leaf maples, and alders, I mused about the word *allow*. Thoughts about the act of allowing and how it affects my quality of life had been swirling through my mind all morning. During my reflections, I defined allowing as the act of being open to, permitting, or being receptive.

After a few minutes of wonderful solitude, I slipped off my tennis shoes and donned my worn water shoes. A short path led me to the Stillaguamish River, where I noticed the river's diminished flow. Due to an unusually hot and dry Northwest summer, a large span of exposed rock extended several yards out from the riverbank.

I sat on the shore for a few minutes, then eased my feet into the cold mountain water. Crawling, hopping, and splashing around downed trees and over boulders, I gradually made my way to the center of the river until I found a large, flat granite rock surrounded by deep, fast-moving water. Sitting down on the rock, I closed my eyes and felt the sun on my face and a gentle breeze playing across my hair. Several different voices of the river serenaded me as water flowed over the boulders, spilled into spiraling vortexes, tinkled across loose rocks, and whooshed through foot-size passages between boulders. My body, mind, and spirit reveled in the moment. It was exactly what I had hoped to find. Yet, as soon as the calmness seeped into my conscious, a quiver of anxiousness seized my gut. Suddenly, I had the urge to move on. It was as if I'd exceeded my contentment quota.

Puzzled by this impulse to leave my dream location, I wondered what would happen if I allowed myself to just be? I calmed myself with a few deep breaths and focused on what was around me rather than what might come next. From a stand of alders, I saw a single yellow leaf glide down onto the river and ride its currents under a nearby bridge. I heard a bee buzz near my ear, while in the distance a truck rumbled down the highway. Whirls of water pushed up against a cluster of rocks, divided, and circled their way to freedom. A blue dragonfly's iridescent wings caught the sunlight as it skimmed the water.

By allowing myself to fully absorb the sights, the sounds, the feel of the hard, cold rock beneath me and the warm sun on my skin, I felt the totality of the experience etch itself into my memory. After about twenty minutes,

I felt an inner serenity. With a deep sense of gratitude, I left the rock and scrambled across the boulders back to the riverbank.

Next, I drove six miles up a logging road to a hiking trail I had never explored. About a quarter mile into my walk, I noticed something unusual—the absence of noise. I paused. The sound of my shoes crunching on the gravel gave way to a silence so intense I could hear my heartbeat. After letting the sound-void sink into my innermost being, I continued at a leisurely pace, pausing periodically to enjoy the quiet stillness. Filled with gratitude, I gave thanks for a day spent bathed in the beauty of nature.

❧ Make it your story

The art of living in the now takes only a moment. When you find yourself getting restless and looking toward the next activity instead of what you are currently doing, stop and pay attention to what is around you. Use your senses to experience your immediate environment. What to do you hear, see, and smell? Observe without putting any value judgments on what you experience.

If you find yourself worrying, let it go. Worry never accomplishes anything. Use your mental energy on something that can affect change.

Ground yourself in the present moment. First, plant your feet firmly on the ground. Feel your whole foot connected with the ground, from the heel to the toes. Some people find this grounding technique helps them be centered, balanced, and connected to the earth. Once you feel the connection between your feet and the ground, imagine roots going from the bottom of your feet into the core of the earth. You may be aware of a sinking feeling as the roots drop down through the layers of earth. Take a moment to focus on this sensation.

When you find yourself paying more attention to where you want to go than where you are, implement these techniques and refocus on the now. Being open and receptive allows for life's most precious gift—the present moment.

The Big Jump

THE SEARING PAIN CAME AS SHOCK. One minute I was working at my computer, and the next, stabbing nerve pain was shooting down my right leg.

In hindsight, I could see the problem had been building, dropping hints with sharp bursts of pain that dissolved as quickly as they came. The occurrences were easy to ignore until the final, infinitesimal shift from health to immobility.

Flash-forward a few weeks, and the pain had a label: a bulging disc in my lower back. A spinal disc, smaller than a marble, had commandeered my life. In an instant, all my to-do lists, deadlines, and plans were pushed to the bottom of my priority list. My new goal boiled down to one word: mobility. Constant gnawing pain severely limited my movements, reducing me to hobbling across the room and butt-bumping down stairs. Only the ability to hold a book and read saved my sanity.

One afternoon, while searching for yet another book to divert my attention, I came across my favorite childhood story, *The Big Jump* by Benjamin Elkin. Taking the slim copy off the living room bookshelf, I reread it.

The story takes place long ago in a faraway kingdom, where only kings are allowed to own dogs. When a young boy named Ben falls in love with one of the King's puppies, he sadly exclaims, "I wish I could be a king."

Reading about Ben's plight, I thought, who hasn't yearned for a treasure or talent someone else possesses? From my housebound perspective, I envied people who could walk and drive.

Upon hearing the young boy's wish, the King told Ben that kings must be able to do many things other people could not, including the Big Jump. Before Ben could ask what that was, the King took a giant leap and landed at the top of his castle. Standing high above his land, the King looked down on Ben and the puppy and proclaimed, "If you jump up here, I can't make you a king, but I can let you keep the puppy."

Ah, the carrot-on-a-stick trick. Tell people they can have the object of their desire if they fulfill a seemingly impossible task. We all know that ploy. From eating the dreaded canned peas in order to get dessert to taking daily runs in hopes of winning a marathon, a strong desire can motivate a person to overcome obstacles in pursuit of a difficult goal.

And so it was with Ben. He really wanted that puppy, and quickly accepted the challenge.

The king allowed Ben to keep the puppy while he tried to accomplish the seemingly impossible quest. With the puppy looking on, Ben practiced jumping onto stacks of boxes. Sadly, he was a terrible jumper. With every jump, no matter how high or short, he fell to the ground.

Thinking about Ben's plight, I felt a kinship with him. Every time I recalled a doctor telling me that putting a bulging disc back in place was like putting toothpaste back in a tube, I felt despair. To resume my normal life without undergoing surgery, I would have to take on a challenge as daunting as Ben's—healing my bulging disc.

As Ben's story continued, he was about to give up when the puppy jumped on one box, then the next, and then the next, until he reached the top of the stack. "Ha, ha," said Ben. "Now I know how to jump."

The next morning, Ben raced to the castle followed by a group of children. He called out to the king, "I can do it, I can do it!" Then, with a smile on his face, Ben jumped up to the top of the castle one step at a time.

The other children laughed and said, "Anyone can jump that way."

"Yes," said the King, handing the dog to Ben. "Anyone can jump this way, but it took Ben to show you it was possible."

How often do we act like those laughing children, thinking there is only one way to succeed? If we are lucky, we have someone like Ben who shows us a way to break our goal down into smaller steps.

Following the wise example Ben set before me, I stopped yearning for a miracle and began taking baby steps toward recovery. Although it took longer than I wanted and required the assistance of healing arts practitioners and daily Jin Shin Jyutsu self-help treatments, I did it. I am not jumping to the top of a castle in one big jump, but I am walking, one step at a time.

⚘ Make it Your Story

Focus on something you want to accomplish. It could be changing careers, committing to meditating ten minutes a day, or trying out a new exercise routine. Your goal can be large or small one. The key is your motivation.

Once you have chosen a task, create a list of small steps needed to fulfill your goal. Checking off items as you move toward your goal will allow you to see measurable progress.

Write down your victories and your failures. Explore how it feels to hit a roadblock. Instead of sticking with tried-and-true ideas, experiment with innovative ways you can triumph over obstacles.

Once you accomplish your goal, celebrate. Give yourself kudos for setting out a challenge for yourself and completing the task. Evaluate and reflect on what you learned and how you can use your success to accomplish more goals.

Rest Stop Trepidations

Leaving behind the miles of pumice and sparse vegetation that surround Oregon's Crater Lake, my partner, Bo, and I wound our way down scenic U.S. Highway 97. Thousands of acres of lodgepole pines, mountain hemlocks, ponderosa pines, and Douglas firs spread out before us, creating a multi-hued patchwork of green. The crowning touch was a soaring pair of eagles circling overhead.

Turning onto Highway 58, we continued our drive back to our home in Washington State. Just outside of Oregon's Willamette Pass, we spotted a sign for a much needed rest stop. Although the sign said Salt Creek Falls, we did not anticipate seeing a real waterfall. Having recently driven through the town of Klamath Falls, which had absolutely no waterfalls, we questioned Oregon's ability to name locations based on their true attributes.

Three miles down the winding road lined with a delicious mix of evergreens, we found the rest area. The parking slots were deserted, except for one with a large double cab red truck. Lounging on the hood of the truck and spread out across the sidewalk was a group of six scowling men with muscular builds, dirty T-shirts, and frayed jeans. Arms crossed, they gave us steely stares as we pulled in several slots away from their truck.

As I looked around I saw no restrooms or picnic tables. The rest stop's lack of amenities and off-the-beaten-path location meant it was unlikely other travelers would be joining the truckload of men and us.

Bo and I sat in the car and assessed the situation. If the men chose to threaten us, we would offer no physical match. They were younger, stronger, and outnumbered us. We struggled with our need to stretch our legs versus the possible danger these men represented. Beyond a potential physical threat, these men challenged us on a deeper level. While our instincts said we needed to be cautious, we did not want fear to rule our actions. After talking it over, we decided to get out and stretch.

As we strolled along the sidewalk, one of the men stepped forward and told us that just down the trail and around the bend was a beautiful waterfall. "You should get your camera out of the car and go see it. You do have a camera, don't you?"

Getting the camera meant opening the car trunk, showing the men our suitcases and mementos from our travels. Not something I felt inclined to do.

We hemmed and hawed, saying we did not think we were interested in the waterfall. In actuality, I wasn't sure there even was a waterfall. All I could hear was the sound of the wind in the trees. Suspicion crept into my mind. *Yeah right,* I thought, *you want us out of the way so you can break into the car, steal our stuff, and maybe even take the car, too. Or maybe you want us to go down the trail so you can bop us on the head and steal our wallets.* None of my scenarios had happy endings.

Our rest break was turning out to be anything but restful. While we could have hopped in the car and continued our journey, an inner struggle kept me from leaving. While acknowledging my uneasiness, I knew it was the perfect opportunity to put my newly-developing set of belief systems into action.

Over the past year, I had begun cultivating a new way of viewing stereotypes and unexamined fear. My new perspective came from two sources. The first was my part-time job at a university's minority center tutoring students from around the world. Over the course of my work, I worked with numerous undergraduates who had fled their countries due to military conflicts. One woman had to leave her mother on a mountainside because she was too ill to continue the journey. Several students shared stories about spending years in impoverished refugee camps where illness and violence were regular occurrences. All the students came to the U.S. with little or no knowledge of what their new lives would hold. These young adults faced fear and uncertainty beyond my comprehension. My work at the tutoring center taught me that it was possible to move forward even when facing life-threatening fears.

Sunny Jacobs was the second source. On the recommendation of a friend, Bo and I had attended a talk by Sunny where she described her 19 years in prison for a murder she did not commit. She spent her first weeks in jail stewing in anger, fear, and worry. Then one day, as she paced her six-foot by five-foot cell, Sunny reached a decisive moment. She understood that she had a choice. She could continue to fill herself with negativity, or take charge of what she could still control. "I decided they could lock my body in a cell, but not my spirit," said Sunny.

Drawing on her knowledge of yoga and meditation, Sunny created a daily routine that incorporated both practices. With her self-initiated program, she consciously let go of fear and anger. Her message to us was that no matter what situation people find themselves in, they always have a choice in how to react.

After finally being exonerated and released from prison, Sunny noticed that people on the outside often allowed fear to trap them. She saw many people on the "outside" who created internal prisons that limited what they did and where they went. To Sunny, they were more imprisoned by their beliefs than she had been by prison walls.

I was still weighing the safety of us being alone in the parking lot with six big men, let alone wandering down the trail, when two more large men came crashing out from behind a cluster of tall bushes. Before they even came to a stop, they started raving about the wonders of the waterfall. "It is just 100 yards down the trail. It will only take you a couple of minutes."

I faced a dilemma. If there truly was a waterfall, I wanted to see it. But I did not want to be stupid and put our safety in jeopardy. I also didn't want to be limited by fear. Between my work experience and remembering Sunny's words, I was inspired to let go of my sense of foreboding. Nodding my head toward the trail, I signaled to Bo.

Side by side, we scurried toward the trailhead. Once on the trail, we agreed to give our excursion two minutes to see if we could hear or view a waterfall. Surely, we said to each other, they could not take our car apart that quickly.

Within a short distance, we came upon an incredibly huge and beautiful waterfall. Torrents of water spilled over a rock shelf mottled with Irish green moss. Falling several hundred feet, the water crashed into a deep, dark pool. Sprays of water filled the air with a misty rain. The waterfall easily surpassed the beauty of other falls that received big billings at tourist information centers.

As we came back up the trail, we saw that our car was still intact. The eight men still stood on the sidewalk, arms folded. Only now they were smiling, as if to say, "See, you didn't need to be afraid of us." Blushing, I thanked them for encouraging us to view the waterfall. "You were right," I said. "It was truly spectacular."

Waving goodbye to the group of eight men, we drove back to the highway. Watching the sun and shadows play in the passing trees, I mentally chewed over what had just happened. *Yes, some fears are important for self-preservation*, I thought. But the waterfall episode showed me how habitual responses could hold me back from pioneering new experiences. At Salt Creek Falls, overriding my initial fear was more rewarding than playing it safe. Although caution kept me from retrieving the camera and snapping a picture of the waterfall, I was coming away with something even more treasured—the knowledge that I always have a choice in how to react.

✧ Make it your story

Fear can feel like an arrow shooting through you—fast, powerful, and seemingly out of your control. Your power comes from deciding what to do after it strikes. Do you hold fear inside and let it engulf you? Or do you release it so its energy dissipates?

It's often difficult to recognize there is a choice. As Sunny Jacobs said, fear can make a person feel imprisoned and powerless.

Do you agree with Sunny Jacobs' observation about people creating internal prisons that limit where they go and what they do? What do you think of the idea that people always have a choice in how to react?

Think back on your life. Have there been situations in your life where you created your own inner prison and imposed arbitrary limits or rules on yourself?

When have you responded to a situation without thinking, and then regretted your action? How did you feel afterwards?

Write down times you have restricted your options or reacted without thinking. Write about times you expanded your thinking, or situations when you were proud of your reaction. What differences do you experience when you react from a limiting belief system versus when you make conscious choices?

Blessed by water

I LEARNED TO SWIM BEFORE I COULD WALK, and thus began my love affair with water. As an adult, swimming is still my passion. While my left brain is busy keeping me afloat, my right brain is free to enter a peaceful, reflective state. It is in these moments that I connect with my soul's essence, my ageless core-self.

Open water is my true love. Oceans, lakes, rivers—any body of water that allows me to stretch out and swim in one direction for at least a mile before heading back. I like water without boundaries, just open water and me.

As a teen, I spent summer days swimming in the warm ocean waters of Southern California. I grew into adulthood testing my strength against the ocean. The hot sands of sunbathing held no allure. Water was my environment and I spent hours immersed in its salty bath, emerging with a salt-encrusted body.

Even before I knew about Yemanjá, the African-Brazilian goddess of the sea and "Mother whose children are the fish," I thought of the ocean as a feminine power.

Although I did not have a name for her, Yemanjá was my teacher. Under her tutelage, I swam out past the breaking waves. My mother's daily admonishments to be careful and to watch out for undertows were dismissed with adolescent scorn. The ocean offered me an escape from my crazed hormones, the sexual glares of teenage boys, and my girlfriends' boy-mania. Psychologically and physically, I was out of touch with the California beach babe mentality, where skimpy bikinis and bright red hickeys were badges of honor. Only in the water was I at peace with my changing body and my changing life.

Out beyond the crowds, I felt strong and powerful. Yemanjá's crashing waves did not tolerate timidness. Leaving my paralyzing shyness on the shore, I gleefully ran into the ocean. Diving under towering waves, I held my breath and waited on the ocean's floor while the waves crashed overhead. The hundreds of pounds of water formed a cloak of security. Inside my watery cocoon, no one could touch me, mentally or physically.

Rising from the bottom after the turbulence had passed, I would swim, stroke after stroke, out past the raucous waves to the open sea. Invariably, saltwater, the ocean's embryonic fluid, would slip through my parted lips. When my muscles ached with tiredness, I turned my back to the water and floated on Yemanjá's rounded swells until my energy was restored. Once renewed, it was time to head back toward civilization. Checking out the waves, I waited for one with the right height and curve for body surfing. Catching the crest of a perfectly shaped wave, I would ride it to shore, where I was usually grounded by a swimsuit full of sand.

Many years have passed since those youthful days. Now the joys of my summers are quick trips to a small suburban lake north of Seattle that most non-swimmers scorn. The neglected stepsister of Seattle's lushly-landscaped lakes, its gravel path leads to a desolate beach with burnt yellow grass and a rocky shore. Only hot-hot days bring a crowd to this beach, and even then other swimmers stay close to shore.

I ignore the park's shoddy condition and focus my attention on the water. Dropping my towel on the shore, I wade into the clear green lake. In the heat of the summer, the water is body temperature and I am at one with its fluid essence.

A dozen strong strokes and I enter a world of solitude. The noise of the landlocked world drifts away. I bask in the sound of water lapping against my arms and the bubbles that play around my face when I exhale. A mouthful of musty-tasting water reminds me of years past, when the saltwater washed through my mouth. Being on the other side of child-bearing, I no longer worry about the glares of teenage boys, but my body continues to undergo changes.

Swimming the crawl stroke, I stretch and pull my arms through the water, gliding more than swimming across the surface. With each stroke, I relax. Feelings of futility, of trying to balance the needs of my family and friends with my personal needs, are washed away and replaced by a deep sense of peace. The yin and yang of life comes into balance. Moving through the water, I see myself as a woman in command of her body and her life.

Shoreside houses and towering trees mark my progress. My mantra, "reach and pull and breathe," carries me past a majestic chestnut tree with burly spiked pods and hand-sized leaves. Past the willows standing proud at the edge of the lake with their shag cut and trimmed ends dipping down into the water.

At the end of the lake, I stop and float. Giving thanks for my buoyant body, I lay resting on the lake's current with my legs stretched out and my arms tucked under my head. Gently bobbing, I gaze skyward, watching the sun and wind transform birch leaves into tiny prisms. The play of light against the leaves and the gentle ripples in the water move me on a cellular level. My deeply shy teen-self mixes and blends with my more confident woman-self. Rejuvenated, I begin swimming back to shore. The rhythm of my strengthened stroke propels me forward.

Every year, as summer folds into fall and the earth slants away from the sun, the water cools. Intuitively, I know my outdoor swimming is coming to an end. Believing it is better to swim within boundaries than not swim at all, I reluctantly pack my gym bag and head for an indoor pool.

Doing laps—back and forth, back and forth—I am lulled into a hypnotic, almost meditative state. Blocking out the chorine smell and other swimmers, I conjure up a lifetime of water-based memories. Instead of blue tile and overhead lights, I summon images of feather-stroke clouds floating above towering cedars and seagulls flying across the sky.

Outdoors or indoors, swimming allows me the time and space to mull over the ebbs and flows of life. When I am struggling with problems at work, family disputes, or melancholy moods, I take to the water the way others take to drink. Immersing myself, stretching out my muscles, and gliding across the water's surface, the weight of life's difficulties dissolve. Through the years and around the globe, water carries my body forward.

✂ Make it your story

Sometimes we need to metaphorically shake ourselves by the shoulders to loosen up our thought processes. To think outside our normal thought patterns can require us to distract the conscious mind with a repetitive task. Housework, gardening, and exercise are three activities that work for me. What techniques help distract your logical conscious mind and help you tap into your intuitive, knowing self?

Engage in one of those activities. Pay attention to ideas that bubble to the surface while your conscious mind is occupied. After you are done with the activity, spend time writing about the ideas that grab your imagination and inspire you.

Soul Connection

HAVE YOU HEARD THE STORY about the astronomer and the guitarist?

The astronomer says, "I scoured the universe with my telescope. I talked to colleagues at the Very Large Array in New Mexico, the Keck Telescope in Hawaii, and people working with the Hubble Telescope. And none of us have found God."

The guitarist replied, "That is absurd. It is like me saying, 'I have taken my guitar apart, inspected each part with a microscope, and found no music."

This story reminds me of the human soul. Like God and music, the existence of the soul is commonly accepted, yet it is impossible to locate.

Surgeons dissecting a cadaver can search every organ and never find it. The lack of a tangible soul leaves room for speculation about the soul's function.

One interpretation of the soul comes from an ancient Jewish mystical teaching called Kabbalah. According to this tradition, the human soul has three different sections, *ruach*, *nefesh*, and *neshama*. Although these parts are intimately linked, each serves a different purpose. Because the soul is not perceptible in the material world, the three sections are actually more like aspects of the soul than anatomical parts. The *ruach* is affected by verbal communication and the *nefesh* by our worldly deeds. The *neshama* is our inner purity.

Ruach is the "spirit of life," breath, or that which animates us. *Nefesh* links us to the material plane (i.e. Earth) through the physical body and contains our personality and identity. Both *ruach* and *nefesh* are affected by how we live our lives. When we perform immoral or wrongful acts, we pick up impurities. After death, these parts of the soul must go through a process of final purification before we can face God.

Neshama, the final section of the human soul, remains pure. This part cannot be blemished, stained, or spoiled in any way, not even by evil deeds. This deep inner kernel is deemed holy and considered the piece of soul that connects people to God.

Mulling over the idea of *neshama*, I imagine it to be a key element of redemption. If everyone possesses this piece of purity or goodness within them, then it is never too late for a person, no matter how immoral, to change his or her ways and embrace salvation. Accepting a religious doctrine is optional. All a person has to do is tune into their inner godliness.

When reading the morning newspaper, I sometimes try to see the *neshama* side of people. But it's difficult to see the pure, God-like side of some people, such as parents who killed their children so they wouldn't have to experience the impending divorce, a man who tried to push a woman off a freeway overpass, or a woman whose road rage caused a traffic fatality. It is even harder to see the holy side of people instigating war, genocide, or torture. Even though I don't understand how purity can exist inside someone committing immoral acts, I hold onto the belief that we all have *neshama* within us.

Occasionally I come across stories about people who committed hideous crimes against humanity, saw the errors of their ways, and changed for the good. One example is John Newton, the author of the hymn "Amazing Grace." As a young man in the 1700s, Newton led an adventure-filled life as a master of a slave ship. Known for hard drinking and blasphemy that shocked even hardened crew members, he was notorious for ridiculing people that held Christian beliefs. Then, after surviving a series of harrowing storms, Newton converted to evangelical Christianity. He gave up profanity, drinking, and gambling, stopped his involvement with the slave trade, and studied to become a minister. As his tombstone says, he spent the last 43 years of his life preaching "the faith he had long labored to destroy."

A more current illustration would be Stanley "Tookie" Williams. As co-founder of the Crips, one of the largest and deadliest gangs in Los Angeles from the 1970s through to the 1990s, he could easily be called evil. After being convicted of four murders that occurred in 1979 (which he denied committing), he was put on death row. There he became an antiviolence crusader. During the next 24 years, before he was put to death in 2005, Williams denounced gang violence, authored books urging children to steer clear of gangs, and was nominated for the Nobel Peace Prize six years in a row.

One might ask if the pure part of Tookie's soul won out or if he was putting on a show to save his own life. While only God can accurately answer that question, Tookie felt redeemed. In one of his last interviews, Tookie said, "Redemption is tailor-made for the wretched. I've been a wretched person, but I've redeemed myself." The millions of people around the world who rallied for his clemency agreed with Tookie.

Even though most of us don't have the power to render life-and-death verdicts, we do pass judgment on each other. We unconsciously criticize other people's clothes, weight, driving habits, and dozens of other nitpicky things. Imagine what it would be like if we took the opposite tactic and focused on the *neshama* aspect of each other. What if, instead of criticizing people's outfits, we paid tribute to the pure soul hidden beneath outward appearances?

There are many ways to acknowledge the blessed kernel within other people. One way is by saying or thinking *namaste*, a Sanskrit greeting that means "The divine in me recognizes the divine within you." Or we can think "There is another pure soul."

Like the astronomer seeking God in the night sky or the guitarist searching for music in his instrument, the praise we send out into the world will be impossible to locate. But perhaps, on some level, our psyche can sense the greetings dancing between senders and receivers on silver threads of intention.

✣ Make it your story

Instead of recognizing the neshama *in other people, we often make negative judgments and direct criticism towards them. If you find yourself putting someone down, whether it is spoken aloud or internal, stop. Change your internal dialogue to "they are doing the best they can in their given situation."*

I have been working with the aforementioned maxim since college, when a professor shared it in a teacher training class. After thinking about the concept for a few decades—many spent fighting its wisdom—I now concede that it is true. My current belief is that I don't know everything going on in anyone's life; what looks like a weak performance to me may be the very best that person can do. In my life, there are plenty of times I am functioning on a subpar level. On those days, I may be doing half as well as I usually do, but I am doing the best I can in that moment.

Make an effort to turn off critical comments and instead send a blessing. Silently say Namaste, blessings on your journey, or another statement that resonates with your belief system. By doing so, you will avoid putting yourself in a superior position and instead offer other people grace.

Reflection

Waiting for the Other Shoe to Drop

HAVE YOU EVER BRACED YOURSELF for an inevitable, life-changing event? Whether it is a divorce, corporate downsizing, a child moving away from home, or losing a loved one to a terminal illness, many people begin grieving their loss before the event actually occurs. This mechanism is called "anticipatory grief."

Sometimes the anticipation period is short. For example, my oldest child went from being unemployed and living at home to being gainfully employed in another state within a three-week period. I only had 21 days to imagine what life would look like once she moved out.

At the other end of the scale, change can be excruciatingly slow. When a loved one is diagnosed with a terminal illness, the decline often lasts for weeks, months, or years. In his book *When Parents Die: A Guide for Adults*, author Edward Myers compares a sudden death to an explosion that knocks you flat. But a slow, protracted death, he says, "arrives more like a glacier, massive and unstoppable, grinding you down."

Death is not the only thing that arrives at glacial speed. Sometimes financial considerations delay divorces or separations. Both parties may know the end has arrived, but neither can afford to move out. Another example is changing jobs. You may be mentally ready to leave a stifling job, but need to pay down your credit card bills before leaving.

No matter what the cause, prolonged anticipatory grief can create tremendous strain in many areas of your life. One way to cope is by practicing mindfulness. This means being present to what you're experiencing from moment to moment, instead of being preoccupied with the past or trying to control the future. Focusing your attention on the sights, scents, and sounds in your environment will give you a mental respite from uncertainty and stress.

Like many people, I find it taxing to wait for a negative event to occur. After my mom was diagnosed with terminal cancer, I jumped every time the phone rang, afraid it was news of her death. A man I know felt similarly when layoff notices were being handed out at work. Whenever he saw his boss coming toward his desk, he panicked.

To deal with my sense of panic surrounding my mom's cancer, I set aside ten minutes of alone time each day for a total meltdown. First, I found a private place (sometimes in my car). Then I gave myself permission to cry, scream, rant, and rave about the unfairness of losing my mom six months after the birth of my first child. My ten-minute tantrums left me feeling calm, as if I'd been washed clean from the inside.

Another tool I have used and seen several friends employ is journaling. A few people I know used journaling to help them through their divorces. When the stress of living with a soon-to-be-ex mounted, these individuals released their frustrations in a torrent of writing. They said it provided a way to release the anger, fear, and negative thoughts that were coursing through their minds. A bonus of journaling was that putting their thoughts down on paper lessened the time they spent ruminating about the death of their marriage. And, they gained insights into how they wanted to rebuild their life once the divorce was final.

✌ Make it your story

When you need relief from anticipatory grief, take a few deep breaths and think about incorporating one or two of these ideas into your life. It may take the anguish out of your pending loss for a few moments, or maybe longer.

1. Practice mindfulness. Pay attention to what is happening in the moment. One way to do this is by focusing on your senses. What can you see, hear, and smell in your immediate environment?

2. Once a day, take ten minutes of alone time and have a full-blown melt-down.

3. Don't put your life on hold. Take time to socialize and attend fun events.

4. Practice good self-care. Reach out to family and friends to talk about what you are going through.

5. Use journaling as way to express and release your feelings of anger, fear, and other negative emotions that are coursing through your mind.

Dreamtime Helper

OVER THE PAST FIVE YEARS, a famous actor has made frequent guest appearances in my dreams. You probably know him. He has been in numerous blockbuster movies, including *Austin Powers 3, Batman Returns,* and *Twins.* Can you guess his identity? It's Danny DeVito.

Until he started showing up in my dreams, I did not think about him very much. But once I began deciphering the meaning behind his dreamtime appearances, I realized Danny's rise to stardom held important pointers I could use to achieve my goals. (After spending so many nights together, I feel comfortable calling him by his first name.)

Before I tell you what I learned, let me share the latest dream in which Danny played my co-star.

In dreamtime, Danny offered to critique my manuscript. As I searched for a copy, all I could find was an old printout with lots of red marks and edits covering the pages. My inability to locate a fresh copy sent me into a state of frustration and embarrassment. While I engaged in self-flagellation, Danny calmly walked over to my computer and printed out a fresh copy.

Having participated in a dream group for many years, I knew the group members could help me decipher my dream by asking me questions to uncover what my dream character represented. That day, the pivotal question was, "If I was from Mars and had never heard of Danny DeVito, how would you describe him to me?"

I immediately said he is not quite 5 feet tall, overweight, balding, and he has a strong New Jersey accent. After rattling off that list, I realized those are not typical traits of a Hollywood actor. He could have easily failed to find work, much less stardom. It took a lot of chutzpah for him to break into acting. He not only overcame the odds of finding acting jobs, he became a star.

As the words tumbled out of my mouth, I understood Danny represented my ability to overcome obstacles that block pathways in my waking life. Having him stroll into my dreamscape was a sign that if I keep moving in the direction of my goals, I can beat the odds and succeed. My job is to mirror Danny's most admirable traits: belief in oneself, a clear focus, and stick-to-itiveness.

Since he began playing a key role in my dream landscape, I did a little research on the Internet. There I learned that Danny has acted in 105 movies and TV shows (remember *Taxi?*), and has produced and directed dozens more. And, although he breaks every stereotype for debonair leading men, he has successfully played that role in movies like *Other People's Money* and *Ruthless People*, among other films.

After processing my dream about the manuscript with my dream group, I saw that Danny's presence also served as a warning sign. I have been giving my inner critic, that part of myself that loves pointing out what is wrong, too much power. Instead of believing her tirades about my "bad" writing, I need to bring a fresh, positive attitude to my work. Rather than dwelling on potential rejection, I should keep writing, rewriting, and submitting my work to editors. Danny's dreamtime visit showed me that if I persevere, I will fulfill my aspirations.

Sometimes, even with my dream version of Danny DeVito at my side, the obstacles to my dream of publishing wildly successful books seem daunting. There are moments when I feel like I am struggling against too many factors. Besides my inner critic, there is the decline of the publishing industry; a dwindling number of publishing houses remain, most with shrinking budgets and agents who only want to represent people who already have successful track records.

During those times, I recall a story of two frogs that fell into a vat of cream. The first frog immediately shouted, "We are going to die!" Then he kicked his legs into the air and sank to the bottom. The second frog said, "I won't give up." And with those words, he began thrashing about in the cream. The more his legs fluttered, the quicker the cream turned into butter. After a time, the butter became so firm the frog was able to hop out.

When despair starts pushing positive thoughts out of my head, I think about Danny's guest appearances in my dreams and the frog story. They have become like talismans for me and inspire me to be optimistic. Tapping into their wisdom, I can usually find a point of calmness, even when part of me feels like a victim skirmishing against factors outside my control. My levelheaded, confident self knows I always have a choice in how I view my situation and what actions I am willing to take.

Drawing lessons from Danny DeVito and the frog story, I know that obstacles are not a sign of failure—they just mean I have not yet succeeded. I just need to have faith in myself and keep taking positive steps toward my goals.

✣ Make it your story

Do you have role models that demonstrate positive ways to move forward on your chosen path? People who inspire you to go beyond what looks possible? Folks who demonstrate by example how to transform tough times into stepping stones that will help you reach your goals?

My helper, Danny, came to me in dreamtime, but I also have people in my family and my circle of friends who act as role models for me. If you are looking for role models, check out the people in your life and read biographies about positive figures such as Walt Disney, Mary Kay, and Eleanor Roosevelt.

Role models are not set in stone. Someone who works for you now may not be the example you need in five or ten years. As time goes by, reevaluate your team of role models; you might want to make a few changes.

Thomas Edison once said, "If I find 10,000 ways something won't work, I haven't failed. I am not discouraged, because every wrong attempt discarded is another step forward." With or without a role model by your side, the truth is you have not failed if you are still trying.

Spirituality of Gardening

The kiss of the sun for pardon,
The song of the birds for mirth,
One is nearer God's heart in a garden
Than anywhere else on earth.
Dorothy Frances Gurney

MY YARD IS A MESS. Weeds lord over what is left of the grass. Without regular mowing, the lawn turns into a carpet of yellow dandelions. When it comes to my flowerbeds, I take the attitude of Ralph Waldo Emerson, who once said, "What is a weed? A weed is a plant whose virtues have not yet been discovered."

The focus of my gardening is more about nourishing my soul than growing plants. Although I tend a tiny vegetable patch with tomatoes, zucchini, and basil, my pleasure in gardening doesn't come just from what I can reap. I am more enamored with how the process keeps me in touch with the life force flowing though all of nature.

Not long ago, I received a newsletter from global vocalist and vocal coach Gina Salá. She had just returned from spending time at the Hopi Reservation in Arizona. Writing about the landscape, Gina said that the moment she reached the Hopi Land, it felt like everything shifted. She suddenly became aware that every aspect of nature was alive and conscious. Gina realized that what she normally thought of as just ground beneath her feet actually felt more like the shoulder of a giant conscious Being resting for a moment. That connection with the life force of mother earth can also come from an appreciation of weeds, garden plants, and trees.

There are some who believe they can literally connect with the heartbeat of nature through trees. In another newsletter, I read about a Jin Shin Jyutsu practitioner who takes the pulses of trees. By gently placing her fingertips against the trunk of trees, she found that pine trees have a pulse similar to the beat of cantering horses, while the pulses of madrona move slowly, like the pulling of saltwater taffy.

The mystery inherent in planting and tending trees and plants is undeniable. Even people I know who ardently avoid the topic of spirituality speak about their connection with the energy of plants in their yard.

One woman feels a sense of communion with her plants and listens for directions from them before planting or thinning. Another friend says digging in the dirt keeps her aware of a power greater than herself. I think both of these women would agree with the quote from cultural historian Thomas Berry, "Gardening is an active participation in the deepest mysteries of the universe."

Maybe it is that participation in the mysteries of the universe that takes me into a meditative state when I garden. Being outside with my hands in the soil transports me. Listening to birds, noticing creepy crawlers, and feeling the wind on my face pulls my thinking away from mundane, everyday issues and I slip into a contemplative frame of mind. Gardening provides the perfect backdrop for solitary reflection. Many times, solutions to problems magically drop into my consciousness while I am working in my yard.

Spending time on my knees digging in the dirt gets me in touch with the essence of life. Sometimes while I am in that traditional prayer position, I recall the biblical parable about the mustard seed. This passage talks about the smallest of all seeds growing into the largest of garden plants and becoming a tree that provides sanctuary for birds. That parable reminds me that great things come from small beginnings, whether it is a seed or an idea.

And, as if the spiritual side of gardening is not enough, there is the harvest at the end of the season, with sun-warmed tomatoes, prolific zucchini, and sweet basil. Gathering luscious produce into a basket fills me with gratitude. My sense of thanks continues through the dark winter months when I pull garden produce that still exudes the essence of warm summer days out of the freezer.

⚘ Make it your story

Whether you live in the city or country, take time to be in nature. It can be as simple as having your morning coffee outside or walking barefoot across a lawn.

What natural environment attracts you? Is it sitting by a river, swimming in the ocean, or hiking in the mountains? Once you have chosen a location, spend some time there silently communing with nature. Notice how you feel when you focus on your connection with nature.

If you are not able to get out of the city, you can connect with nature by visiting a local park, bringing flowers into your home, or wearing earthy scented essential oils. Another way to connect with nature is to grow a plant from seed. Each seed is like an individual. Treat it with respect, nurture it, and witness its growth.

Wabi-Sabi: Everything Old Is New Again

There is a crack, a crack in everything
That's how the light gets in.
Anthem *by Leonard Cohen*

RECENTLY, I CAME ACROSS a Japanese philosophy called Wabi-Sabi that celebrates my imperfections . . . and yours. At its essence, Wabi-Sabi is the Japanese art of finding beauty and acceptance in the transitory states of nature and in the natural cycle of growth, decay, and death.

Instead of treasuring things that are in perfect condition, it embraces flaws. While there are no set rules, there are three main tenets of Wabi-Sabi: all things are temporary; all things are imperfect; all things are incomplete.

The first tenet, impermanence, points out the obvious: no matter how well you reinforce the structure of a building, secure a treasured item, or take care of your body, it will not last forever. Everything, from belongings to thoughts to actions, are impermanent. Scores of people spend vast resources on anti-aging, exfoliating moisturizers to reduce wrinkles. But we can no more stop the aging process than we can stop fall leaves from dropping off trees. As much as we may wish the colors of fall would stay forever, we would have to give up winter's snow-blanketed mountains, the riot of spring colors, and warm summer evenings. The same is true for our bodies. Each season of life brings its unique gifts.

Many states of being appear to be permanent, but in reality they are just periods of inactivity or of things momentarily being in equilibrium. In time, adjustments will occur, sometimes by degree and at other times in one colossal swoop. Even though we wonder, as Dr. Seuss did, "How did it get so late so soon? It's night before it's afternoon. December is here before it's June," we know the only certainty in life is change.

Embracing the second tenant, imperfections, may be a little bit more difficult. After all, imperfection is the antithesis of our youth-worshiping, consumeristic culture. Instead of focusing on botoxing, sanding, and repairing, Wabi-Sabi celebrates marks of time, including age lines, cracks, rust, and frayed edges. Imperfections are honored, not hidden.

One joy that comes with embracing imperfection in our lives is that we can accept ourselves for who we are, not who we think we should be or how others "expect" us to be. There is certain liberation in dropping out of the eternal quest for perfection. Instead of whitewashing our personalities, we can embrace our idiosyncrasies, knowing that our endearing quirks are what make us unique and memorable. The same thing applies to old buildings with sloping floors and chipped paint. No one voluntarily drives even a mile off their route to see communities with identical homes all painted varying shades of white. But in Europe, tourists flock to see the charm and history found in ancient Roman, Greek, and Gothic architecture.

Tenet three, the idea that things are always incomplete, is reminiscent of early twentieth-century author Gertrude B. Stein's famous quote, "There is no there there." Over the years, I have encountered people who say they will be happy when _____ (fill in the blank). Some people believe happiness is assured after they acquire wealth. For others, it is after they marry their soul mate. A lot of folks think happiness is guaranteed after they retire. Wabi-Sabi teaches us that all the beauty and knowing in life is not "out there" to be discovered. It is in this moment, right in front of us. The key to happiness is living with what is, not the life that is just out of reach. There is only the now. The future is not yet here; the past is gone. We only have the present.

❧ Make it your story

Wabi-Sabi recognizes that trying to obtain and maintain perfection is fruitless. Whether it is our own aging process or the wearing down of material things, over time everything develops blemishes.

Impermanence or change is an integral part of life. Seasons, fashions, politics, and weather change on a regular basis. As the saying goes, "The only constant is change." Instead of fighting what is inevitable, strive to attain ease and grace in the world of change.

Imperfections in objects tend to be more acceptable than in people. Many people find blemishes on antiques beautiful, but wrinkles on people undesirable. While it's possible to shore up defects or cosmetically cover up blemishes, whitewashing the perceived problem only changes its outward appearance. There is an opportunity to improve our acceptance of ourselves and the world around us by celebrating cracks and stains and other marks that age and weather and use leave in their wake.

Things that are incomplete are often devalued. However, that is not necessarily a true assessment. An unfinished degree may have given a person the exact knowledge and skills necessary to do her dream job. A house that is still under construction can still provide adequate shelter. Things and tasks do not need to be complete to provide value. Just as the joy of travel is in the journey, not arriving at the destination, the joy of living is in the process.

Think about actions you can take to embrace the three main tenets of Wabi-Sabi: impermanence, imperfection, and incompleteness. What is your response to each of these tenets? How does your attitude toward these tenets influence your acceptance of changes in yourself, in others, and in your environment? Imagine what your life would look like if you embraced Wabi-Sabi as a way of life.

Try New Things

HAVE YOU EVER WATCHED a child's wobbly attempts at walking and chuckled?

As an adult, it is easy to forget the trials and errors it takes to master the many challenges children face growing up. I think it's safe to assume most adults don't remember the diligent work it took to toddle across the living room for the first time. Or how acquiring new skills in an area where you haven't had prior successes can be downright scary.

I relearned what it's like to try something new and scary when my two children were in elementary school and the three of us bought secondhand roller skates. As a child I never skated, so my kids and I were learning this new skill together. First, we rolled around the house. With lots of ledges to hang onto, we did alright. Then we moved out onto the patio before eventually making our way to a deserted school parking lot.

Out in the open, with nothing to grab onto, I was seized by the fear of twisting my ankle or breaking a bone. Suddenly, the encouraging words I had spewed out over the years about learning by falling took on new meaning. In the school parking lot my attitude toward my children's struggles with new physical skills changed. To stand on the sidelines and encourage them to try new things was one thing. Quaking in my skates, facing a potential face-plant onto the concrete, was totally different. Suddenly I remembered how much courage it took to acquire proficiency in new sports.

Sadly, I did not draw a parallel between learning new physical skills with mental challenges until I attended a ten-day training session for a new job. My assumption that computers made schoolwork easier was dashed when I suffered a case of mind-freeze while learning computer codes for an archaic system that could have been designed by the creator of Rubik's cubes. My inability to digest a nonstop flow of information gave me a new perspective on my kids' plight with schoolwork. After my learning failure, I had more sympathy for my kids' overtaxed minds when they plodded through new concepts.

Inspired by my kids' ability to constantly learn new skills, I regularly push myself past my comfort zone. The payoff is twofold. By staying in touch with how it feels to learn new things, I celebrate my children's accomplishments and praise their hard work more often. And, by refusing to be complacent, I learn I can do more than I initially think I can. In my quest to push beyond my comfort zone, I've taken a few solo camping trips and overcome my terror of public speaking.

The lessons I learned from my children have also helped me within my larger community. Whether or not I understand why a person finds something to be challenging or scary, I can offer an ear for listening and words of encouragement.

✧ Make it your story

Leaving your comfort zone can put you in a vulnerable position, a situation where the outcome is unknown. That feeling can turn into a fear of the unfamiliar and result in putting the brakes on attempts to try something new. One cure for that is to start with something small. Visit a suburb in your city that you have not been to before. Try a new ethnic cuisine. Watch a new movie or read a book in a new genre, such as mystery or western.

Once you have increased your confidence, try something a little bit bigger. You could sign up for a class in an unfamiliar subject at your local community college, go on a vacation to a new location, or try a new sport or hobby. The opportunities are endless.

By stepping out of your comfort zone, you gain new perspectives that allow you to experience beginner's mind. What is beginner's mind? It is the act of dropping your expectations and seeing life with fresh eyes and an open mind. What you learn through this new mind-set can open you up to fresh ways to look at routine aspects of your life.

Meditating with Ocean Yogis

MY FASCINATION WITH DOLPHINS began at age nine, when my fourth grade class studied these playful mammals. Over the years, I kept up with dolphin research, learning about their ability to follow complex commands, understand abstract concepts, and recognize themselves in a mirror. In celebration of my fiftieth birthday, I took my dolphin fascination a step further and swam with wild dolphins in Hawaii.

It wasn't until three years after my Hawaiian dolphin adventure that I realized dolphins and I both did a form of breathwork. This idea first flashed across my brain when I was halfway through a twelve-week meditation class.

As dusk made its inevitable transition to night, I sat at home in my comfortable blue recliner, reading the weekly assignment in the meditation textbook. Scanning a section about a meditation technique involving breathwork, it suddenly occurred to me; yogis aren't the only ones to have mastered that technique. Dolphins are born with a capacity for breathwork that meditation devotees spend years trying to master. After years of meditating on a daily basis, I finally understood that meditation was teaching me to mimic this critical trait of ocean yogis.

At first, it seemed like a startling realization. But, the more I compared the yogic practice of breathwork with dolphins' breathing, the more correlations I found. All meditation practices I had studied or read about involved breathwork, a simple term that covers a variety of methods for focusing on one's breathing.

Meditation and breathwork go together like a candle and flame. It is possible to have a candle and not light it. But in order to get the most out of the candle, it is best to strike a match and enjoy the candle's flame. Similarly, it is possible to meditate without doing breathwork. However, to go into a deep meditative state, it's important to pay attention while inhaling and exhaling.

Many meditation practices apply the same technique to meditative breathwork: closing the mouth and focusing on the nostrils as the breath comes in and goes out. By concentrating on this process, it is possible to detect a temperature change between the air being inhaled and exhaled air. The air is cool on the inhale and warm on the release.

In addition to being a meditative focus, breathing plays an important role in human survival. Inhaling provides oxygen the body and its various organs require. Exhaling rids the body of waste products, such as carbon dioxide. Although most people consider the kidneys and digestive system to be the body's major waste removal systems, research has shown that they only release a tiny portion of the waste produced by the body. Breathing, in contrast, removes more than fifty percent. The rest of the waste is removed via the body's largest organ, the skin.

Throughout the ages, yogic disciples have believed that breath is more than "just the air" humans breathe. According to yogic tenets, air is full of "prana"—energy, or the spirit of life. The word inspire is based on the roots "in" and "spire," or literally, to breathe in. To be inspired is to be full of the breath of life. People can live without food for up to thirty days, and without water for several days, but breathing is so essential people cannot live without oxygen for more than a few minutes. After twenty minutes without sufficient oxygen, the brain dies.

A typical adult has a resting breathing rate of 12 to 18 breaths per minute. By practicing breathwork during meditation, it is possible learn how to slow breathing down to ten breaths or less per minute.

Slow, deep breathing improves health by calming the mind and reducing stress. That is why, during times of stress, people are often advised to "take a deep breath." Shallow breathing, the use of only the upper portions of the lungs, reduces the amount of oxygen taken into the body. That in turn leads to a lack of concentration and emotional imbalance. Shallow breathing is so common many people rarely use the bottom third of their lungs. In contrast, deep breathing—where the belly expands outward, the ribs expand, and the chest slightly rises—increases lung capacity, aids digestion, and strengthens the immune system.

People have subconscious breathing mechanisms that allow us to breathe automatically or unconsciously. Dolphins, on the other hand, are conscious breathers, aware of each breath they take. Instead of breathing continuously, like people, dolphins can take a breath through a crescent-shaped blowhole on the top of their heads, dive beneath the water, and hold that breath for approximately ten minutes until they resurface. Dolphins must think to breathe rather than think to hold their breath, whereas we breathe automatically and have to think to hold our breath.

Without giving it any conscious thought, we depend on our subconscious breathing mechanisms to keep working as we snooze. Because dolphins are conscious breathers, they cannot sink into a deep slumber the way we do. If they slept the way people do, they would suffocate. Part of their brain must remain awake to take conscious breaths.

Dolphins sleep by turning off one half of their brain at a time. The "awake" side is in charge of breathing and staying alert to predators and obstacles. While sleeping, dolphins swim slowly and surface every now and then for a breath or to rest at the surface of shallow water with their blowhole exposed. After about two hours, dolphins allow the side of their brain that has been active to sleep, and reactivate the rested side.

In many ways, dolphins' method of sleeping is similar to the wakeful rest I achieve during meditation. I remain in the waking state of consciousness, gently focusing on my breath, while allowing thought patterns, emotions, sensations, and images to arise and release. Furthermore, dolphins keep one eye open when they sleep, while I strive to open my third eye, or spiritual center, at the center of my forehead while meditating.

Recognizing the similarities between meditators and dolphins strengthens my incentive to meditate daily. I feel a connection with these sleek friends when I sit quietly and focus on my breathing. And, in those blessed moments when I reach a still point where monkey mind subsides and human limitations melt away, I swim with dolphins in the ethereal waters of my imagination.

✺ Make it your story

The first step in practicing breathwork is determining how you currently breathe. Begin by exhaling. Then place one hand on your abdomen, one hand on your chest, and inhale deeply. Notice which one of your hands moves the most. If you felt your abdomen move outward, you are already on the right track. However, if you felt your abdomen pull inward and your lungs expand, you are taking shallow breaths.

To practice the deep breathing used in breathwork, place a hand on your abdomen. Sit up straight. With your mouth closed, breath through your nose.

As you inhale, expand your abdomen four to six inches. About halfway through your inhale, you may feel a slight expansion in your chest. That's fine. Keeping your mouth closed, exhale through your nose. As your abdomen deflates, imagine your belly button touching your spine. It may help to picture a flower opening on the inhale and closing on the exhale.

In the beginning, expanding your abdomen with each breath may feel a bit awkward. But over time it can become your natural way of breathing. Consciously practice deep breathing in a variety of situations. Pay attention to how it affects the way you feel. If you are irritated while driving, try taking several deep breaths. Experiment with deep breathing at work, when you are feeling tired, or facing a problem that needs resolution.

The Story Behind the Story

READING THIS BOOK, YOU DON'T SEE the anguish I suffered through choosing just the right words. Nor do you see the drafts I took to my critique group. Specifically, the one that came back dripping with so much red ink it needed emergency triage. All you see is a polished published book. Allow me to give you a peek into the world behind my words.

Like most writers, my inner critic (or IC for short) is my consistent companion. After 20-plus years as a professional freelance writer, my IC still raises her voice in horror every time I submit a new piece for publication. She doesn't care that I have published hundreds of articles and a book. Her criticism is consistent and unrelenting. "Your writing doesn't deserve to be read, much less published," she declares.

At this very moment, she is deploying all her negative tactics to keep me from sharing this piece with you. She says you will think I am stupid. But what she really fears is that I will tell you my secrets. And she is right, that is exactly what I intend to do.

I don't claim to have overcome all of my IC's negative criticism. Some of her comments still sting and inflict emotional pain. But I have learned a couple of things I'd like to share with you.

First, there is no silencing a ticked-off IC. When your IC has something to say, stop and listen to her tactless rant. The key is to hear the words, but not heed them. Let her speak her piece, but don't take what she says personally.

After years of trying to argue with my IC, I have finally stopped. There was no winning the argument. She is much more ruthless than I am and she holds tight to her convictions no matter what counter-arguments I present. So, I got sneaky. Now I agree with her.

A typical interaction goes something like this: I am about to email a submission to my critique group or editor and I hear my inner critic say, "That article stinks. If you send that out you'll be the laughing stock of the writing community." Then I respond by saying, "You are absolutely right. If I send this out everyone will know I don't have an ounce of talent. And (here is the important part) I am going to send it out anyway." I agree with my IC and then do what I want to do. Judging from her lack of response, she doesn't know what to do when I concur with her opinion but refuse to back down.

I found this technique to be so effective with my inner writing critic, I have begun using it with all forms of negative self-talk. When my IC lets loose with discouraging criticism regarding my desire to sing, practice healing arts, and create artwork, I listen, acknowledge I may be called a fool, and continue implementing my plans.

In addition to defusing my IC by agreeing with her, I also use another method to triumph over her rants; I impersonate the person I want to be. Let's say I want to be a public speaker (which I do). My IC tells me it is a dumb idea because I will never make a living wage speaking. Plus, there are thousands of people who are better trained. And on and on she goes, dishing out insult and disagreement.

After listening to my IC's views about my aspirations (ah, right now she is calling them delusions), I do the things it takes to become the person I want to be. In this case, I spend time planning and presenting workshops in a variety of venues. Sometimes I have a small turnout at speaking engagements. And, while it is tempting in those moments to agree with my IC's assessment of my talent (or, as she says, "lack of ability"), I continue to hone my speaking skills.

Whether I like it or not, my inner critic is in my life to stay. If I picture my life in 20 years, I can envision her still harassing me any time I try something new. In response, I will agree with her, then continue pursuing my dreams.

⤷ Make it your story

Think about the influence your inner critic has on your life. Does it interfere with your ability to fulfill dreams and ambitions? What is its favorite modus operandi: negative self-talk, anxiety attacks, or self-sabotage? What tricks do you use to outsmart your inner critic?

Agreeing with the self-critic and doing what I want works for me, but it does not work for everyone. You may want to talk back and counter the nasty comments. Here are a few examples of how to talk back: "Stop talking to me like that," "No more put downs," or "That is enough negativity." You can also challenge each negative comment with a positive one. For example, if your inner critic says you are stupid, name the ways you are smart.

Another name for the critical inner voice is S.O.S.—same old stuff. The critic may be persistent, but it is not very original. Usually the same themes are rehashed over and over. Once you discover the most effective way to talk to your critic, start developing responses you can use whenever a frequently-used insult surfaces.

To delve deeper into origins of your critic's voice, try this project. Using pictures and words from magazines, newspapers, photographs, and calendars, create a collage of your inner critic. Then write uninterrupted for five minutes. When you are finished, circle the phrases that stand out. Create a "found poem" using those phrases. Write about ideas that arise from this process.

Colleen Foye Bollen is a professional writer and award-winning author. She has published hundreds of articles in national and regional publications and a how-to writing book, *Shorts: A Gateway into New Markets.*

Spirituality is an intricate part of Colleen's daily life. Dream work, meditation, and prayer help her navigate everyday situations. Colleen is also a Jin Shin Jyutsu practitioner and owner of a healing arts practice called Flowing Stillness.

Combining her years of teaching with decades of writing, she conducts workshops about writing, spirituality, and creativity. Colleen lives in the Pacific Northwest.

Praise for
Savoring Life's Spiritual Moments

Colleen Bollen has written a lovely primer for turning ordinary moments into spiritual check-ins with yourself. I love her invitation to take her story example and "make it your story," which turns this book into an active romp into your journal, your life, and a deeper self-awareness.

—**Tama Kieves**, author of *This Time I Dance!: Creating the Work you Love, Thriving Through Uncertainty: Moving Beyond Fear of the Unknown* and *Making Change Work for You* and others.

~

Colleen's personal stories demonstrate that spirituality is a fact of life and she shows us how we can find meaning in the passing moments of our days. Her stories also demonstrate how she has taken spiritual teachings and applied them to her daily life. Thus, she provides us with a meaningful blueprint of how to walk our talk.

—**Sharlyn Hidalgo**, MA, author of *The Healing Power of Trees: Spiritual Journeys Through the Celtic Tree Calendar, Nazmy—Love is My Religion: Egypt, Travel and a Quest for Peace* and others.

~

With a title, Savoring Life's Spiritual Moments, *I can honestly say that for me, this book was a very savoury morsel. Colleen writes with verve and humour, literally carrying the reader into her many stories before unveiling their insight with minimum words and fuss. I like her style. I like her writing. I like the obvious honesty of her stories. She is a brilliant storyteller.*

—**Michael J. Roads**, author of *Through the Eyes of Love—Journeying with Pan—Books One, Two and Three, Entering the Secret World of Nature* and others.

Made in the USA
Coppell, TX
23 December 2020